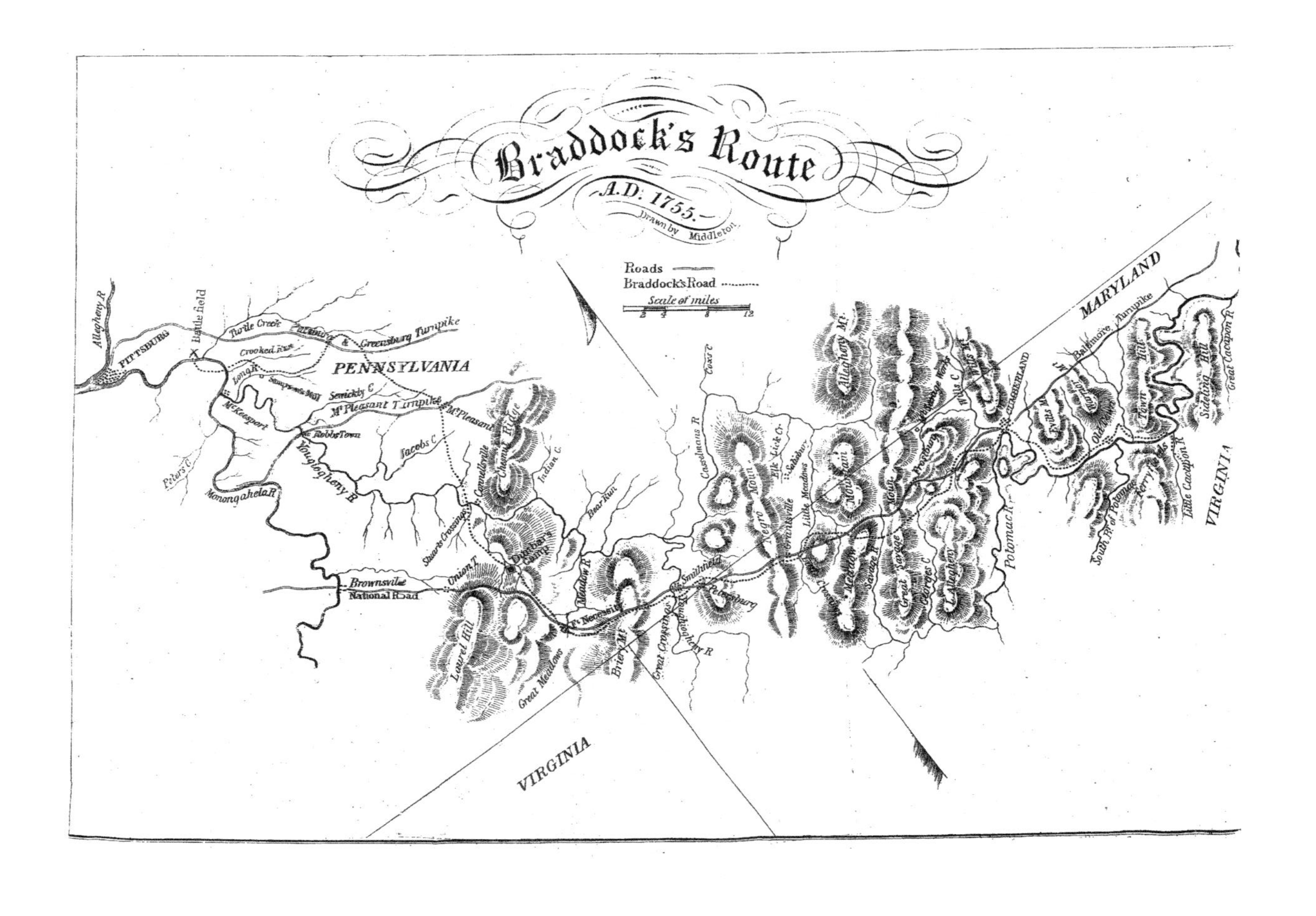

Braddock's Route
A.D. 1755.
Drawn by Middleton.
Roads
Braddock's Road
Scale of miles
2 4 8 12
PENNSYLVANIA
MARYLAND
VIRGINIA
VIRGINIA
Allegheny R
PITTSBURG
Battle field
Turtle Creek
Greensburg Turnpike
Crooked Run
Peters C.
Monongahela R
Mc Keesport
Sewickly C.
Mt Pleasant Turnpike
Mt Pleasant
Youghiogheny R
Jacobs C.
Connellsville
Chesnut Ridge
Indian C.
Bear Run
Brownsville
National Road
Union T.
Dunbar's Camp
Laurel Hill
Great Meadows
Meadow R
Briery Mt
Great Crossings
Youghiogheny R
Smithfield
Petersburg
Casselmans R
Coxs C.
Negro Moun.
Elk Lick C.
Grantsville
Little Meadows
Allegheny Mt.
Savage R
Great Savage
Georges C.
L. Allegheny
Potomac R
Wills C.
Wills Mt.
CUMBERLAND
Evitts Mt.
Old Town
Baltimore Turnpike
Town Hill
Sideling Hill
Great Cacapon R
Little Cacapon R
South Br. of Potomac

THE

HISTORY OF PITTSBURGH,

WITH

A BRIEF NOTICE OF ITS

FACILITIES OF COMMUNICATION,

AND OTHER ADVANTAGES FOR

Commercial and Manufacturing Purposes.

WITH TWO MAPS.

By NEVILLE B. CRAIG, Esq.

PITTSBURGH:
PUBLISHED BY
JOHN H. MELLOR, BOOKSELLER & STATIONER, 81 WOOD ST.
PRINTED BY KENNEDY & BROTHER, THIRD STREET.
1851.

PREFACE.

A PREFACE to a book is a queer affair, a kind of work of supererogation, a production which is rarely useful to any person except the printer, and not always so to him. When the body of the work does not exactly make up a form, it is convenient for the printer to have a page, or perhaps more, written about something to make out the necessary space. Webster says a Preface is intended to inform the reader of the main design of that to which it is prefixed. The book itself, is surely the best exposition of its own purpose, but a preface may do the same thing briefly.

The title page of our book does this very briefly; but we will make out a preface by saying that our design in preparing our book was to give, from the scanty and scattered materials within our reach, a plain narrative of the steps by which the heavily timbered land, at the head of the Ohio, was converted into thriving and populous cities and villages, and to point out the advantages which the inhabitants of this location enjoy, such as cheap fuel, salubrity of climate, fine and pure water, and very easy access to the various parts of the country around.

ERRATA.

Page 25, last word but one, for "*were*" read "*was.*"
" 207, for "1789," read "1787."
" 253, in the extract from "Hildreth's History," for "*Pitt,*" read "*Fayette.*"
" 297, in line 18, after the word "*to,*" read "*noxious.*"
" 303, for "*activity,*" read "*actively.*"
" 397, 6th line from bottom for "*enjoyed*" read "*enjoys.*"

GENERAL INDEX.

A

B

G

H

I & J

K

L

M

T

W

Y

INTRODUCTORY.

In writing the history of American towns, there exist not those materials for giving interest and variety to the narrative which can be found in older countries, where distance lends enchantment to the view and gives room for the play of fancy. If, however, our own history affords less opportunity for the introduction of romantic incidents, it, at least, gives us the means of detailing with greater accuracy the events which have actually occurred. In regard to this section of country, there is one point in which the narrative must differ widely from those of some older countries. Of Rome, for instance, from its foundation, we have a continued narrative partly true, partly fictitious, down through twelve centuries or more; while of the country in which we dwell, we have for many years after its first occupancy only occasional and very brief glimpses. This latter circumstance naturally gives to the account of the first occupancy and settlement, the form of lean and occasional sketches; but even these glimpses of the steps by which this region of country passed from a wilderness to a rich and highly cultivated land, thickly populated with an enterprising, active people, can scarcely fail to be interesting.

The annals of Pittsburgh, however, present greater variety of incidents than most American towns. A writer in speaking of Detroit uses the following language. "How numerous and diversified are the incidents compressed within the history of this settlement. No place in the United States presents such "a series of events interesting in themselves, and "permanently affecting, as they occurred, its prosperity. Five times its flag has changed, three different sovereignties have claimed its allegiance, and "since it has been held by the United States, its "government has been thrice transferred. Twice it "has been besieged by the Indians, once captured in "war and once burned to the ground."

We think that the history of Pittsburgh, will present no less variety of incident. Great Britain, France, Great Britain again, Virginia, the United States and Pennsylvania have each in turn exercised sovereignty here. Twice it has been captured in war. First by Contrecœur in 1754 and by Forbes in 1758. Once besieged by Indians, in 1763, once blown up and burned by the French in 1758, it was the field of controversy between neighboring States in 1774, and finally the scene of civil war in 1794.

In the following book a brief notice of each of these events and various others in our history will be given; and our progress thus traced, from the period when the roving Iroquois or Delawares were the only tenants of the forest here, down to the present day of steam power, telegraphs and railroads.

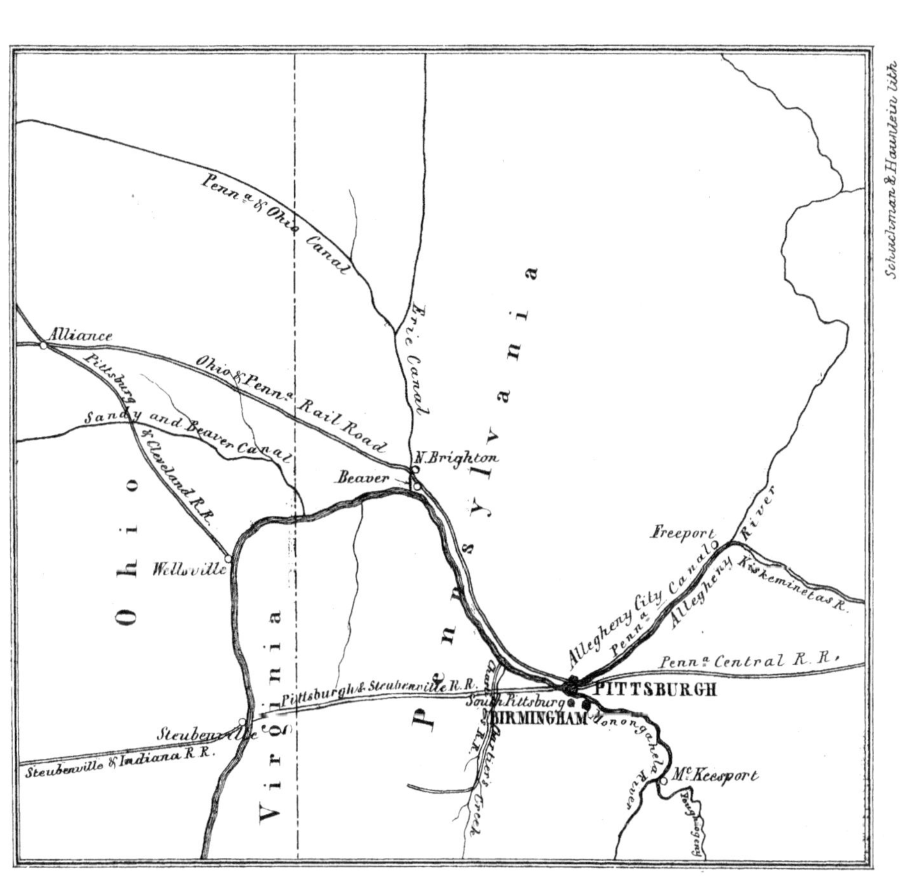

Penn.a & Ohio Canal
Erie Canal
Alliance
Ohio & Penn.a Rail Road
Pittsburg & Cleveland R.R.
Sandy and Beaver Canal
N. Brighton
Beaver
Ohio
Wellsville
Virginia
Pennsylvania
Freeport
Allegheny River
Allegheny City Canal
Penn.a
Kiskeminetas R.
Penn.a Central R.R.
PITTSBURGH
Pittsburgh & Steubenville R.R.
South Pittsburg
BIRMINGHAM
Monongahela River
Mc Keesport
Steubenville
Steubenville & Indiana R.R.
Chartier's Creek
Schuchman & Haunlein lith

THE

HISTORY OF PITTSBURGH.

CHAPTER I.

EARLIEST known occupants of this region. Six Nations or Iroquois, Delawares, Shawanese, European claimants, French, English. Captain Celeron. English grant to Ohio company. Washington's first visit and notice of "the Forks." Shingiss. Captain Trent arrives. Monsieur Contrecœur descends the Allegheny, takes Ensign Ward prisoner, Fort Duquesne built. Operations of Washington and the French, Jumonville killed, taking of Fort Necessity.

AT the time the white man first appeared in the region around the head of the Ohio, the only occupants of the soil, were the six nations called *Iroquois* by the French, *Magua* by the Dutch; *Mingoes* by the English; and *Mengwe* by the other Indian nations; The *Lenni-Lenape* or Delawares, and the *Shawanos* or the Shawanese.

The Six Nations were originally *five*, viz: the Mohawks, the Oneidas, the Onondagoes, the Cayugas and the Senecas; subsequently, however, the Tuscaroras upon being driven from North Carolina, applied for admission into the Five Nations, and since their admission in 1712, the union has been styled the Six Nations. The home of the Five Nations was in New York, but they were a very warlike people and their conquests had extended, as we are told, by Colden in his history of the Five Nations, from New York to Carolina, and from New England to the Mississippi. To manage their common concerns they had a Council composed of Sachems of different nations, who met annually, it is said, at Onondaga. This council has been compared to the Wittenagemot of the Saxons.

Mingoes were found scattered through Western Pennsylvania and in Ohio. Washington in 1753 found *Tanacharison*, the Half King of the Six Nations at Logstown, and a portion of them settled in the rich bottom on the Ohio, below Steubenville, have left their name there.

The Delawares, another nation of Indians occupying this region of country, were once the formidable enemies of the Iroquois, but about two hundred years ago their condition was greatly altered. The mediators among the Indians were women. It is deemed disgraceful for a warrior to speak of peace while war exists. About 1617 the Iroquois had, by their own account, conquered the Delawares and forced them to put on petticoats and assume the character of women. The Delawares admit the fact, of the assumption of the new character, but say the Iroquois accomplished their purpose by artifice; by persuading them that it would be magnanimous for a great and heroic nation like the Delawares to assume the character of a mediator. The ceremony of the metamorphosis was celebrated with great pomp at Albany, in presence of the Dutch, whom the Delawares accused of conspiring with their enemies, the Mengwe, to degrade them.

The cause of the Delawares, and their explanation of this strange occurrence, is zealously advocated by the Rev. Mr. Heckewelder; but that view of the matter seems far from satisfactory. The Iroquois, upon several subsequent occasions, assumed that dictatorial or authoritative tone to the Delawares, which might be expected from a conqueror, but not from a treacherous deceiver. The submissiveness, too, of the Delawares under such treatment, seems rather to resemble the timidity of a conquered, than the fierce resentment of a deceived people. A single instance will elucidate this point. In 1736 there was a dispute between the Delawares and the proprietors of Pennsylvania arising out of what was called the *walking* purchase of land, in the forks of the Delaware river. In 1742 a new treaty was to be made with Governor Thomas, at Philadelphia. He solicited the influence of the Six Nations, who sent down two hundred and thirty warriors. After the Council had assembled, *Cannassatego*, an Iroquois chief, told the Governor "That they saw the Delawares had been an unruly people, and were altogether in the wrong; that they had concluded to remove them, and oblige them to go over the river Delaware and quit all claim to any lands on this side for the future, since they had received pay for them, and it is gone through their guts long ago." "They deserved to be taken by the hair of the head and shaken severely until they recovered their senses." "We conquered you and made women of you, and you know you can no more sell lands than women." "For all these reasons we charge you to remove instantly; we don't give you liberty to think about it. You are women. *Don't deliberate, but remove away.*"

The Delawares dared not disobey. They left the

Council immediately, and soon after removed from the forks of the Delaware; some to Shamokin and Wyoming, the places assigned them by *Canassatego*, and some to Ohio.

Certainly the language of the Iroquois resembled that of a conqueror, rather than that of a mere deceiver, and the conduct of the Delawares was not such, as we would expect from persons who were shamefully deceived and imposed upon.

Again, at a Treaty held at Fort Pitt, in May, 1768, a little incident occurred, which showed that the Shawanese also submitted very patiently to the rebukes of the Iroquois, and tended to prove that the latter well deserved the name given them by the late De Witt Clinton, of the *Romans of America*. *Nymwha*, a Shawanese, addressing the Pennsylvania Commissioners and the English present, said: "We desired you to destroy your forts, &c. We also desired you not to go down the river," &c. Next day *Keyashuta*, a Seneca chief, (one of the Indians, by the way, who accompanied Washington from Logstown, to Le Bœuf in 1753, and whom the writer well recollects,) rose with a copy of the Treaty of 1764 with Col. Bradstreet, in his hand, and addressing the Commissioners, said: "By this Treaty we agreed that you had a right to build forts and trading-houses where you pleased, and to travel the road of peace from the sun rising to the sun setting. At that Treaty the Shawanese and Delawares were with me, and know all this well, and I am surprised they should speak to you as they did yesterday." Two days afterwards, *Kissinaughta*, a Shawanese chief, rose, and said: "You desired us to speak from our hearts, and tell you what gave us uneasiness of mind, and we did so. We are very sorry we should have said any thing to give offence, and we acknowledge we were wrong."

At the time of the charter to William Penn, the Delawares occupied New Jersey, the valley of the Delaware river, and the entire basin of the Schuylkill. Subsequently they removed to the Ohio, and in 1753, Washington found *Shingiss*, their King, near McKee's Rocks, and Queen *Aliquippa* at the mouth of the Youghiogany, now McKeesport.*

The *Shawanos*, or Shawanese, are described as a restless people, who were constantly engaged in war with some of their neighbors. They were originally from the South; the French say from the Cumberland river; Mr. Heckewelder was told by other Indians that they were from Florida, and Mr. Johnson, United States Agent of Indian affairs, at Piqua, in Ohio, states that they came from the Suwaney river, Florida, and that it derived its name from them. He also states, that they, and they only, of all the Indian tribes, have a tradition that their ancestors crossed the sea. He also says, that until lately they kept a yearly sacrifice for their safe arrival.

About 1698, they first appeared in Pennsylvania, as Mr. Heckewelder states, at Montour's Island, six miles below Pittsburgh, some advanced to Conestoga, and others settled on the head waters of the Susquehanna and Delaware. In 1728, they were again in motion to the West, and located themselves near the Allegheny and Ohio. In 1732, of seven hundred warriors in the State, three hundred and fifty were Shawanese.

*Another Delaware town, called Shannopin's town was situated near the Allegheny river, from the two mile run downwards.

They had several villages within the limits of the present counties of Allegheny and Beaver. Christian Frederic Post passed through three Shawanese villages between Fort Duquesne and *Sawcunk*, which, we believe, was near the mouth of Beaver, about where Beaver town now stands. Their principal residence was afterwards on the Scioto.

Of the Six Nations, the Senecas were the most western in geographical position, their homes extended from the head waters of the Allegheny river some distance down the Ohio; and to this nation belonged Tanacharison, Guyasutha and Cornplanter.

These various nations, strangely mixed together and yet preserving their distinctive and separate organizations, were dwelling here in peace, when the white man appeared among them. The Englishman claiming title under a charter by a distant king, strengthened by a treaty with the Iroquois; the Frenchman resting upon the first discovery. It is useless now to inquire, which had the better or which the worse title. Certainly it was easy enough for either claimant to find sufficient flaws in his adversary's title; to excuse his resistance to it; especially in a case where only a plausible pretext was needed.

France then held extensive possessions in North America. Canada and Louisiana belonged to her, and she was anxious to strengthen herself, and circumscribe her adversary, by establishing a line of posts from her northern to her southern colony. The point at the junction of the Monongahela and Allegheny rivers, at once became a commanding position in this great scheme.

In 1749 Capt. Celeron, a French officer, was detached from Canada to take possession of the country along the Allegheny and Ohio rivers. He performed his task and deposited leaden plates at different points. Three of these have been found, one at the mouth of French creek, as we have been told, one at Marietta, and one at the mouth of Big Kenhawa. Of the latter, a very accurate *fac simile* was engraved for, and published in the *Olden Time*, a periodical issued in Pittsburgh in 1846.

In the year 1748 Thomas Lee, one of the King's council in Virginia, formed a plan for a settlement on lands west of the mountains; a company was formed of persons in Maryland and Virginia, and Mr. Hanbury, of London, by the name of the Ohio Company; to whom a half a million acres of land, principally on the south side of the Ohio, between the Monongahela and Kenhawa, were granted.

We learn from Washington's journal of his visit to the French at Le Bœuf, that the Ohio Company, intended to lay off their fort near McKee's Rocks; this, however, was not done, we know not why.

On the 24th day of November, 1753, George Washington arrived here, on his way to the French commandant at Le Bœuf. His journal contains the following notice of this place, where, at that time, we presume, there was no human being residing.

"As I got down before the canoe, I spent some time in viewing the rivers, and the land in the fork, which I think extremely well situated for a fort, as it has the absolute command of both rivers. The land at the point is twenty-five feet above the common surface of the water; and a considerable bottom of flat well timbered land all around it very convenient for building. The rivers are each a quarter of a mile across, and run here very nearly at right angles; Allegheny, bearing north-east; and Monongahela, south-east. The former of these two is a very rapid and swift running water, the other deep and still, without any perceptible fall.

"About two miles from this, on the south-east side of the river, at the place where the Ohio company intended to erect a fort, lives Shingiss,* king of the Delawares. We called upon him, to invite him to a council at Logstown.

"As I had taken a good deal of notice yesterday of the situation at the fork, my curiosty led me to examine this more particularly, and I think it greatly inferior, either for defence or advantages, especially the latter. For a fort at the fork would be equally well situated on the Ohio, and have the entire command of the Monongahela, which runs up our settlement, and is extremely well designed for water carriage, as it is of a deep, still nature. Besides, a fort at the fork might be built at much less expense, than at the other place."

Washington proceeded from Logstown to Le Bœuf, where he received a very unsatisfactory reply; immediately after his return arrangements were made to send troops to this point.

One company under the command of Capt. Trent, were first ready to march. On the 17th day of Feb-

* Of this man, (Shingiss,) the reverend Mr. Heckewelder says, "were his war exploits all on record, they would form an interesting document, though a shocking one! Conacocheaque, Big Cove, Sherman's valley and other settlements along the frontier felt his strong arm sufficiently, that he was a bloody warrior,—cruel his treatment, relentless his fury. His person was small, but in point of courage and activity, savage prowess, he was said never to be exceeded by any one."

ruary, 1754, a memorable day in our history, Mr. Trent arrived at the Forks to meet Mr. Gist and others; they expected the rest of the company, to the number of seventy or eighty in a few days, and then intended to lay the foundation of the new fort. We know not precisely when the work was begun, but it must have been prior to the 17th April, for on that day Monsieur Contrecœur with sixty batteaux, three hundred canoes, eighteen pieces of cannon, and one thousand men, Indians and Frenchmen, arrived here from Venango, and, by the following document, summoned Ensign Ward, who commanded in the absence of Captain Trent, to surrender:

A SUMMONS,

BY ORDER OF MONSIEUR CONTRECŒUR, CAPTAIN OF ONE OF THE COMPANIES OF THE DETACHMENT OF THE FRENCH MARINE, COMMANDER-IN-CHIEF OF HIS MOST CHRISTIAN MAJESTY'S TROOPS, NOW ON THE BEAUTIFUL RIVER, TO THE COMMANDER, OF THOSE OF THE KING OF GREAT BRITAIN, AT THE MOUTH OF THE RIVER MONONGAHELA.

SIR—Nothing can surprise me more than to see you attempt a settlement upon the lands of the King, my master, which obliges me now, Sir, to send you this gentleman, Chevalier Le Mercier, Captain of the Artillery of Canada, to know of you, Sir, by virtue of what authority you are come to fortify yourself within the dominions of the King, my master. This action seems so contrary to the last Treaty of Peace, at Aix La Chapelle, between his Most Christian Majesty and the King of Great Britain, that I do not know to whom to impute such an usurpation, as it is incontestable that the lands situated along the Beautiful River belong to his Most Christian Majesty.

"I am informed, Sir, that your undertaking has been concerted by none else than by a Company, who have more in view the advantage of a trade, than to endeavor to keep the union and harmony which subsists between the two crowns of France and Great Britain, although it is as much the interest, Sir, of your nation as ours, to preserve it.

"Let it be as it will, Sir, if you come out into this place, charged with orders, I summon you in the name of the King, my master, by virtue of orders which I got from my General, to retreat peaceably with your troops from off the lands of the King, and not to return, or else I will find myself obliged to fulfil my duty, and compel you to it. I hope, Sir, you will not defer an instant, and that you will not force me to the last extremity. In that case, Sir, you may be persuaded that I will give orders that there shall be no damage done by my detachment.

"I prevent you, Sir, from asking me one hour of delay, nor to wait for my consent to receive orders from your Governor. He can give none within the dominions of the King, my master. Those I have received of my General are my laws, so that I cannot depart from them.

"On the contrary, Sir, if you have not got orders, and only come to trade, I am sorry to tell you, that I can't avoid seizing you, and to confiscate your effects to the use of the Indians, our children, allies and friends, as you are not allowed to carry on a contraband trade. It is for this reason, Sir, that we stopped two Englishmen, last year, who were trading upon our lands; moreover, the King, my master, asks nothing but his right; he has not the least intention to trouble the good harmony and friendship which reigns between his Majesty and the King of Great Britain.

"The Governor of Canada can give proof of his having done his utmost endeavors to maintain the perfect union which reigns between two friendly Princes. As he had learned that the Iroquois and the Nipissingues of the Lake of the two Mountains, had struck and destroyed an English family, towards Carolina, he has barred up the road, and forced them to give him a little boy belonging to that family, and which Mr. Ulerich, a merchant of Montreal, has carried to Boston; and what is more, he has forbid the savages from exercising their accustomed cruelty upon the English, our friends.

"I could complain bitterly, Sir, of the means taken all last winter to instigate the Indians to accept the hatchet and to strike us, while we were striving to maintain the peace. I am well persuaded, Sir, of the polite manner in which you will receive M. Le Mercier, as well out of regard to his business as his distinction and personal merit. I expect you will send him back with one of your officers, who will bring me a precise answer. As you have got some Indians with you, Sir, I join with M. Le Mercier, an interpreter, that he may inform them of my intentions upon that subject.

"I am, with great regard, Sir,

"Your most humble and most ob't serv't,

"CONTRECŒUR.

"Done at our Camp, April 16, 1754."

Resistance by about forty men, even with the aid of an unfinished stockade, to several hundred French and Indians, with several pieces of cannon, were out of the question. Ward had no brother officer to consult with, but *Tanacharison,* the half King of the Six Nations of Indians, a zealous friend of the English was present, and advised him to inform the French commandant, that he was not an officer of rank, nor was he invested with authority to answer the demand, and to request time until the arrival of Captain Trent, who was at Turtle Creek. He went to the French camp; Tanacharison, in company, with this reply. Contrecœur, however, refused to wait, and demanded an immediate surrender. A capitulation of course followed, and on the succeeding day, Ward, with his party, ascended the Monongahela to Redstone, now Brownsville, where a store house had previously been erected.

A full narrative of the whole affair was given, under oath, by Ensign Ward, to Mr. Dinwiddie, Governor of Virginia, who forwarded it to the British Government. Ward, in his statement, mentions that Contrecœur invited him to supper, after the capitulation. Poor Ward, probably, had but little appetite that night, and had Contrecœur foreseen all the consequences of the doings of that day, his happiness would, also, have been greatly clouded.

This affair of the 17th of April, 1754, has been regarded, as the commencement of that memorable war, whose operations extended over continental Europe, Asia, Africa and America. On that day French dominion extended from the eastern shores of Nova Scotia, by the St. Lawrence, the Great Lakes and the Ohio and Mississippi rivers to the Gulf of Mexico. In Africa she owned Senegal and Goree. In India she held extensive possessions, guarded and defended by fortifications and troops. We will, hereafter, see how she was left, by the treaty of Paris which put an end to the war, begun here by Contrecœur.

That officer having thus obtained possession of this place proceeded at once to erect a fort, which he called Fort *Du Quesne*, after the Governor of Canada, the Marquis *Du Quesne* de Menneville.

Ensign Ward arrived at Willis' Creek, where Cumberland now stands, on the 22d of April, where Washington had arrived with three companies. Expresses were immediately sent to the Governors of Pennsylvania, Maryland and Virginia, asking for reinforcements. Washington, then, had a consultation with his officers and determined to advance, and, if possible, to reach the Monongahela, at Redstone, and there erect a fortification.

Active operations between Washington and the French, now ensued in Fayette county; which are not directly connected with the annals of Pittsburgh, and yet, cannot be entirely overlooked in performing our task. We shall, therefore, notice these operations as briefly as possible; referring our readers to the *Olden Time*, or any history of the United States, for fuller information.

On the 9th of May, Washington was at Little Meadows, where he received information that Contrecœur had been reinforced with eight hundred men. On the 18th he was encamped on the Youghiogany, near where Smithfield, in Fayette county, now stands. A few days after he moved forward to the Great Meadows.

That same night, (May 27th,) about nine o'clock, an express arrived from *Tanacharison*, who was then encamped with some of his warriors about six miles off, with information that the French were near his encampment. Col. Washington, immediately started with forty men to join the Half-King. The night was dark, the rain fell in torrents, the woods were intricate, the soldiers often lost their way groping in the bushes and clambering over rocks and logs, but at length they arrived at the Indian camp just before sunrise, (May 28th.) A Council with *Tanacharison* was immediately held, and joint operations against the French were determined on. Two Indian spies discovered the enemy's position in an obscure place, surrounded by rocks, and a half mile from the road. Washington was to advance on the right, *Tanacharison* on the left. Thus they approached in single file, until they were discovered by the French, who immediately seized their arms and prepared for action. The action commenced by a brisk firing on both sides, which was kept up for a quarter of an hour, when the French ceased to resist. Monsieur Jumonville, the commandant, and ten of his men were killed, and twenty-two were taken prisoners, one of whom was wounded. A Canadian escaped during the action. Washington had one man killed and two wounded. No harm happened the Indians. The prisoners were sent to Governor Dinwiddie.

Among the prisoners taken on the 28th of May, were Messieurs Drouillon and La Force, and two cadets. La Force was described as a bold, enterprising man, of great subtlety and cunning, and we will hereafter find Captain Stobo, while a prisoner at Fort Duquesne, speaking of his absence as a great loss to the French. Washington, in a letter to Governor Dinwiddie, thus speaks of him: "Besides, La Force would, if released, I really think, do more disservice than fifty other men, as he is a person whose active spirit leads him into all parties, and has brought him acquainted with all parts of the country. Add to this a perfect use of the Indian tongue and great influence with the Indians."

The Canadian who escaped at the time of Jumonville's death would, of course, carry the news of that affair to Fort Duquesne, and Washington, anticipating that a larger force would be sent against him, set his troops to work to enlarge and strengthen the work he had prepared at the Great Meadows, and called it *Fort Necessity.*

The Indians began to flock in around him, Tanacharison and his followers, Queen Aliquippa and her son, and others to the number of forty or fifty families. Captain Mackay, with an independent company of one hundred men from South Carolina, also joined him. That officer had a royal commission, which he thought placed him over Washington. He, however, was a prudent man, and no disagreement occurred. On the 10th of June, nine deserters from the French arrived at Washington's camp, and confirmed intelligence previously received by a messenger sent from Logstown to Tanacharison, that the Shawanese had agreed to take up the hatchet against the English. These deserters also stated that the Fort at the Forks was completed. They stated that there were not above five hundred men in the Fort when they left, but supposed that two hundred had since arrived. The same deserters also stated, as Washington said in his letter, that Jumonville's party were sent out as spies.

On the 11th of June, Washington, leaving Captain

Mackay at Fort Necessity, marched with his troops, intending to advance to Redstone. After two weeks of toil he reached Gist's farm, only thirteen miles from Fort Necessity. Here information was received that reinforcements had arrived at Fort Duquesne from Canada, and that a large detachment would soon be sent against the English. A retreat was then decided upon.

Washington intended to retreat to Will's creek, but when he arrived at the Great Meadows he found his men so exhausted by their exertions and by the scarcity of provisions that they could neither draw the swivels farther nor carry their baggage. They had been eight days without bread, and found only a few bags of flour at the Great Medows. It was, therefore, concluded to remain there, erect a fortification, and wait until supplies and reinforcements could reach them. It was now the first of July. Expresses were sent to hasten on aid; while the men were set to work to fell trees and collect the logs to erect a breast work and a fort, which was called *Fort Necessity*.

"On the 3d of July, early in the morning, an alarm was received from a sentinel who had been wounded by the enemy; and at nine o'clock intelligence came that the whole body of the enemy, amounting, as was reported, to nine hundred men, was only four miles off. At eleven o'clock they approached the fort and began to fire at a distance of six hundred yards, but without effect. Colonel Washington had drawn up his men on the open and level ground outside of the trenches, waiting for the attack, which he presumed would be made as soon as the enemy's forces emerged from the woods; and he ordered his men to reserve their fire till they should be near enough to do execution. The distant firing was supposed to be a stratagem to draw Washington's men into the woods, and thus to take them at a disadvantage. He suspected the design, and maintained his post till he found the French did not incline to leave the woods and attack the fort by an assault, as he supposed they would, considering their superiority of numbers. He then drew his men back within the trenches, and gave them orders to fire according to their discretion, as suitable opportunities might present themselves. The French and Indians remained on the side of the rising ground, which was nearest to the fort, and, sheltered by the trees, kept up a brisk fire of musketry, but never appeared in the open plain below. The rain fell heavily through the day, the trenches were filled with water, and many of the arms of Colonel Washington's men were out of order, and used with difficulty.

"In this way the battle continued from eleven o'clock in the morning till eight at night, when the French called and requested a parley. Suspecting this to be a feint to procure the admission of an officer into the fort, that he might discover their condition, Colonel Washington at first declined listening to the proposal, but when the call was repeated, with the additional request that an officer might be sent to them, engaging at the same time their parole for his safety, he sent out Captain Vanbraam, the only person under his command that cou'd speak French, except the Chevalier de Peyrouny, an ensign in the Virginia regiment, who was dangerously wounded and disabled from rendering any service on this occasion. Vanbraam returned, and brought with him from M. de Villiers, the French commander, proposed articles of capitulation. These he read and pretended to interpret, and some changes having been made by mutual agreement, both parties signed them about midnight.

"By the terms of the capitulation, the whole garrison was to retire, and return without molestation to the inhabited parts of the country, and the French commander promised, that no embarrassment should be interposed, either by his own men or the savages. The English were to take away every thing in their possession, except their artillery, and to march out of the fort the next morning with the honors of war, their drums beating and colors flying. As the French had killed all the horses and cattle, Colonel Washington had no means of transporting his heavy baggage and stores; and it was conceded to him that his men might conceal their effects, and that a guard might be left to protect them till horses could be sent up to take them away. Colonel Washington agreed to restore the prisoners who had been taken at the skirmish with Jumonville; and as a surety for this article two hostages, Captains Vanbraam and Stobo, were delivered up to the French, and were retained till the prisoners should return. It was moreover agreed that the party capitulating should not attempt to build any more establishments at that place, or beyond the mountains, for the space of a year.

CHAPTER II.

Vanbraam and Stobo, hostages, detained some time in Fort Du Qnesne; letter from the latter; notice of Stobo. Braddock's expedition; persons engaged in it. T. C. Atkinson's delineation of his route, account of his defeat by one who was present; list of killed and wounded officers. James Smith's account of the burning of prisoners at Fort Du Quesne next day.

Vanbraam, one of the persons delivered up as hostages, was a Dutchman; the other, Robert Stobo, a Scotchman. Of the former we know but little, of the latter we have learned something more, though still much less than we would desire to know. The distinguished historian, David Hume, in a letter to Smollet, dated 21st September, 1768, speaks of Stobo as the friend of the latter and says: "he has surely had the "most extraordinary adventures in the world." We shall take occasion to make some allusion to him in a short time.

These hostages were both detained in Fort Duquesne some time. While there, Stobo wrote the two following letters to the Governor of Virginia:

LETTER FROM CAPTAIN STOBO, JULY 28, 1754.

"The Indians are greatly alarmed at a report said to be brought up by an Indian named Tuscarora John. He reports that the Half-King, Monecatootha, and a Shawanese King, &c., to the number of 37, were confined by the English and carried as prisoners. That John Meinors, alias Jacob Cork, of Montour's company, told him so soon as they got them to the inhabitants they would hang them all, and advised him to make his escape. This was industriously reported the day before the Shawanese counselled with the French and their Indians. The French made them a very long and eloquent speech; telling them they did not come to make war with any but the English would not let them alone. That they expected their children would not see their father abused in his old age; but that if they had a mind to join the English they might; if not and to live in peace with all, there were goods for them. This was all I could pick up. The French gave two very large belts of Wampum and as many strings. Their Indians gave an equal number. The French gave them likewise a large present, viz: 16 very fine guns, 2 barrels of gunpowder, and bullets in proportion, 16 fine suits of clothes, several of a meaner kind, blankets, strouds, &c. The Shawanese made no answer at that time, nor have I heard they have as yet. 'Tis now reported for certain, that the Half-King, &c., are killed, and their wives and children given up to the barbarity of the Cherokees and Catawbas, of whom they say there are 300 at the new store. True or false, it has greatly alarmed them, and had it not been for that report, I believe: a great many Indians and of several nations would have been with you now. If true (which I cannot think,) there will be no farther dependence on any Indians this way, and will make our return very hazardous, but that is not to be considered. The Shawanese, Picts and Delawares have had a grand council by themselves; what they have determined I know not; but I have persuaded some of them to venture to see you, by assuring them they will be used in the best manner, and there is large presents at the new store. A present well timed now, will be of great service. If peace be made with the Indians, Catawbas and Cherokees, I hope all will go well. I assure you there was not any of those Indians we call ours at the battle, except six or seven. I believe of the Mingo nation, two fellows not regarded by them, particularly one English John; he was at Gist's with those that were suspected as spies. I am informed he intends to see you with some of the rest. Take care of them. I send this by Monecatootha's brother-in-law: a worthy fellow, and may be trusted. On the other side, you have a draft of the Fort, such as time and opportunity would admit of at this time. The garrison consists of 200 workmen, and all the rest went in several detachments to the number of 1000, two days hence. Mencin, a fine soldier, goes; so that Contrecœur, with a few young officers and cadets, remain here. A Lieut. went off some days ago, with 200 men, for provisions. He is daily expected. When he arrives, the garrison will. La Force is greatly wanted here—no scouting now—he certainly must have been an extraordinary man amongst them—he is so much regretted and wished for. When we engaged to serve the country, it was expected we were to do it with our lives. Let them not be disappointed. Consider the good of the expedition, without the least regard to us. For my part, I would die a thousand deaths, to have the pleasure of possessing this Fort but one day. They are so vain of their success at the Meadows, it is worse than death to hear them. Strike this fall as soon as possible. Make the Indians ours. Prevent intelligence. Get the best, and 'tis done. 100 trusty Indians might surprise this Fort. They have access all day, and might lodge themselves so that they might secure the guard with the tomahawks; shut the sally gate, and the Fort is ours. None but the guard and Contrecœur, stay in the Fort. For God's sake communicate this to but few, and them you can trust. Intelligence comes here unaccountably. If they should know I wrote, I would loose the little liberty I have. I should be glad to hear from you. But take no notice of this in your's. Excuse errors, bad diction, &c. Pray be kind to this Indian. Springes and Delaware George have been here." [Here follows a plan of the Fort.]

SECOND LETTER DATED FORT DUQUESNE, JULY 29, 1754.

"SIR—I wrote you yesterday by an Indian named the Long or Mono; he will be with you in seven days. This goes by Delaware George. If these discharge their trust they ought to be well rewarded. The purport of yesterday's letter was to inform you of a report, and I hope false, which greatly alarms the Indians; that the Half-King, and Monecatootha are killed, their wives and children given to the Cherokees. I wish a peace may be made up between the Catawbas and the nations here; they are much afraid of them. Many would have joined you ere now had it not been for that report. You had as just a plan of the fort as time and opportunity would allow. The French manage the Indians with the greatest artifice. I mentioned yesterday a council the Shawanese had with the French, the present they gave, and if they made the French a speech yesterday, the bearer, who was present, will inform you to what purport. If yesterday's letter reaches you it will give you a particular account of most things. I have scarce a minute; therefore can only add one more thing: there are but 200 men here at this time, 200 more expected in few days;. the rest went off in several detachments to the amount of 1000, besides Indians. The Indians have great liberty here; they go out and in when they please without notice. If 100 trusty Shawanese, Mingoes and Delawares were picked out, they might surprise the Fort, lodging themselves under the platform behind the palisadoes by day, and at night secure the guard with the tomahawks. The guard consists of 40 men only, and 5 officers. None lodge in the Fort but the guard, except Contrecœur—the rest in bark cabins around the Fort. All this you have more particular in yesterday's account. Your humble servant, &c. La Force is greatly missed here. Let the good of the expedition be considered preferable to our safety. Haste to strike.

"A list of deserters and prisoners at the French Fort:

"Mercer's company.—John Smith, John Baker. Did not get here till after the detachment of deserters.

"Vanbraam's do.—Barnabas Deven.

"Mercer's do.—Jacob Arants, John Ramsey. This man is the cause of all our misfortunes. He deserted the day before the battle. The French got to Gist's at dawn of day, surrounding the Fort, imagining that we were still there, gave a general fire. But when they found we were gone, they were determined to return with all expedition, thinking we had returned to the inhabitants — when up comes Mr. Rascal, told them he had deserted the day before, and the regiment was still at the Meadows, in a starving condition, which caused his deserting, and hearing they were coming, deserted to them. They confined him—told him if true he should be rewarded, if false, hanged. This I had from the English interpreters.

"Mechas' do.—John Stuerdfages, wounded in the right arm.

"Montour's do.—Daniel Laferty, Henry O'Brien, prisoners.

"Taken at Guest's by an Indian named English John, Lowrey's traders, Andrew M'Briar, Nehemiah Stevens, John Kennedy, Elizabeth Williams.

"The Indians offered their prisoners for sale. Enquired the price—40 pistoles for each. A good ransom.

"All sent to Canada in custody of the Indian who took them, except John Kennedy: he was given to the Owl to weigh upon while his leg was curing. He was wounded with ten others, and four Indians. All are recovering but one, who died after having his arm cut off. Four were shot on the spot. That is all the loss I can hear of. On the 23d three of their people deserted. I hope they are got with you by this time. I hear more intend it soon. I spoke to the commander several times concerning the prisoners, telling him as long as we came to a capitulation, he had no right to make them prisoners—he told me they were the Indian's, and he could not get them from them."

The extraordinary zeal for the service of his country, and the self-devoting spirit manifested in these letters, attracted the admiration of the writer of this history many years ago, and he has long labored to get fuller information about Stobo. The letter of Hume next attracted his attention, and subsequently Mr. Draper furnished some notices of his adventures for the Olden Time. Some three years ago a friend saw in an English catalogue of books, "*The Memoirs of Major Robert Stobo, of the Virginia Regiment.*" An order was immediately sent for its purchase, but before it arrived the book had disappeared. Since that time repeated searches have been made for it, but in vain, until very recently, when, through the kindness of Mr. James McHenry, of Liverpool, England, the writer obtained from the British Museum a manuscript copy of the book preserved there.

From this work we learn, that Robert Stobo was the only son of William Stobo, a merchant of Glasgow, in which city Robert was born in the year 1727. His father and mother both died when he was young, and he was then, with his own consent, sent to Virginia to serve in a store owned by some Glasgow merchants. Subsequently he sold his property in Glasgow and entered into mercantile business himself in Virginia. He, however, lead a very gay life and the business seemed not likely to prosper much in his hands. But he became a great favorite of the Governor, Dinwiddie, who, in 1754, when apprehensions began to be entertained of a frontier war, appointed him the oldest Captain of the Virginia Regiment, then raised. After being detained some time he was sent to Quebec. Not, however, as a close prisoner, but having the privilege of going about the neighboring country until some time after Braddock's Defeat, when a great change took place in his situation. When General Braddock began his expedition against Fort Duquesne, copies of the foregoing letters and the accompanying plan of that fort were given to him and at the time of his defeat they fell into the hands of the enemy, and were published. The consequence was that Stobo was immediately ordered into close confinement. Subsequently he was tried and sentenced to be executed, the sentence, however, was deferred, though his confinement was rendered still more rigorous. At length, however, he effected his escape, and after some most extraordinary adventures indeed, arrived at Louisburgh, on the island of Cape Breton, shortly after General Wolfe had sailed for Quebec. He immediately returned to Quebec, afforded that General much information and pointed out the place of landing.

We have thought proper to give this brief notice of the "extraordinary adventures" of the man who was the first English prisoner in Fort Duquesne, and who gave the first description of it.

The writer of this work will probably in a short time republish the whole "Memoir of Robert Stobo."

From the date of Stobo's letters, we have no information of proceedings here, until the advance of Braddock towards this place in July 1755.

The defeat of General Braddock on the 9th of July, 1755, was a very important event in the history of the colonies. It was, perhaps, the most disastrous affair that had ever befallen them, and laid open very large portions of the territory of Pennsylvania, Maryland and Virginia to the ravages of the Indians. It was an interesting event too, in another respect. Many persons who afterwards figured in our revolution were engaged in that action and gained some experience in the art of war. General Gage, who subsequently commanded the British army at Bunker Hill, led the advanced party at Braddock's Field; Gates, the conqueror of Burgoyne, and Morgan, the hero of the Cowpens, and Mercer, and Stephens, and Neville, and many others, and above all George Washington, the greatest and the best, was there.

We have, therefore, concluded to give full accounts of the march of Braddock and his defeat. Fortunately for our present purpose, it so happened that while the compiler of these annals was publishing the Olden Time, he received from Mr. T. C. Atkinson, civil engineer, (who had been employed in making surveys for a railroad through the country traversed by Braddock,) a very satisfactory account of the march of the army from Cumberland to the field of battle. It is a document eminently worthy of preservation and we have concluded to insert it in full as a part of our work. Mr. Atkinson proceeds as follows:

BRADDOCK'S ROUTE TO THE BATTLE OF THE MONONGAHELA.

The interest with which the routes of celebrated expeditions are regarded, and the confusion which attends them after the lapse of years, is well exemplified in the case of Hannibal, whose march towards Rome, in order to divert their army from the siege of Capua, was totally lost in the course of a few centuries. The constant blunders of Livy in copying first from one writer, and then from another, who made him take a different path, justify a recent English historian who went to Italy to see the ground for himself, in saying that the Punic War was almost as hard in the writing as the fighting.

As the time is coming when the road by which the unfortunate Braddock marched to his disastrous field, will be invested with antiquarian interest, akin to that attending Hannibal's route, or rather the *via scelerata*, by which the Fabian family marched out of Rome, I have thought it time not idly spent to attempt to pursue its scattered traces as far as it is in my power, among more pressing occupations. In this sketch, I do not design to pursue it to its extent, but only to identify it in those parts where it has been convenient for me to visit it, and in others to shadow out its general direction. Where it is obscure, I hope to have opportunities to examine it at a future day.

Of the well conducted expedition of Col. Bouquet, and its precise path, the publications of Mr. Hutchins, the geographer, who was one of the engineers, leaves us very well informed. It is presumable that similar details would be found of the march of 1755 if it had had a successful termination. The three engineers who were in the field were wounded; and it is probable their papers fell into the hands of the enemy, or were lost in the fight.

General Braddock landed at Alexandria on the 20th of February, 1755. The selection of this port for the debarkation of the troops, was censured at the time, though it is probable it had the approval of Washington. The two regiments he brought with him were very defective in numbers, having but about 500 men each, and it was expected their ranks would be recruited in America. It is shown by the repeated requests on this point made by the General at Cumberland, that this expectation was vain. After numerous delays, and a conference with the Royal Government, we find Gen. Braddock *en route* on the 24th of April, when he had reached Fredericktown, in Maryland. Passing thence through Winchester, Va., he reached Fort Cumberland about the 9th of May. Sir John

Sinclair, Deputy Quarter Master General, had preceded him to this point about two weeks.*

The army struck the Little Cacapehon, (though pronounced Cacapon, I have used for the occasion the spelling of Washington, and various old documents,) about six miles above its mouth, and following the stream, encamped on the Virginia side of the Potomac, preparatory to crossing into Maryland. The water is supposed to have been high at the time, as the spot is known as the Ferry-fields, from the army having been ferried over. This was about the 4th or 5th of May.

The army thence pursued the banks of the river, with a slight deviation of route at the mouth of the South Branch, to the village of Old Town, known at that time as the Shawnee Old Town, modern use having dropped the most characteristic part of the name. This place, distanced about eight miles from the Ferry-fields, was known at that early day at the residence of Col. Thomas Cresap, an English settler, and the father of the hero of Logan's speech. The road proceeded thence parallel with the river and at the foot of the hills, till it passed the narrows of Will's Moun-

* Many misstatements are prevalent in the country adjacent to the line of march, especially east of Cumberland, the traditionary name of Braddock's route being often applied to routes we know he did not pursue. It is probable the ground of the application consists in their having been used by the Quarter Master's men in bringing on those Pennsylvania wagons and pack horses procured by Dr. Franklin, with so much trouble, and at so great expense of truth. Sir John Sinclair wore a Hussar's cap, and Franklin made use of the circumstance to terrify the German settlers with the belief that he was a Hussar who would administer to them the tyrannical treatment they had experienced in their own country, if they did not comply with his wishes. It is singular that a small brook and an obscure country road in Berkley County, Va., bear the name of Sir John's Run, and Sir John's Road, supposed to be taken from the name of this officer.

tain, whence it struck out a shorter line coincident with the present county road, and lying betwen the railroad and the mountain, to Fort Cumberland.

From the Little Cacapehon to this point the ground was comparatively easy, and the road had been generally judiciously chosen. Thenceforward the character of the ground was altered, not so much in the general aspect of the country, as that the march was about to abandon the valleys, and now the real difficulties of the expedition may be said to commence.

The fort had been commenced the previous year, after the surrender at the Great Meadows, by Col. Innes, who had with him the two independent companies of New York and South Carolina. It mounted ten four pounders, besides swivels, and was favorably situated to keep the hostile Indians in check.*

The army now consisted of 1000 regulars, 30 sailors, and 1200 provincials, besides a train of artillery. The provincials were from New York and Virginia; one company from the former colony was commanded by Capt. Gates, afterwards the hero of Saratoga. On the 8th of June, Braddock having, through the interest and exertions of Dr. Franklin, principally, got 150 wagons and 2000 horses from Pennsylvania, was ready to march.

Scaroodaya, successor to the Half-King of the Senecas, and *Monacatootha*, whose acquaintance Washington had made on the Ohio, on his mission to Le Bœuf, with about 150 Indians, Senecas and Delawares, ac-

* The original name of Cumberland was Cucucbetuc, and from its favorable position on the Potomac, it was most probably the site of a Shawnee village, like Old Town; moreover, it was marked by an Indian name, a rare occurrence in this vicinity, if any judgment may be drawn from the few that have been preserved.

companied him. George Croghan, the Indian agent of Pennsylvania, and a friendly Indian of great value, called Susquehanna Jack, were also with him.

The first brigade under Sir Peter Halket, led the way on the 8th, and on the 9th the main body followed. Some idea of the difficulties they encountered may be had when we perceive they spent the third night only five miles from the first. The place of encampment, which is about one-third of a mile from the toll-gate on the National Road, is marked by a copious spring bearing Braddock's name.

For reasons not easy to divine, the route across Will's Mountain first adopted for the National Road was selected, instead of the more favorable one through the narrows of Will's Creek, to which the road has been changed within a few years, for the purpose of avoiding that formidable ascent. The traces are very distinct on the east and west slopes, the modern road crossing it frequently. From the western foot, the route continued up Braddock's Run to the forks of the stream, where Clary's tavern now stands, 9 miles from Cumberland, when it turned to the left, in order to reach a point on the ridge favorable to an easy descent into the valley of George's Creek. It is surprising that, having reached this high ground, the favorable spur by which the National Road accomplished the ascent of the Great Savage Mountain, did not strike the attention of the engineers, as the labor requisite to surmount the barrier from the deep valley of George's Creek, must have contributed greatly to those bitter complaints which Braddock made against the Colonial Governments for their failure to assist him more effectively in the transportation department.

Passing then a mile to the south of Frostburg, the road approaches the east foot of Savage Mountain, which it crosses about one mile south of the National Road, and thence by very favorable ground through the dense forests of white pine peculiar to this region, it got to the north of the National Road, near the gloomy tract called the *Shades of Death*. This was the 15th of June, when the dense gloom of the summer woods, and the favorable shelter which these enormous pines would give an Indian enemy, must have made a most sensible impression on all minds of the insecurity of their mode of advance.

This doubtless had its share in causing the council of war held at the Little Meadows* the next day. To this place, distant only about twenty miles from Cumberland, Sir John Sinclair and Maj. Chapman had been dispatched on the 27th of May, to build a fort; the army having been 7 days in reaching it, it follows as the line of march was upwards of three miles long, the rear was just getting under way when the advance were lighting their evening fires.

* This interesting locality lies at the west foot of the Meadow Mountain, which is one of the most importaut of the Allegheny Ridges, in Pennsylvania especially, where it constitutes the dividing ridge between the eastern and western waters. A rude entrenchment, about half a mile north of the Inn on the National Road, kept by Mr. Huddleson, marks the site of this fort. This is most probably the field of a skirmish spoken of in frontier history, between a Mr. Paris, with a scouting party from Fort Cumberland, and the Sieur Donville, commanding some French and Indians, in which the French officer was slain. The tradition is distinctly preserved in the vicinity, with a misapprehension of Washington's participation in it, arising probably from the partial resemblance between the names of Donville and Jumonville. From the positiveness of the information, in regard to the battle ground, conflicting with what we know of Jumonville's death, it seems probable enough that this was the scene of this Indian skirmish; and as such, it possesses a classic interest, valuable in proportion to the scarcity of such places. For a notice of Mon. Donville's death, see vol, 1, page 75, Olden Time.

Here it may be well enough to clear up an obscurity which enters into many narratives of these early events, from confusing the names of the *Little Meadows* and *Great Meadows*, *Little Crossings* and *Great Crossings*, which are all distinct localities.

The *Little Meadows* have been described as at the foot of Meadow Mountain; it is well to note that the *Great Meadows* are about 31 miles further west, and near the east foot of Laurel Hill.

By the *Little Crossings* is meant the Ford of Casselman's River, a tributary of the Youghiogheny; and by the *Great Crossings*, the passage of the Youghiogheny itself. The Little Crossings is 2 miles west of the Little Meadows, and the Great Crossings 17 miles further west.

The conclusion of the council was to push on with a picked force of 1200 men and 12 pieces of cannon; and the line of march, now more compact, was resumed on the 19th. Passing over ground to the south of the Little Crossings, and of the village of Grantsville, which it skirted, the army spent the night of the 21st at the Bear Camp, a locality I have not been able to identify, but suppose it to be about midway to the Great Crossings, which it reached on the 23d. The route thence to the Great Meadows or Fort Necessity, was well chosen, though over a mountainous tract, conforming very nearly to the ground now occupied by the National Road, and keeping on the dividing ridge between the waters flowing into the Youghiogheny on the one hand, and the Cheat River on the other. Having crossed the Youghiogheny, we are now on the classic ground of Washington's early career, where the skirmish with Jumonville, and Fort Necessity, indicate the country laid open for them in the previous year. About one mile west of the Great Meadows, and near the spot now marked as Braddock's Grave, the road struck off more to the north-west, in order to reach a pass through Laurel Hill, that would enable them to strike the Youghiogheny, at a point afterwards known as Stewart's Crossing, and about half a mile below the present town of Connellsville. This part of the route is marked by the farm known as Mount Braddock. This second crossing of the Youghiogheny was effected on the 30th of June. The high grounds intervening between the river and its next tributary, Jacob's Creek, though trivial in comparison with what they had already passed, it may be supposed, presented serious obstacles to the troops, worn out with previous exertions. On the 3d of July a council of war was held at Jacob's Creek, to consider the propriety of bringing forward Col. Dunbar with the reserve, and although urged by Sir John Sinclair with, as one may suppose, his characteristic vehemence, the measure was rejected on sufficient grounds. From the crossing of Jacob's Creek, which was at the point where Welchhause's Mill now stands, about 1½ miles below Mount Pleasant, the route stretched off to the north, crossing the Mount Pleasant turnpike near the village of the same name, and thence by a more westerly course, passing the Great Sewickley near Painter's Salt Works, thence south and west of the Post Office of Madison and Jacksonville, it reached the Brush Fork of Turtle Creek. It must strike those who examine the map, that the route for some distance, in the rear and ahead of Mount Pleasant, is out of the proper direction for Fort Duquesne, and accordingly we find on the 7th of

July, General Braddock in doubt as to his proper way of proceeding. The crossing of Brush Creek which he had now reached, appeared to be attended with so much hazard, that parties were sent to reconnoitre, some of whom advanced so far as to kill a French officer within half a mile of Fort Duquesne.

Their examinations induced a great divergence to the left, availing himself of the valley of Long Run, which he turned into, as is supposed, at Stewartsville, passing by the place now known as Samson's Mill, the army made one of the best marches of the campaign, and halted for the night at a favorable depression between that stream and Crooked Run, and about two miles from the Monongahela. At this spot, about four miles from the battle ground, which is yet well known as Braddock's Spring, he was rejoined by Washington on the morning of the 9th of July.

The approach to the river was now down the valley of Crooked Run to its mouth, where the point of fording is still manifest, from a deep notch in the west bank, though rendered somewhat obscure by the improved navigation of the river. The advance, under Col. Gage, crossed about 8 o'clock, and continued by the foot of the hill bordering the broad river bottom to the second fording, which he had effected nearly as soon as the rear had got through the first.

The second and last fording near the mouth of Turtle Creek, was in full view of the enemy's position, and about one mile distant. By 1 o'clock the whole army had gained the right bank, and was drawn up on the bottom land, near Frazier's house, (spoken of by Washington, as his stopping place, on his mission to Le Bœuf,) and about three fourths of a mile distant from the ambuscade.

The advance was now about to march, and while a part of the army was yet standing on the plain, the firing was heard. Not an enemy had yet been seen.

The following account of the proceedings of the army for a few days before and after the battle, is taken from the Diary of a person, who was evidently a participator in all those transactions, and is the best narrative we have seen; for which reason we insert it in full:

GENERAL BRADDOCK'S EXPEDITION, 1755.—KING'S LIBRARY VOL. 212, P. 87, TO THE END.

July 4th.—We marched about six miles to Thicketty-run; the country was now less mountainous and rocky, and the woods rather more open, consisting chiefly of white oak.

From this place two of our Indians were prevailed upon to go for intelligence towards the French fort, and also (unknown to them,) Gist, the General's guide.

The Indians returned on the 6th and brought in a French officer's scalp, who was shooting within half a mile of the Fort. They informed the General that they saw very few men there or tracks, nor any additional works; that no pass was possessed by them between us and the Fort, and that they believed very few men were out upon observation. * * * * They saw some boats under the Fort, and one with a white flag coming down the Ohio. [Allegheny.]

Gist returned a little after, the same day, whose account corresponded with theirs, excepting that he saw a smoke in a valley between our camp and Duquesne. He had concealed himself with an intent of getting close under the Fort in the night, but he was discovered and pursued by two Indians who had very near taken him.

At this camp the provisions from Colonel Dunbar, with a detachment of a Captain and 100 men, joined us, and we halted here one day.

On the 6th of July we marched about six miles to Monakatuca Camp, which was called so from an unhappy accident that happened upon the march.

Three or four people loitering on the rear of the Grenadiers were killed by a party of Indians and scalped. Upon hearing the firing, the General sent back the Grenadier company, on whose approach the Indians fled. They were discovered again a little after by our Indians in the front, who were going to fire upon them, but were prevented by some of our outrangers, who mistaking these, our Indians, for the enemy, fired upon them and killed Monakatuca's son, notwithstanding they made the agreed countersign, which was holding up a bough and grounding their arms. When we came to our grounds, the General sent for the father and the other Indians, condoled with and made them the usual presents, and desired the officers to attend the funeral, and gave an order to fire over the body.

This behavior of the General was so agreeable to the Indians, that they afterwards were more attached to us, quite contrary to our expectations.

The line of carrying horses extending very often a prodigious length, it was almost impossible to secure them from insults, though they had yet marched without any interruption. Every Bat-man having been ordered to carry his fire-lock, and small parties having kept constantly on their flanks. The disposition of march for these horses had varied almost every day according to the nature of the country, but the most common was to let them remain upon the ground an hour after the march of the line, under the guard of a captain and one hundred men, by which means there was no confusion in leaving the ground, and the horses were much eased. They were now ordered, when the roads would permit, to march upon the flanks, between the subaltern's picket and the line; but whenever the country was close or rocky, they were then to fall in the rear, and a strong guard marched thither for their security, which was directed to advance or fall back in proportion to the length of the line of carrying horses, taking particular care always to leave parties upon the flanks.

ORDERS AT MONAKATUCA CAMP.

If it should be ordered to advance the van, or send-back the rear guard, the advanced parties detached from them are to remain at their posts facing outwards.

Whenever there is a general halt, half of each of the subaltern's advanced parties are to remain under arms with fixed bayonets, facing outwards, and the other half may sit down by their arms.

On the 7th July we marched from hence, and quitting the Indian path, endeavored to pass the Turtle Creek about twelve miles from the mouth, to avoid the dangerous pass of the Narrows. We were led to a precipice which it was impossible to descend. The General ordered Sir John St. Clair to take a captain and one hundred men, with the Indians, guides, and some light horse, to reconnoitre very well the country. In about two hours he returned and informed the General he had found the ridge which led the whole way to Fort Duquesne, and avoided the Narrows and Frazier's, but that some work which was to be done would make it impossible to move further that day; we therefore encamped here, and marched the next morning about eight miles to the camp near the Monongahela.

When we arrived here, Sir John St. Clair mentioned, (but not to the General,) the sending a detachment that night to invest the Fort; but being asked whether the distance was not too great to reinforce that detachment in case of an attack, and whether it would not be more advisable to make the Pass of the Monongahela, or the Narrows, whichever was resolved upon, with our whole force, and then to send the detachment from the next camp, which would be six or seven miles from the fort. Sir John immediately acquiesced, and was of opinion that would be a much more prudent measure.

The guides were sent for, who described the Narrows to be a narrow pass of about two miles, with a river on the left, and a very high mountain on the right, and it would require much repair to make it passable by carriages. They said the Monongahela had two extreme good fords, which were very shallow, and the banks not steep. It was, therefore, resolved to pass this river the next morning, and Lieut. Col. Gage was ordered to march before the break of day, with the two companies of Grenadiers, 160 rank and file, of the 44th and 48th, Capt. Gates' Independent

Company, and two six pounders, with proper guides, and he was instructed to pass the fords of the Monongahela, and to take post after the second crossing, to secure the passage of that river. Sir John St. Clair was ordered to march at four o'clock, with a detachment of 250 men, to make the roads for the artillery and baggage, which was to march with the remainder of the troops at five.

ORDERS AT THE CAMP NEAR MONONGAHELA.

All the men are to draw and clean their pieces, and the whole are to load to-morrow on the beating of the General, with fresh cartridges.

No tents or baggage are to be taken with Lieut. Col. Gage's party.

July 9th.—The whole marched agreeably to the orders before mentioned, and about eight in the morning, the General made the first crossing of the Monongahela by passing over about 150 men in the front, to whom followed half the carriages; another party of 150 men headed the second division; the horses and cattle then passed, and after all the baggage was over, the remaining troops which till then possessed the heights, marched over in good order.

The General ordered a halt, and the whole formed in their proper line of march.

When we had moved about a mile, the General received a note from Lieut. Col. Gage, acquainting him with his having passed the river the second time without any interruption, and having posted himself agreeably to his orders.

When we got to the other crossing, the bank on the opposite side not being yet made passable, the artillery and baggage drew up along the beach, and halted till one, when the General passed over the detachment of of the 44th, with the pickets of the right. The artillery wagons and carrying horses followed, and then the detachment of the 48th with the left pickets, which had been posted during the halt upon the heights.

When the whole had passed, the General again halted till they formed according to the annexed plan.

It was now near two o'clock, and the advanced party under Lieut. Col. Gage, and the working party under John St. Clair, were ordered to march on till three. No sooner were the Pickets upon their respective flanks and the word given to march, but we heard an excessive quick and heavy firing in the front. The General imagining the advanced parties were very warmly attacked, and being willing to free himself from the incumbrance of the baggage, ordered Lieut. Col. Burton to reinforce them with the van guard, and the line to halt. According to this disposition, eight hundred men were detached from the line, free from all embarrassments, and four hundred were left for the defence of the artillery and baggage, posted in such a manner as to secure them from any attacks or insults. The General sent forward an aid-de-camp to bring him an account of the nature of the attack, but the fire continuing, he moved forward himself, leaving Sir Peter Halket with the command of the baggage. The advance detachment soon gave way, and fell back upon Lieut. Col. Burton's detachment, who was forming his men to face a rising ground upon the right. The whole were now got together in great confusion. The colors were advanced in different places to separate the men of the two regiments. The General ordered the officers to endeavor to form the men, and tell them off into small divisions, and to advance with them, but neither entreaties nor threats could prevail.

The advanced flank parties, which were left for the security of the baggage all but one ran in. Their baggage was then warmly attacked, a great many horses and some drivers were killed, the others escaped by flight. Two of the cannon flanked the baggage, and for some time kept the Indians off; the other cannon which were disposed of in the best manner, and fired away most of their ammunition, were of some service, but the spot being so woody, they could do little or no execution.

The enemy had spread themselves in such a manner that they extended from front to rear, and fired upon every part. The place of action was covered with trees and much underwood upon the left, without any opening but the road, which was only about twelve feet wide. At the distance of about 200 yards in front, and upon the right, were two rising grounds covered with trees.

When the General found it impossible to persuade them to advance, and no enemy appeared in view; and nevertheless a vast number of officers were killed by exposing themselves before the men, he endeavored to retreat them in good order; but the panic was so great that he could not succeed. During this time they were loading as fast as possible, and firing in the air. At last, Lieut. Col. Burton got together about 100 of the 48th regiment, and prevailed upon them, by the General's order, to follow him toward the rising ground on the right, but he being disabled by his wounds, they faced about to the right and returned.

When the men had fired away all their ammunition,

and the General and most of the officers were wounded, they, by one common consent, left the field, running off with the greatest precipitation. About fifty Indians pursued us to the river, and killed several men in the passage. The officers used all possible endeavors to stop the men, and to prevail upon them to rally; but a great number of them threw away their arms and ammunition, and even their clothes, to escape the faster. About a quarter of a mile on the other side the river, we prevailed upon near 100 of them to take post upon a very advantageous spot, about two hundred yards from the road· Lieut. Col. Burton posted some small parties and sentinels. We intended to have kept possession of that ground till we could have been re-inforced. The General and some wounded officers remained there about an hour, till most of the men run off. From that place the General sent Mr. Washington to Col. Dunbar, with orders to send wagons for the wounded, some provisions and hospital stores, to be escorted by the two youngest grenadier companies, to meet him at Gist's plantation, or nearer if possible. It was found impracticable to remain here, as the General and the officers were left almost alone; we therefore retreated in the best manner we were able. After we had passed the Monongahela the second time, we were joined by Lieut. Col. Gage, who had rallicd near 60 men. We marched all that night, and the next day, and about 10 o'clock that night we got to Gist's Plantation.

July 11th.—Some wagons, provisions and hospital stores arrived. As soon as the wounded were dressed, and the men had refreshed themselves, we retreated to Col. Dunbar's camp, which was near Rock Port. The

General sent a Sergeant's party back with provisions to be left on the road on the other side of the Yoxhio Geni for the refreshment of any men who might have lost their way in the woods. Upon our arrival at Col. Dunbar's camp, we found it in the greatest confusion. Some of his men had gone off upon hearing of our defeat, and the rest seemed to have forgot all discipline. Several of our detachment had not stopped till they had reached this camp.

It was found necessary to clear some wagons for the wounded, many of whom were in a desperate situation, and as it was impossible to remove the stores, the howitzer shells, some 12 pound shot, powder, and provisions, were destroyed, or buried.

July 18th.—We marched from hence to the camp near the Great Meadows, where the General died.

The following is a list of the officers killed and wounded on that day:

STAFF.

Major General Braddock,		died of his wounds.
Robert Orme, Esq., Roger Morris, Esq.,	Aids de Camp,	wounded.
William Shirley, Esq., Secretary,		killed.
Sir John St. Clair, Deputy Quarter Master General,		wounded.

LATE SIR PETER HALKET'S REGIMENT.

Sir P. Halket, Colonel,	killed.	Captain Tatton,	killed.
Lieut. Col. Gage,	wounded.	Captain Gethins,	"

SUBALTERNS.

Lieutenant Littleler,	wounded.	Lieutenant Lock,	wounded.
" Dunbar,	"	" Disney,	"
" Halket,	killed.	" Kennedy,	"
" Treeby,	wounded.	" Townsend,	killed.
" Allen,	killed.	" Nartlow,	"
" Simpson,	wounded.	" Pennington,	wounded.

COLONEL DUNBAR'S REGIMENT.

Lieut. Col. Burton,	wounded.	Captain Rowyer,	wounded.
Major Sparkes,	"	Captain Ross,	"
Captain Cholmley,	"		

SUBALTERNS.

Barbut,	wounded.	Brereton;*	killed.
Walsham,	"	Hart,	"
Crimble,	killed.	Montreseur,	wounded.
Widman,	"	Macmullen,	"
Hanford,	"	Crow,	"
Gladwin,	wounded.	Sterling.	"
Edmeston,	"		

ARTILLERY.

Lieutenant Smith,	killed.	Lieutenant M'Cloud,	wounded.
Lieutenant Buchanon,	wounded.	" M'Culler,	"

ENGINEERS.

Peter McKeller, Esq.,	wounded.	—— Williamson, Esq.,	wounded.
Robert Gordon, Esq.,	"		

DETACHMENT OF SAILORS.

Lieutenant Spendelow,	killed.
Mr. Talbot, Midshipman,	"
Captain Stone, of General Lascelle's Regiment,	wounded.
Captain Floyer, of General Warburton's Regiment,	"

INDEPENDENT COMPANIES OF NEW YORK.

Captain Gates,	wounded.	Lieutenant Howarth,	wounded.
Lieutenant Sumain,	killed.	" Gray,	"

VIRGINIA TROOPS.

Captain Stevens,	wounded.	Captain Peronie,	killed.
" Poulson,	killed.		

SUBALTERNS.

Hamilton,	killed.	Stuart,	wounded.
Wright,	"	Wagoner,	killed.
Splitdorff,	"		

Terrible as was the slaughter of troops on that day, a scene presented itself here on the ensuing day of a more horrible character. Our account is taken from the Narrative of Colonel James Smith. We might hope, for the credit of humanity, that such transactions never took place; but Colonel Smith was a man of good character, well known here by some persons still living. He removed to Kentucky and was there elected to the legislature. That he was a prisoner among the Indians, there is no doubt; the Colonial Records at Harrisburgh prove it.

Before giving his narrative of that shocking scene, we give from a work published in Kentucky, a brief account of his own capture and adventures.

"In the spring of the year 1755, James Smith, then a youth of eighteen, accompanied a party of three hundred men from the frontiers of Pennsylvania, who advanced in front of Braddock's army, for the purpose of opening a road over the mountain. When within a few miles of Bedford Springs, he was sent back to the rear to hasten the progress of some wagons loaded with provisions and stores for the use of the wood cutters. Having delivered his orders, he was returning, in company with another young man, when they were suddenly fired upon by a party of three Indians, from a cedar thicket which skirted the road. Smith's companion was killed upon the spot; and although he himself was unhurt, yet his horse was so much frightened by the flash and report of the guns, as to become totally unmanageable, and after a few plunges threw him with violence to the ground. Before he could recover his feet, the Indians sprang upon him, and, overpowering his resistance, secured him as a prisoner. One of them demanded, in broken English, whether 'more white men were coming up,' and upon his answering in the negative, he was seized by each arm and compelled to run with great rapidity over the mountain until night, when the small party encamped and cooked their suppers. An equal share of their scanty stock of provisions was given to the prisoner, and in other respects, although strictly guarded, he was treated with great kindness. On the evening of the next day, after a rapid walk of fifty miles through cedar thickets, and over very rocky ground, they reached the western side of the Laurel mountain, and beheld, at a little distance, the smoke of an Indian encampment. His captors now fired their guns and raised the *scalp* halloo! This is a long yell for every scalp that has been taken, followed by a rapid succession of shrill, quick, piercing shrieks—shrieks somewhat resembling laughter in the most excited tones. They were answered from the Indian camp below by a discharge of rifles, and a long whoop, followed by shrill cries of joy, and all thronged out to meet the party. Smith expected instant death at their hands, as they crowded around him; but, to his surprise, no one offered him any violence. They belonged to another tribe, and entertained the party in their camp with great hospitality, respecting the prisoner as the property of their guests. On the following morning Smith's captors continued their march, and on the evening of the next day arrived at Fort Duquesne—now Pittsburgh. When within half a mile of the fort they again raised the scalp halloo, and fired their guns as before. Instantly the whole garrison was in commotion. The cannons were fired—the drums were beaten, and the French and Indians ran out in great numbers to meet the party and partake of their triumph. Smith was again surrounded by a multitude of savages, painted in various colors, and shouting with delight; but their demeanor was by no means as pacific as that of the last party he had encountered. They rapidly formed in two lines, and brandishing their hatchets, ramrods, switches, &c., called aloud for him to run the gauntlet. Never having heard of this Indian ceremony before, he stood amazed for some time, not knowing what to do; but one of his captors explained to him that he was to run between the two lines and receive a blow from each Indian, as he passed, concluding his explanation by exhorting him to 'run his best,' as the faster he ran the sooner the affair would be over. The truth was very plain—and young Smith entered upon his race with great spirit. He was switched very handsomely along the lines for about three-fourths of the distance, stripes only acting as a spur to greater exertions, and he had almost reached the extremity of the line, when a tall chief struck him a furious blow with a club upon the back of the head, and instantly felled him to the ground. Recovering himself in a moment, he sprung to his feet and started forward again, when a handful of sand was thrown in his eyes, which, in addition to the great pain, completely blinded him. He still attempted to grope his way through, but was again knocked down and beaten with merciless severity. He soon became insensible under such barbarous treatment, and recollected nothing more until he found himself in the hospital of the fort, under the hands of a French surgeon, beaten to a jelly, and unable to move a limb. Here he was quickly visited by one of his captors—the same who had given him such good advice when about to commence his race. He now inquired, with some interest, if he felt 'very sore.' Young Smith replied that he had been bruised almost to death, and asked what he had done to merit such barbarity. The Indian replied that he had done nothing, but that it was the customary greeting of the Indians to their prisoners—that it was something like the English 'how d'ye do,' and that now all ceremony would be laid aside, and he would be treated with kindness. Smith enquired if they had any news of General Braddock. The Indian replied that their scouts saw him every day from the mountains—that he was advancing in close columns through the woods—(this he indicated by placing a number of red sticks parallel to each other, and pressed closely together)—and that the Indians would be able to shoot them down 'like pigeons.'

"Smith rapidly recovered, and was soon able to walk upon the battlements of the fort, with the aid of a stick. While engaged in this exercise, on the morning of the 9th ——, he observed an unusual bustle in the Fort. The Indians stood in crowds at the great gate, armed and painted. Many barrels of powder, balls, flints, &c., were brought out to them, from which each warrior helped himself to such articles as he required. They were soon joined by a small detachment of French regulars, when the whole party marched off together. He had a full view of them as they passed, and was confident that they could not exceed four hundred men. He soon learned that it was detached against Braddock, who was now within a few miles of the Fort; but from their great inferiority in numbers, he regarded their destruction as certain, and looked joyfully to the arrival of Braddock in the evening, as the hour which was to deliver him from the power of the Indians. In the afternoon, however, an Indian runner arrived with far different intelligence. The battle had not yet ended when he left the field; but he announced that the English had been surrounded, and were shot down in heaps by an invisible enemy; that instead of flying at once or rushing upon their concealed foe, they appeared completely bewildered, huddled together in the centre of the ring, and before sun down there would not be a man of them alive. This intelligence fell like a thunderbolt upon Smith, who now saw himself irretrievably in the power of the savages, and could look forward to nothing but torture or endless captivity. He waited anxiously for further intelligence, still hoping that the fortune of the day might change. But about sunset, he heard at a distance the well known scalp halloo, followed by wild, quick, joyful shrieks, and accompanied by long continued firing. This too surely announced the fate of the day. About dusk, the party returned to the Fort, driving before them twelve British regulars, stripped naked, and with their faces painted black! an evidence that the unhappy wretches were devoted to death. Next came the Indians, displaying their bloody scalps, of which they had immense numbers, and dressed in the scarlet coats, sashes and military hats of the officers and soldiers. Behind all came a train of baggage horses, laden with piles of scalps, canteens, and all the accoutrements of British soldiers. The savages appeared frantic with joy, and when Smith beheld them entering the Fort, dancing, yelling, brandishing their red tomahawks, and waving their scalps in the air, while the great guns of the Fort replied to the incessant discharge of the rifles without, he says that it looked as if h—l had given a holiday, and turned loose its inhabitants upon the upper world. The most melancholy spectacle was the band of prisoners. They appeared dejected and anxious. Poor fellows! They had but a few months before left London, at the command of their superiors, and we may easily imagine their feelings at the strange and dreadful spectacle around them. The yells of delight and congratulation were scarcely over, when those of vengeance began. The devoted prisoners (British regulars,) were led out from the Fort to the banks of the Allegheny, and to the eternal disgrace of the French commandant, were there burnt to death, with the most awful tortures. Smith stood upon the battlements, and witnessed the shocking spectacle. The prisoner was tied to a stake, with his hands raisen above his head, stripped naked, and surrounded by Indians. They would touch him with red hot irons, and stick his body full of pine splinters, and set them on fire—drowning the shrieks of the victim in the yells of delight with which they danced around him. His companions in the mean time stood in a group near the stake, and had a foretaste of what was in reserve for each of them. As fast as one prisoner died under his tortures, another filled his place, until the whole perished. All this took place so near the Fort, that every scream of the victims must have rang in the ears of the French commandant!

"Two or three days after this shocking spectacle, most of the Indian tribes dispersed, and returned to their homes, as is usual with them after a great and decisive battle. Young Smith was demanded of the French by the tribe to whom he belonged, and was immediately surrendered into their hands."

From the date of the above horrible occurrences until the taking of Fort Duquesne by General Forbes, we have only occasional and very transient glances at this place.

CHAPTER III.

Action between scouting parties; Death of Monsieur Donville; Humane instructions of Dumas, the successor of Contrecœur at Fort Duquesne. Extensive influence of Braddock's defeat; Col. Armstrong's expedition against Kittaning. John McKinney's description of Fort Duquesne in 1756. Lieut. Baker takes a French officer near Fort Duquesne; Captain Lignery, commandant at Duquesne 1757. Discouraging aspect of the war at that time. France every where triumphant; Desponding letters of Walpole and Chesterfield. William Pitt prime minister; new life infused into British councils. Amherst succeeds Earl of Loudoun, as commander-in-chief in America; Wolfe and Forbes under him; character of Forbes; Expedition against Fort Duquesne; Army assembled at Ray's town, now Bedford. Discussion about route between Washington and Col. Bouquet, probable reasons in favor of the Pennsylvania route; Grant's defeat; Official report of Forbes' Army; Attacks on Fort Ligonier; Advance of Forbes, capture of Fort Duquesne; First Fort Pitt built; Forbes' return to Philadelphia and death. Col. Hugh Mercer left in command; the rest of the army return to the settlements; prominent part of Scotchmen in the early history of this region.

About the first of April, 1756, a Mr. Paris, with a scouting party from Fort Cumberland, fell in with a small body of Indians commanded by Monsieur Donville; an action took place, the French commandant was killed, and the following instructions were found upon him:

"FORT DUQUESNE, 23d March, 1756.

"The Sieur. Donville, at the head of fifty savages, "is ordered to go and observe the motions of the "enemy in the neighborhood of Fort Cumberland. "He will endeavor to harass their convoys and burn "their magazines at Gonococheaque, should this be "practicable. He must use every endeavor to take "prisoners who may confirm what we already know of "the enemy's designs. The Sieur. Donville will use "all his talents and all his credit, to prevent the "savages from committing any cruelties upon those "who may fall into their hands. Honor and humani- "ty ought, in this respect, to serve as our guide.

"DUMAS."

By this order it would appear, that Contrecœur was no longer in command at this place; and we may reconcile the humanity evinced in the above order, with the cruelty manifested on the 9th of July 1755, by supposing that the commanders had in the interim been changed.

The extent to which Pennsylvania and Maryland were laid open to the ravages of the enemy, by Braddock's defeat, is shown in the suggestion that Donville might destroy magazines on Conecocheaque.

In September, 1756, Colonel John Armstrong made a dashing expedition from Fort Shirley, where Shirleysburg, in Huntington county, now stands, against Kittaning, at that time occupied by Delaware Indians, under Capt. Jacobs. The prisoners taken there, stated that the number of French, then at Fort Duquesne, was about four hundred, and that the principal part of the provisions used by them came from the Mississippi.

In February, 1756, John McKinney was taken prisoner by the Indians, and carried first to Fort Duquesne and thence to Canada, from whence he made his escape and came to Philadelphia, where he gave the following description of the Fort:

"Fort Duquesne is situated on the east side of the Monongahela, in the fork between that and the Ohio.

It is four square, has bastions at each corner; it is about fifty yards wide—has a well in the middle of the Fort, but the water bad—about half the Fort is made of square logs, and the other half next the water of stockadoes; there are intrenchments cast up all around the Fort about 7 feet high, which consists of stockadoes drove into the ground near to each other, and wattled with poles like basket work, against which earth is thrown up, in a gradual ascent; the steep part is next the Fort, and has three steps all along the intrenchment for the men to go up and down, to fire at an enemy—these intrenchments are about four rods from the Fort, and go all around, as well on the side next the water as the land; the outside of the intrenchment next the water, joins to the water. The Fort has two gates, one of which opens to the land side, and the other to the water side, where the magazine is built; that to the land side is, in fact, a draw-bridge, which in day-time serves as a bridge for the people, and in the night is drawn up by iron chains and levers.

"Under the draw-bridge is a pit or well, the width of the gate, dug down deep to water; the pit is about eight or ten feet broad; the gate is made of square logs; the back gate is made of logs also, and goes upon hinges, and has a wicket in it for the people to pass through in common; there is no ditch or pit at this gate. It is through this gate they go to the magazine and bake-house, which are built a little below the gate within the intrenchments; the magazine is made almost under ground, and of large logs and covered four feet thick with clay over it. It is about 10 feet wide, and about thirty-five feet long; the bake-house is opposite the magazine; the waters sometimes rise so high as that the whole Fort is surrounded with it, so that canoes may go around it; he imagines he saw it rise at one time near thirty feet. The stockadoes are round logs better than a foot over, and about eleven or twelve feet high; the joints are secured by split logs; in the stockadoes are loop holes made so as to fire slanting towards the ground. The bastions are filled with earth solid about eight feet high; each bastion has four carriage guns about four pound; no swivels, nor any mortars that he knows of; they have no cannon but at the bastions. The back of the barracks and buildings in the Fort are of logs placed about three feet distance from the logs of the Fort; between the buildings and the logs of the Fort, it is filled with earth about eight feet high, and the logs of the Fort extend about four feet higher, so that the whole height of the Fort is about 12 feet.

"There are no pickets nor palisadoes on the top of the Fort to defend it against scaling; the caves of the houses in the Fort are about even with the top of the logs or wall of the Fort; the houses are all covered with boards, as well the roof as the side that looks inside the Fort, which they saw there by hand; there are no bogs nor morasses near the Fort, but good dry ground, which is cleared for some distance from the Fort, and the stumps cut close to the ground; a little without musket shot of the Fort, in the fork, is a thick wook of some bigness, full of large timber.

"About thirty yards from the Fort, without the intrenchments and picketing, is a house, which contains a great quantity of tools, such as broad and narrow axes, planes, chisels, hoes, mattocks, pickaxes, spades, shovels, &c., and a great quantity of wagon-wheels and tire. Opposite the Fort, on the west side of the Monongahela, is a long, high mountain, about a quarter of a mile from the Fort, from which the Fort might very easily be bombarded, and the bombarder be quite safe; from them the distance would not exceed a quarter of a mile; the mountain is said to extend six miles up the Monongahela, from the Fort; Monongahela, opposite the Fort, is not quite musket shot wide; neither the Ohio nor Monongahela can be forded, opposite the Fort. The Fort has no defence against bombs. There was about 250 Frenchmen in this Fort, besides Indians, which at one time amounted to 500; but the Indians were very uncertain; sometimes hardly any there; that there were about 20 or 30 ordinary Indian cabins about the Fort.

"While he was at Fort Duquesne, there came up the Ohio from the Mississippi, about thirty batteaux, and about 150 men, loadened with pork, flour, brandy, tobacco, peas, and Indian corn; they were three months in coming to Fort Duquesne, and came all the way up the falls without unloading."

On the 8th of June, 1757, Lieut. Baker, with five soldiers and fifteen Cherokee Indians, returned from an expedition towards Fort Duquesne. They had fallen in with a party of three French officers and seven men on the head waters of Turtle Creek, about twenty miles from that Fort. They killed five of the Frenchmen and took one officer prisoner. This officer gave the information that Captain Lignery, then commanded at the Fort, and that there were at that place six hundred French troops and two hundred Indians. This is the latest information we have from Duquesne prior to the fall of the next year, 1758.

The war between Great Britain and France, up to the end of the year 1757, had been an unfortunate and disgraceful one to the former power. On the Ohio, British power and trade was extinct; while the incursions of the French and their savage allies extended almost to the scite of the present seat of our State Government. In the East Indies British power was almost annihilated and British subjects were cruelly sacrificed in the black hole at Calcutta. In the Mediterranean, whither the Marquis De la Galissoniere had gone from Canada, Admiral Byng was foiled and Minorca taken, and in Germany thirty thousand Hanoverian troops, under the command of the brother of George the 2d, had been disgracefully surrendered as prisoners to the French commandant there.

Some of the wisest men of England were greatly discouraged. Horace Walpole in a letter said, "it is time for England to slip her cables and float away into some unknown ocean;" and Lord Chesterfield wrote, "whoever is in, or whoever is out, I am sure we are "undone both at home and abroad; at home, by our "increasing debt and expenses, abroad by our incapa-"city and ill luck. I never yet saw so dreadful a "prospect."

Such were the opinions of some of the most eminent persons of England, when that extraordinary man, from whom our city received its name, was called upon to direct the affairs of Government. Three years of disaster, disgrace and despondency, were succeeded by years of triumph and success.

In America, the commander-in-chief, the Earl of Loudoun, a bustling *do-nothing*, of whom it was wittily remarked, "he reminds me of St. George, on a sign; he is always on horseback but never advances," was succeeded by General Amherst, under whom were Wolfe and Forbes. Under their command the enemy was swept from the continent, and the star of England was placed once more in the ascendant. Among the first of these brilliant successes was the capture of this place by an army under the command of General John Forbes. This gallant soldier was a native of Fifeshire, in Scotland, and was at the time he was selected to command the army, destined to this quarter of the country, in his 49th year. He had seen much service on the continent of Europe. He was bred to the profession of medicine, but at an early day inclined to prefer a military career, he purchased a commission into the Scotch Gray Dragoons, and rapidly rose to the rank of a Lieutenant Colonel. His zeal and ability soon recommended him to the favor of the celebrated Earl of Stair, Lord Ligonier and other distinguished military characters. In the preceding war, he was employed in the post of Quarter Master General under the Duke of Cumberland, which office he filled with great ability.

A large portion of his army was collected together at Philadelphia, from whence he marched in July, 1758, to join Colonel Bouquet, with an advance party at Ray's town, now Bedford. Most lamentable delays occurred in the preparations to move from that place. It was not until September that the Virginia troops, under the command of Colonel Washington, were ordered from Cumberland, to join the British troops.

Here a warm discussion ensued between Washington and Bouquet, as to the route to be pursued. The former advocated Braddock's route; the latter a new route through Pennsylvania. In favor of Braddock's road, Washington urged the fact that it had already been opened to within ten miles of Fort Duquesne. The Virginians always believed that a Pennsylvania influence induced Forbes to prefer the other road.

Yet we, who know this country, the character of our climate and the habits of our rivers, can readily perceive that, although the southern route was preferable for an army landed in Virginia and advancing at mid summer; yet it might be very different with an army assembled in Pennsylvania and not expecting to reach Fort Duquesne until November. In June and July when Braddock crossed the Youghiogany and the Monongahela, those rivers were probably very low and easily fordable; while in November the waters would be high, gelid and impassable, except in boats, which would require much time for construction.

We have, also, lately seen a few sheets of an orderly book of Forbes' army, while at Ray's town, by which we learn that on the 19th of September, a Sergeant and twelve men were ordered to march as an escort of provisions for Fort Cumberland. The fact that provisions had to be sent from Pennsylvania, was, no doubt, very influential on the mind of Forbes against the Cumberland route.

On the 11th of September, while the main body of the army was still at Ray's town and an advanced corps near where Ligonier now stands; Major Grant was detached from the latter place towards Fort Duquesne. Of the result of this movement the following letter which we find in the Pennsylvania Gazette gives the fullest account we have any where seen:

"ANNAPOLIS, October 5th, 1758.

"We are informed by a letter from Frederick county, that on Monday, the 11th of September, Major Grant, of the Highland regiment, marched from our camp on the waters of the Kiskiminitas, with 37 officers and 805 privates, taken from the different regiments that compose the Western Army, on an expedition against Fort Duquesne.

"The third day after their march, they arrived within eleven miles of Fort Duquesne, and halted till three o'clock in the afternoon; then marched within two miles of Fort Duquesne, and left their baggage there, guarded by a captain, two subalterns, and fifty men, and marched with the rest of the troops, and arrived at eleven o'clock at night upon a hill, a quarter of a mile from the Fort. Major Grant sent two officers and fifty men to the Fort, to attack all the Indians, &c., they should find lying out of the Fort; they saw none, nor were they challenged by the centries. As they returned, they set fire to a large store house, which was put out as soon as they left it. At break of day, Major Lewis was sent with 400 men, (royal Americans and Virginians,) to lie in ambush a mile and a half from the main body, on the path on which they left their baggage, imagining the French would send to attack the baggage guard and seize it. Four hundred men were posted along the hill facing the Fort, to cover the retreat of Capt. M'Donald's company, who marched with drums beating toward the Fort, in order to draw a party out of the Fort, as Maj. Grant had some reason to believe there were not above 200 men in the Fort, including Indians; but as soon as they heard the drums, they sallied out in great numbers, both French and Indians, and fell upon Captain M'Donald, and two columns that were posted lower on the hill to receive them. The Highlanders exposed themselves without any cover, and were shot down in great numbers, and soon forced to retreat. The Carolinians, Marylanders, and Lower Countrymen, concealing themselves behind trees and the brush, made a good defence; but were overpowered by numbers, and not being supported, were obliged to follow the rest. Major Grant exposed himself in the thickest of the fire, and endeavored to rally his men, but all to no purpose, as they were by this time flanked on all sides. Maj. Lewis and his party came up and engaged, but were soon obliged to give way, the enemy having the hill of him, and flanking him every way. A number were drove into the Ohio, most of whom were drowned. Major Grant retreated to the baggage, where Captain Bullet was posted with fifty men, and again endeavored to rally the flying soldiers, by entreating them in the most pathetic manner to stand by him, but all in vain, as the enemy were close at their heels. As soon as the enemy came up to Capt. Bullet, he attacked them very furiously for some time, but not being supported, and most of his men killed, was obliged to give way. However, his attacking them stopped the pursuit, so as to give many an opportunity of escaping. The enemy followed Major Grant, and at last separated them, and Captain Bullet was obliged to make off. He imagines the major must be taken, as he was surrounded on all sides, but the enemy would not kill him, and often called to him to surrender. The French gave quarters to all that would accept it."

The following is a return of Forbes' Army on the 25th of September, just two months before the taking of this place:

Names of Corps.	Field Officers.	Co. Officers.	Total.	
Division of 1st Battalion of Royal Americans,	1	12	363	
Highland or 62d Regiment,	3	37	998	1267
Division of do.	3	12	269	
1st Virginia Regiment,	3	32	782	1484
2d do. do.	3	35	702	
3d North Carolina Companies,	1	10	141	
4th Maryland Companies	1	15	270	
1st Battallion Pennsylvania Troops,	3	41	755	2192
2d do.	3	40	666	
3d do.	3	46	771	
Three Lower Counties, now State of Delaware,	"	"	263	
Total,			5980	

Detachments on the frontiers of Pennsylvania and the road of communication:

	Major.	Captains.	Subalterns.	Total.
From the Penn'a Reg't,	1	10	17	563
" N. Carolina do.	1	3	61	624

On the 14th of October, the rear division of the army moved from Ray's town towards Loyal Hanna; and on the same day a letter was written at the latter place stating that the advanced party there, had been attacked on the 12th inst., by twelve hundred French and two hundred Indians, that the attack continued from 11 o'clock, A. M., until 3 o'clock, P. M., when the enemy retreated. The attack was renewed at night, but was speedily repulsed.

	Killed.	Wounded.	Missing.
The Highlanders had	1	0	0
" Virginians	4	6	0
" Pennsylvanians	5	5	17
" North Carolinians	0	0	3
" Marylanders	2	6	12
	12	17	31

On the 18th of November, General Forbes advanced with the rear division of the army, from Loyal Hanna, and on the 25th of November, 1758, took possession of the remains of Fort Duquesne.

John Ormsby, the father of the late Oliver Ormsby and Mrs. Sidney Gregg, was a Commissary in that army, and in a brief biography gives the following statement:

"When the army arrived at Turtle Creek, a council "of war was held, the result of which was, that it was "impracticable to proceed, all the provisions and for- "age being exhausted. On the General being told of "this he swore a furious oath, that he would sleep in "the Fort or a worse place the next night. It was a "matter of indifference," says Mr. Ormsby, "to the "emaciated General, where he died, as he was carried "the whole distance from Philadelphia and back, on a "litter. About midnight a tremendous explosion was "heard, from the westward, on which Forbes swore "that the French magazine was blown up by design or "accident, which revived our spirits. The above con- "jecture of the *head of iron*, was soon confirmed by a "deserter from Fort Duquesne, who said that the In-

"dians who had watched the English Army, reported "that they were as numerous as the trees in the woods. "This so terrified the French that they set fire to their "magazines, barracks, &c. and pushed off in their "boats, some up and some down the Ohio; so that the "next morning, we got peaceable possession of the "remains of the Fort. The place had a most desolate "appearance, as all the improvements made by the "French had been burnt to the ground. You may "judge our situation," says Mr. Ormsby, "when I "assure you, that we had neither flour, meat nor liquor "in store. The only relief offered was plenty of "venison and bear meat, which the hunters brought "in, and which our people devoured without bread or "salt. General Forbes was a brave soldier but afflict-"ed with a complication of disorders."

This point, which was the original bone of contention, thus again passed into the possession of the Anglo-Saxon race, and it became necessary to adopt measures to secure its possessions against an enemy, who were not prepared to abandon all hope of retaking it. It was then too late in the season to construct a formidable work here, and provisions were so scarce, that a large force could not be supported during the winter. The enemy and their savage allies, were still not very far distant, some being on Big Beaver and some on French Creek, eagerly watching movements here, and prepared to make another descent, in case a suitable opportunity presented itself. The army was, therefore, set to work to build a small military work on the bank of the Monongahela at the South end of West street, such as could well accommodate, and be safely garrisoned by, two hundred men. As soon as this was completed, Colonel Hugh Mercer, of Virginia, was placed in command of it, with two hundred men, and then the army marched back to the settlements. We know not when the army or General Forbes left this place, but he arrived in Philadelphia on the 17th of January, 1759, on which occasion guns were fired and bells rang. On the 11th of March, 1759, this resolute and indomitable soldier died in that city, and on the 14th his remains were interred in the chancel of Christ Church. Col. Hugh Mercer, who was left in command here, was a Scotchman by birth, a gallant soldier, who subsequently laid down his life at Princeton, in our struggle for independence. It is quite remarkable how prominent Scotchmen were in the early history of this country. Stobo was long confined in Fort Duquesne. Forbes drove the French from this place, and Mercer was the first officer in command in the first Fort Pitt. Sir Peter Halket and his son, with several other Scotchmen, fell at Braddock's field. While at Grant's defeat, four officers of the name of Mackenzie, three McDonalds, a Munro and a Campbell, all of the Highland Regiment, were killed, while Major Grant himself was wounded and taken prisoner, and one hundred and thirty one soldiers were killed or missing.

CHAPTER IV.

General Stanwix appointed in place of General Forbes. List of officers in Fort Pitt July 1759. Threatened attack on Fort Pitt; providential deliverance; notices of the building of the new and enlarged Fort Pitt; notice of that work and its cost; departure of General Stanwix; notice of his death. General Monckton arrives; movement of troops to Presqu isle. Peace in 1763 of short duration here. Pontiac, the great Ottawas chief, already arranging a combined attack upon the frontiers. War commenced; Le Bœuf, Venango, Presqu isle and various other Forts taken. Fort Pitt beseiged; Col. Henry Bouquet selected to relieve it. Troops assemble at Carlisle. Two days fighting with the Indians at Brushy run. Indians defeated. Fort Pitt relieved. Bouquet Redoubt built and the military plan of Pittsburgh made; Bouquet's expedition to the Muskingum.

We know not precisely when the First Fort Pitt was completed, but it was probably about the 1st of January, 1759; a letter from Colonel Mercer, dated 8th January, 1759, says: "This garrison now consists of two hundred and eighty men, and is capable of some defence, though huddled up in a very hasty manner, the weather being extremely severe.

A letter from General Amherst, dated March 15th, 1759, announces the death of General Forbes and the appointment of General JOHN STANWIX, as his successor.

The following is a list of the officers at this place on the 9th of July, 1759.

Colonel.—Hugh Mercer.

Captains.—Waggoner, Woodward, Prentice, Morgan, Smallman, Ward and Clayton.

Lieutenants.—Mathews, Hydler, Biddle, Conrod, Kennedy, Sumner, Anderson, Hutchins, Dangerfield, and Wright of the train.

Ensigns.—Crawford, Crawford and Morgan.

About this time Fort Pitt was threatened with a very formidable descent of French and Indians from Venango. Col. Mercer, in a letter dated July 17th, 1759, gives the following account of it. Two Indians of the Six Nations returned here on the 15th, from Venango, where they had gone to spy a few days previous. They found there about seven hundred Frenchmen and four hundred Indians. The commanding officer told them that he expected six hundred Indians more in a short time, and that as soon as they arrived, he would come and drive us from this place. Next day two hundred came and the succeeding day as many more, and on the third day they were all fitted off for the expedition by eleven o'clock at night. Three pieces of cannon were brought from Le Bœuf and others expected hourly, with a large number of batteaux loaded with provisions. In the morning of the 12th a grand council was held, in which the Commandant thanked the Indians for attending, threw down the belt and told them he would start next day. Soon after messengers arrived with a packet for the Commandant, at the contents of which the French officer appeared much concerned. At length he said to the Indians: "Chil-"dren, I have bad news, the English have gone against "Niagara. We must give over thoughts of going "down the river, till we have cleared that place of the "enemy. If it is taken our road to you is stopped "and you must become poor." Orders were immediately given to proceed with the provisions, artillery and troops up French creek, which the spies saw set off, and the Indians making up their bundles to follow. The spies think there were over one thousand Indians at Venango. So much for Col. Mercer's statement. We will complete the narrative of the providential means, by which this place was relieved from any further alarm from the French.

In this year, 1759, three expeditions were planned by General Amherst. The first under General Wolfe, against Quebec, the second under Amherst himself, against Ticonderoga and Crown Point, the third against Niagara under General Prideaux. It was the last whose influence was so timeously felt at Venango.

General Prideaux advanced towards Niagara, and landed near it on the 6th of July. He immediately invested it but was soon after killed, and the command then devolved on Sir William Johnson, who pressed the siege with great vigor. Having intelligence of the approach of the French and Indians from Venango, he made arrangements for their reception. On the 24th of July an action took place in which the French were defeated, D'Aubry, their Commandant, taken prisoner, and the next day Fort Niagara surrendered.

There is something so frank, and so full of *naivete*, in John Ormsby's account of this matter, that we cannot overlook it—

"Very few incidents occurred during the early part of the year 1759. Towards the close of it, however, fresh troubles commenced. The French in Canada began to raise an army at Niagara, to attack our small garrison (now called Fort Pitt,) which was in an ill state for defence, when our commandant, Col. Mercer, was informed by express that there were 1500 regulars and a strong body of Indians at Venango, making ready for an expedition against our post, which would attack us within three days.

"This information, you may be sure, struck a panic into our people, being 300 miles from any aid, and surrounded by the merciless savages, from whom no expectation of mercy was in view, but immediate destruction by the tomahawk, or lingering starvation.

"I must own I made my sincere application to the Almighty, to pardon my sins and extricate us from this deplorable dilemma. Our prayers were heard, and we extricated from the dreaded massacre; for day before the expected attack, an Indian fellow arrived from Niagara, informing Col. Mercer that General Johnson laid siege to Niagara, with a formidable English army, so that the attack upon Fort Pitt was countermanded, and the French and Indians ordered to return towards Niagara with the utmost haste. This was done, and when they arrived within a day's march of Niagara, the brave Irish General Johnson ordered an ambuscade to a difficult pass, through which the above troops were to march, and thus they were all killed or taken, to the great joy of poor Ormsby and his associates."

Niagara was then regarded as one of the most important military positions on this continent. Through it alone, could France supply the Indians on the upper Ohio and the Lakes. Well had the French commandant at Venango said: "If it (Niagara) is taken our road to you is cut off and you must become poor." While, therefore, the British held Niagara, there was but little reason to fear the French at Fort Pitt. Still, however, the British government resolved to erect here a formidable work, which would insure their dominion for all time. We cannot fix the precise date of the arrival here of General Stanwix, but it must have been after the 9th July, 1759, as on that day Colonel Mercer was the commandant; and we judge from the following letter that it must have been before the 1st September:

EXTRACT OF A LETTER FROM PITTSBURGH, SEPT. 24.

"It is now near a month since the army has been employed in erecting a most *formidable fortification;* such a one as will, *to latest posterity, secure the British empire on the Ohio.* There is no need to enumerate the abilities of the chief engineer, nor the spirit shown by the troops, in executing the important task; the fort will soon be a *lasting monument* of both. Upon the General's arrival, about 400 Indians, of different nations, came to confirm the peace with the English, particularly the Ottawas and Wyandotts, who inhabit about Fort Detroit; these confessed the errors they had been led into by the perfidy of the French; showed the deepest contrition for their past conduct, and promised not only to remain fast friends to the English, but to assist us in distressing the common enemy, whenever we should call on them to do it. And all the nations that have been at variance with the English, said they would deliver up what prisoners they had in their hands to the General, at a grand meeting that is to be held in about three weeks. As soon as the Congress was ended, the head of each nation presented the calumet of peace to the General, and showed every token of sincerity that could be expected, which their surrender of the prisoners will confirm. In this, *as in every thing that can preserve the lasting peace and happiness of these colonies, the General is indefatigable.*"

Smollet, in his history of England, also mentions that General Stanwix spent the winter of 1759 and 1760 at this place, strengthening it by fortifications, and cultivating peace and friendship with the Indians. He says: "The happy consequences of these measures were soon apparent in the production of a considerable trade between the natives and the merchants of Pittsburgh, and in the perfect security of about four thousand settlers, who now returned to the quiet possession of lands, from whence they had been driven by the enemy on the frontiers of Pennsylvania, Maryland and Virginia."

The work, erected by Gen. Stanwix, was five sided, though not all equal, as Washington erroneously stated in his journal in 1770. Washington also had the following remarks, "two (sides) of which near the land are of brick, the others stockade."

The earth around the proposed work was dug and thrown up so as to enclose the selected position with a rampart of earth. On the two sides facing the country, this rampart was supported by what military men call a *revetment*,—a brick work, nearly perpendicular, supporting the rampart on the outside, and thus presenting an obstacle to the enemy not easily overcome. On the other three sides, the earth in the rampart had no support, and, of course, it presented a more inclined surface to the enemy—one which could readily be ascended. To remedy, in some degree, this defect in the work, a line of pickets was fixed on the outside of the foot of the slope of the rampart. Around the whole work was a wide ditch which would, of course, be filled with water when the river was at a moderate stage.

In summer, however, when the river was low the ditch was dry and perfectly smooth, so that the officers and men had a ball-alley in the ditch, and against the revetments.

This ditch extended from the salient angle of the north bastion—that is the point of the fort which approached nearest to Marbury street, back of the South end of Hoke's row,—down to the Allegheny where Marbury street strikes it.

This part of the ditch was, during our boyhood, and even since, called Butler's Gut, from the circumstance of General Richard Butler and Col. Wm. Butler residing nearest to it,—their houses being the same which now stand at the corner on the south side of Penn and east side of Marbury. Another part of the ditch extended to the Monongahela, a little west of West street, and a third debouche into the river was made just about the end of Penn street.

The redoubt, which still remains near the point, the last relic of British labor at this place, was not erected until 1764. The other redoubt, which stood at the mouth of Redoubt Alley, was erected by Col. Wm. Grant; and our recollection is, that the year mentioned on the stone tablet was 1765, but we are not positive on that point.

Judge Brackenridge, in a communication in the first number of the Pittsburgh Gazette, on the 29th of July, 1786, stated that this Fort cost the British Government *sixty thousand pounds sterling.*

We have been enabled to gather a few more scraps in relation to transactions here in 1759 and 1760, and insert them as we find them.

"FORT AT PITTSBURGH, March 21st, 1760.

"This day Major General Stanwix set out for Philadelphia, escorted by thirty-five chiefs of the Ohio Indians and fifty of the Royal Americans. The presence of the General has been of the utmost consequence at this post during the winter, as well as for cultivating the friendship and alliance of the Indians, as for continuing the fortifications and supplying the troops here and on the communications. The works are now quite perfected, according to the plan, from the Ohio to the Monongahela, and eighteen pieces of artillery mounted on the bastions that cover the isthmus; and casemates, barracks and storehouses are also completed for a garrison of 1000 men and officers, so that it may now be asserted with very great truth, that the British dominion is established on the Ohio. The Indians are carrying on a vast trade with the merchants of Pittsburgh, and instead of desolating the frontiers of these colonies, are entirely employed in increasing the trade and wealth thereof. The happy effects of our military operations are also felt by about *four thousand* of our poor inhabitants, who are now in quiet possession of the lands they were driven from on the frontiers of Pennsylvania, Maryland and Virginia."

"On Saturday last his Excellency General Stanwix arrived in town, (Philadelphia,) accompanied by a number of gentlemen of the army."—*Pennsylvania Gazette, April 17th*, 1760.

When General Stanwix left Fort Pitt there were present as a garrison, 150 Virginians, 150 Pennsylvanians and 400 of the 1st battallion of Royal Americans, all commanded by Major Tulikens.

We know but little more about this General, who seems to have been highly esteemed and respected.

A London paper of July 29th, 1760, says: "Thursday last Major General Stanwix arrived from America, waited on his Majesty, and was most graciously received."

The following article, which we find in the Seventh Volume of Hazard's Pennsylvania Register, is the last notice of him which we have seen:

"PHILADELPHIA, 2d January, 1767.

"*Shipwreck.*—It is with much regret that we announce the loss of the Eagle, on board of which was General Stanwix, his lady and only daughter, a relative and four servants, who all untimely perished."*

EXTRACT OF A LETTER DATED PITTSBURGH, JULY 4TH, 1760.

"General Monckton arrived here the 29th ult., and immediately gave orders for the march of a large detachment of the army to Presqu'ile, (now Erie.) The troops are to march on Monday."

"PHILADELPHIA, July 24th, 1760.

"On the 7th instant, four companies of the Royal Americans, under command of Col. Bouquet, marched from Pittsburgh towards Presqu'ile, as did also Captain McNeil's company of the Virginia Regiment. On the Wednesday following, Col. Hugh Mercer, with three

* From a law book, Fearne's Posthumous works, we learn, that the vessel was bound from Ireland to England; also, that the lady of Stanwix was a step-mother of the daughter. Litigation took place between those who would have been the heirs of the General, of his daughter and of his wife. The question turned upon the presumption of which was the last survivor. Ingenious arguments were presented on each side, and the Court found the matter so difficult, that it recommended a compromise, which was adopted.

companies of the Pennsylvania Regiment, under Captains Biddle, Clapham and Anderson, and two days after two other companies of the same Regiment, under Captains Atlee and Miles, were to follow."

"PHILADELPHIA, July 31st, 1760.

"From Pittsburgh, we learn that Major Gladwin had arrived at Presqu'ile with 400 men from the northward, and that our troops from Pittsburgh would be at the same place by the 15th of this month."

These movements were all made for the purpose of taking possession of Detroit and Mackina, which had been surrendered along with Montreal on the 8th September, 1759.

The completion of Fort Pitt, in the spring of 1760, preceded as it had been by the surrender of Montreal, and with it the whole of Canada, held out a promise of permanent peace in the interior of this country. The promise, however, proved delusive. The preliminaries of a treaty of peace between France, Spain, and Great Britain were signed and interchanged on the 3d of November, 1762, and the definitive treaty on the 10th of February, 1763, and it is highly probable that at that very time *Pontiac*, the great chief of the Ottawa Indians, was arranging that grand confederacy of Indian tribes, which scattered death and desolation along the frontier from Niagara and Fort Pitt to Mackina.

We have but glimpses at Fort Pitt from the summer of 1760 until 1763. In August 1760 Gen. Monckton held a treaty here with the Six Nations, and Shawanese, and Delawares, at which he delivered to them a speech from Sir Jeffrey Amherst, commander-in-chief of his majesty's forces in North America, in which it was stated that the King did not intend to deprive them of any of their lands, except as necessity obliged him to take posts and build forts in some parts of the country, *to prevent the enemy from taking possession of their lands.* He also added that he would give them some presents, as a consideration for the lands where the forts and trading houses should be built. He also said to them that if they would lay off a space of land adjoining each fort, to raise corn, they might fix the limits and should receive such consideration, as should be agreed between them, *to their satisfaction.*

A Philadelphia paper of November 5th, 1760, says: "Last night the honorable General Monckton arrived "here from Pittsburgh."

In the same paper of December 11th, 1760, it is stated: "On Monday last, the honorable Sir John St. "Clair, Deputy Q. M. General of his Majesty's forces, "arrived from Pittsburgh with several other gentlemen. "All well there."

In the latter part of the spring of 1763, broke out that famous Indian war usually known as *Pontiac's* war, though sometimes called *Guyasutha's* war, after a distinguished Seneca Indian, well known in this quarter.

In this war the Shawanese, Delawares and other Ohio Indians took a leading part. Their plan seems to have been well arranged. All the out posts were attacked about the same time, and the following soon fell into the hands of these ruthless foes. Le Bœuf, Venango and Presqu'ile, on and near Lake Erie; La Bay, upon Lake Michigan; St. Joseph's upon the river of that name; Miamis on the Miami river; Ouachtanon, Sandusky and Mackina. Only Fort Pitt, Detroit and Niagara escaped. The latter, owing to its great strength, was not attacked. Major Gladwin, who commanded at Detroit, distinguished himself greatly by his conduct and firmness.

Fort Pitt was very vigorously assailed. The Indians had at an early period surrounded it and cut off all communication. Though they had no cannon, yet with great boldness they posted themselves under the banks of both rivers, and harassed the garrison incessantly with musquetry and fire arrows, hoping, at length, by famine, by fire or fatigue, to overcome the garrison.

Captain Ecuyer, of the Royal American regiment, who commanded, though he wanted several things necessary to sustain a siege and though the defences had been injured by a recent flood in the river, took all precautions which art and judgment could suggest for the defence of the fort. The garrison aided by the inhabitants and the surviving traders who had taken refuge there, seconded his efforts. But still the situation of the fort was alarming. No relief could be sent, except after a march of nearly two hundred miles beyond the settlements.

Colonel Henry Bouquet, a Swiss by birth, who had seen much service in Europe, and who had acted a prominent part under General Forbes, in taking Fort Duquesne, was selected to command the force intended to relieve Capt. Ecuyer. The troops were assembled at Carlisle; on the 28th of July, 1763, they left Fort Bedford, and on the 5th of August they had arrived near Bushy run, about twenty-two miles east of Pittsburgh. Having marched seventeen miles that day and being much fatigued, they were about to encamp, when they were suddenly attacked by the Indians, the attack was, however, repulsed; but the moment pursuit terminated, the attack was renewed. Night, at length, separated the combatants. Next day the action was recommenced, when Col. Bouquet, by a very skilful movement, succeeded in giving the Indians an effective repulse. About fifty of Bouquet's detachment were killed, and sixty wounded, and forty Indians, including several chiefs, were killed.

The Indians being thus foiled in all their plans, abandoned the siege of Fort Pitt and dispersed. Col. Bouquet had not a sufficient force to pursue the enemy beyond the Ohio, and was compelled to delay further action until some future time; he, therefore, after supplying Fort Pitt and other posts with sufficient provisions, &c. dispersed his troops to the best advantage for quartering through the winter. In the mean time he was busily engaged in making the necessary preparations for a campaign against the Delawares, Shawanese, Mohickons, and other Indians. The 42d and 60th regiments were ordered on that service. The Virginians were to raise one regiment, the Pennsylvanians another, and two hundred friendly Indians were to join. The Pennsylvanians alone complied in part with their engagements; the others failed entirely. Arrangements advanced slowly, and it was not until the 5th of August, 1764, that the troops assembled at Carlisle, and not until the 17th of September did they arrive at Fort Pitt.

In this summer of 1764, was erected here, the sole existing monument of British dominion; the Redout, now standing between Penn street and Duquesne Way, with the inscription on a stone tablet in the wall, of the words: "*Col. Bouquet, A. D.*, 1764."

In this same year, also, Col. John Campbell laid out that part of the city of Pittsburgh which lies between Water and Second streets, and between Ferry and Market streets, being four squares. We have never been able to learn what authority Campbell had to act in this case. But when the Penns afterwards authorised the laying out the town of Pittsburgh, their agent recognized Campbell's act, at least, so far as not change his plan of lots. We know not precisely at what time of the year Col. Bouquet's redout was built, nor when Campbell's lots were laid out; but certainly the last step in perfecting this place as a military post and the first step in building up a town here, were taken in the same year.

Col. Bouquet having completed his arrangements as well for the security of this place, as for the proper supply of his army, commenced his march against the Indian towns on the Muskingum, by crossing the Allegheny river on the 3d of October, and pursuing his course along the banks of the Ohio, through Log's town, and by the mouth of Big Beaver, to near the forks of the Muskingum. Here six Indians came to inform the Colonel that all their chiefs were assembled about eight miles from his camp and were ready to treat for peace. On the 17th of October, their conference began. The Indians present were Senecas, Delawares and Shawanese. The proceedings come not within the purview of our task, we shall, therefore, merely state that the Indians agreed to deliver up all the prisoners in their hands and that by the 9th of November two hundred and six persons, males, females and children were delivered up. Many of these were reluctant to leave their Indian friends; but everything being at length arranged, the army decamped on the 19th of November, and arrived at Fort Pitt on the 28th of that month. Peace now prevailed throughout the country.

CHAPTER V.

Rev. Charles Beatty at Pittsburgh, kindly treated by the Commandant, and all the officers; ascends Coal Hill, his account of the fire in the hill; curious legislation and barbarous proclamation; encroachments of the whites along the Youghiogany and Monongahela; complaints of the Indians; efforts of the authorities, British and colonial, to stop the encroachments; conference at Pittsburgh with the Delawares, Shawanese, Munsies and Mohiccans; Congress at Fort Stanwix: present Sir Wm. Johnson, Commissioners from New Jersey, Pennsylvania and Virginia, and chiefs of each of the Six Nations and of the Shawanese and Delawares; several cessions made; terms of cession to the Penns; measures taken by the Penns for the sale of the newly purchased lands; bounds of the new cession included Pittsburgh. Manor of Pittsburgh surveyed; boundaries of the Manor; question for speculation. Washington's third visit here; extract from his journal. Population of Pittsburgh in 1770; orders for the abandonment of Fort Pitt; reflections.

In the summer of 1766, the Reverend Charles Beatty, the grand-father of the Rev. C. C. Beatty, of Steubenville, was appointed by the Synod of New York and Philadelphia, to visit the frontier inhabitants, in order that a better judgment might be formed, what assistance might be necessary to afford them, in their present low circumstances, in order to promote the gospel among them, and also to visit the Indians, in case it could be done safely. On Friday the 5th September, late in the evening he arrived at Fort Pitt. He immediately waited on Capt. Murray, the commandant, who received him and his companion, Mr. Duffield, politely, and introduced them to the Rev. Mr. McLagan, the chaplain to the 42d regiment. The officers were all very kind to them, invited them to their tables, gave them a room in the fort, and supplied them with bedding, so that they were as comfortable as could be expected. On Sabbath, 7th September, Mr. McLagan invited him to preach in the garrison, which he did; while Mr. Duffield preached to the people who live in *some kind of a town, without the fort,* to whom Mr. Beatty also preached in the afternoon.

We infer from the expression "some kind of a town," that Pittsburgh must have been a poor affair indeed.

The following is a note to Mr. Beatty's journal of Monday, September 8th:

"In the afternoon we crossed the *Mocconghehela* "river, accompanied by two gentlemen, and went up "the hill opposite the fort, by a very difficult ascent, "in order to take a view of that part of it more parti-"cularly from which the garrison is supplied with coals, "which is not far from the top. A fire being made by "the workmen not far from the place where they dug "the coal, and left burning when they went away, by "the small dust communicated itself to the body of "the coals and set it on fire, and has nowbeen burn-"ing almost a twelve month entirely under ground, "for the space of twenty yards or more along the face "of the hill or rock, the way the vein of coal extends, "the smoke ascending up through the chinks of the "rocks. The earth in some places is so warm, that "we could hardly bear to stand upon it; at one "place where the smoke came up we opened a hole in "the earth till it was so hot as to burn paper thrown "into it; the steam that came out was so strong of "sulphur that we could scarce bear it. We found "pieces of matter there, some of which appeared to "be sulphur, others nitre, and some a mixture of both. "If these strata be large in this mountain it may be-"come a volcano. The smoke arising out of this "mountain appears to be much greater in rainy wea-"ther than at other times. The fire has already "undermined some part of the mountain, so that great "fragments of it, and trees with their roots are fallen "down its face. On the top of the mountain is a very "rich soil covered with a fine verdure, and has a very "easy slope on the other side, so that it may be easily "cultivated."

This is the first and only evidence, we have ever seen, confirmatory of a tradition, that coal hill was once on fire; we presume, however, that the combustion could never have extended very far.

Messrs. Beatty and Duffield were the first Presbyterian ministers, so far as we have any testimony, who ever preached at the head of the Ohio.

The following items in the history of our State, though not immediately connected with our subject, are introduced as interesting evidences of an improved state of public opinion and of increasing civilization, and when regarded in connection with the abolition of slavery here, are quiet encouraging.

In 1763, acts were passed by the Legislature of this

State granting *lotteries* to aid the following churches: the Episcopal churches at York, Reading and Carlisle, St. Peter's and St. Paul's in Philadelphia, St. Paul's at Chester, St. John's in Concord township, Chester county, St. Martin's at Marcus Hook; also to aid a Lutheran church and a Presbyterian meeting house in Lancaster county.

In 1764, Governor John Penn, by proclamation proposed the following rewards for the scalps or capture of Indians. For every male above ten years captured, $150, or for his scalp being killed $134. For every female, or male under ten years old captured $130, or for the scalp of such female killed $50.

Immediately after the conclusion of the peace of 1763, the white men commenced encroaching on the lands west of the mountains, and along the Youghiogany and Monongahela rivers. The Indians complained about these encroachments. The British government and the government of this State labored to check these invasions of Indian territory. The history of this section of the country from 1764, down to 1774, presents but little of general interest. To continue the connection it is necessary we should give a brief notice of the spirit of encroachment on the part of the whites, of the complaints of the Indians and of the exertions of the various authorities to prevent these encroachments, and to allay these complaints.

EXTRACT FROM MR. CROGHAN'S JOURNAL, DATED FORT PITT, MAY 22, 1766.

"Major Murray informed me that there were several chiefs of the Shawanese, Delaware, Six Nations and

Hurons from Sandusky, with a considerable number of warriors, who had waited a long time to see me.

"24th of May. I had a meeting with the Six Nations, Delawares and Huron chiefs, when they made great complaints about several of their people being murdered on the frontiers of the several provinces. Say they have lost five men on the frontiers of Virginia, one near Bedford in Pennsylvania, and one in the Jerseys. This conduct of their *Fathers*, they say, does not look as if they were disposed to live in peace with their children, the Indians. Besides that, as soon as peace was made last year, contrary to our engagements, a number of our people came over the great mountain and settled at Redstone Creek, and on the Monongahela, before they had given the country to the King their father."

At an early period of 1764, instructions from the king of Great Britain were sent to John Penn, which recited that several persons from Pennsylvania and the back parts of Virginia, had migrated west of the Allegheny Mountains, and seated themselves on lands near the Ohio in express disobedience of the proclamation of the 7th of October, 1763, and therefore enjoined upon the Governor to use all means in his power to prevent such encroachments, and to cause those to remove who had seated themselves on those lands.

A letter from General Gage, the commander-in-chief of the British forces in America, dated July 2d, 1766, assures Governor John Penn, that if he will take proper steps, "as I presume Redstone is within your government, the garrison at Fort Pitt shall assist to drive away the settlers, and it seems proper that a number of the chiefs should be present to see our desire to do them justice."

A letter from Governor Penn to Governor Fauquier of Virginia, dated 23d of September 1766, asks his aid for the removal of the settlers, states that as the boundary line between the two States had not been settled, such settlers might take shelter under an unsettled jurisdiction.

Reply of Governor Fauquier, dated Williamsburg, December 11, 1766, states that the commander-in-chief had taken "more effectual measures, by giving orders to an officer and party to summon the settlers to remove, and in case of refusal to threaten military execution."

Letter from John Penn to Earl Shelbourne, January 21st, 1767, recites what had been done by himself, by Governor Fauquier, and by General Gage, and says, "I am at a loss to know what more can be done by the civil power."

Letter from General Gage, dated New York, December 7, 1767, says: "You are a witness how little attention has been paid to the proclamations that have been published, and that even the removing these people from the lands last summer by the garrison of Fort Pitt, had been only a temporary expedient; as they met with no punishment, we learn they are returned again to Redstone Creek and Cheat river. Recommends that more effective laws should be passed."

On the 3d of February, 1768, an act was passed inflicting death without benefit of clergy upon any person settled upon lands *not* purchased of the Indians, who shall refuse after — day's notice to quite the same, or having removed, shall return to the same or other unpurchased lands; Provided, however, that this law shall not extend to persons who now are, or may hereafter be, settled on the main communications leading to Fort Pitt, under the permission of the commander-in-chief, or to a settlement made by Geo. Croghan, Esq., Deputy Superintendant under Sir William Johnson, upon the Ohio above said fort.

24th February, 1768. Proclamation issued in pursuance of the above act, 250 copies printed, and J. Burd, John Steel, J. Allison, Chr. Lemer, and Capt. James Potter of Cumberland, requested to go to the Monongahela, Youghiogany and other places west of the Allegheny, where such forbidden settlement were made, to set up proclamations, to explain them to the people, and to endeavor to induce them to remove.

In April and May 1768, a conference was held at this place with the Six Nations, the Delawares, Shawanese, Munsies and Mohickons. Total number of Indians present, eleven hundred and three, besides women and children. They, no doubt, created quite a bustle in the little village, which our city must have been at that time. The Indians complained of the encroachments on their lands along the Youghiogany and Monongahela. But nothing more effectual was done than we have before stated, the passing of severe laws and the removal of those who encroached, by the troops from Fort Pitt. Those who were removed by force returned again as soon as the troops were withdrawn. Up to this time the Indian title to the country east of the Allegheny river had not been extinguished.

On the 24th of October, 1768, a Congress was held at Fort Stanwix, New York, present, Sir William Johnson, Superintendant of Indian affairs, the Governor of New Jersey, a Commissioner from Virginia, and Richard Peters and James Tilghman of Pennsylvania, also chiefs from each of the Six Nations of Indians, and from the Shawnese and Delawares.

Sir William Johnson, in his opening address, stated that Lieut. Governor of Pennsylvania had been there several days waiting, but that business called him away.

Several cessions of land were made by the Indians, but we confine ourselves to the one to the Penns, as follows:

"We, *Tyanhasare*, or *Abraham*, sachem or chief of the Indian nation called Mohocks; *Senaghsis*—of the Oneydas; *Chenughiata*—of the Onondagoes; *Gaustrax*—of the Senecas; *Sequarisera*—of the Tuscaroras; *Tagaaia*—of the Cayugas, in general council of the Six Nations at Fort Stanwix, assembled for the purpose of settling a general boundary line between the said Six Nations, and their confederates and independent tribes, and his majesty's middle colonies, send greeting, &c. In consideration of ten thousand dollars, they grant to Thomas Penn and Richard Penn, all that part of the province of Pennsylvania, not heretofore purchased of the Indians, within the said general boundary line, and beginning the said boundary line, on the east side of the east branch of the river Susquehannah, at a place called *Owegy*, and running with the said boundary line, down the said branch on the east side thereof till it comes opposite the mouth of a creek called by the Indians *Awandac*, (*Tawandee*) and across the river and up the said creek on the south side thereof, along the range of hills called *Burnett's* hills by the English, and by the Indians , on the north side of them, to the heads of a creek which runs into the west branch of Susquehannah, which creek is by the Indians called *Tiadaghton*, and down the said creek on the south side thereof, to the said west branch of Susquehannah, then crossing the said river, and running up the same on the south side thereof, the several courses thereof to the fork of the same river which lies nearest to a place on the river Ohio, called the *Kittanning*, and from the said fork by a straight line to Kittanning aforesaid, and then down the said river Ohio by the several courses thereof to where the western bounds of the said province of Pennsylvania crosses the same river, and then with the said western bounds to the south boundary thereof, and with the south boundary aforesaid to the east side of the Allegheny hills, and with the said hills on the east side of them to the west line of a tract of land purchased by the said proprietors from the Six Nation Indians, and confirmed October 23d, 1758, and then with the northern bounds of that tract to the river Susquehannah to the northern boundary line of another tract of land purchased of the Indians by deed, (August 22d, 1749,) and then with that northern boundary line to the river Delaware at the north side of the mouth of a creek called Lechawachsein, then up the said river Delaware on the west side thereof to the intersection of it, by an east line to be drawn from Owegy aforesaid to the said river Delaware, and then with that line to the beginning at Owegy aforesaid."

Some doubts arose as to what stream it was that was called *Tiadaghton*, and what hills were meant by "Burnett's Hills." At a subsequent treaty held in 1784, questions on these points were put to the Indians, and they replied that the creek was Pine Creek, which enters the west branch of the Susquehannah above Jersey Shore, and that Burnett's Hills were by them called the Long Mountains.

It is a singular circumstance of history of this treaty, that although Virginia claimed a very considerable portion of the territory ceded to the Penns; yet her commissioner Thomas Walker, Esq., was present, saw the money paid to the Indians, and their chiefs executing a deed for a territory which embraced Pittsburgh, the very bone of contention, between those colonies, and yet made no objection, so far as we can learn.

The title being thus acquired, measures were immediately taken to prepare the new purchased lands for sale. On the 23d of February, 1769, an advertisement was published for general information that the Land Office would be opened on the third day of the ensuing April, at 10 o'clock, A. M. to receive applications from all persons inclined to take up lands in the new purchase upon the terms of five pounds sterling per hundred acres, and one penny per acre, per annum, quit rent. This quit rent was afterwards abolished by the act, vesting in the Commonwealth the title of the Penns, commonly called the Divesting act, passed on the 27th of November, 1779. In Washington county, and in that portion of Allegheny, west of the Monongahela river, many settlements were also made under Virginia titles, so that there was a rapid increase of the population from 1770 until 1775. Much of the very best land in that quarter is held by titles based on Virginia entries; which by the Compromise of 1779 are recognized as equally good as a Pennsylvania warrants. A large portion of the lands along Chartier's Creek is thus held by entries made between 1769 and 1779. The place spoken of in the deed as the fork nearest to the Kittanning is now the north west corner of Cambria county.

This cession of 1768 gave to the Penns all the territory in Pennsylvania, south of the west branch of the Susquehannah and of a straight line from the north west corner of Cambria county to Kittanning, and all the territory east of that part of the Allegheny river below Kittanning, and all the country south of the Ohio. So that Pittsburgh and the country eastward of it was ceded while the country west of the Allegheny and north of Ohio was still *Indian* country, and preserved that name until within the memory of the writer.

While the proprietaries prepared to sell the other lands within their recent purchases; they also made provision to reserve certain favorite portions as their own private property. The country around Fort Pitt was regarded as being very favorably located, it was, therefore, determined to withdraw it from market and reserve it to the private use of the proprietaries.

On the 5th day of January, 1769, a warrant issued for the survey of the "Manor of Pittsburgh." On the 27th of March the survey was completed and returned the 19th of May, 1769. It embraced within its bounds five thousand seven hundred and sixty-six acres, and allowance of six per cent. for roads, &c. The survey began at a spanish oak on the south bank of the Monongahela, thence south 800 perches to a hickory, thence west 150 perches to a white oak, thence north 35 degrees west 144 perches to a white oak, thence west 518 perches to a white oak, thence north 758 perches to a post, thence east 60 perches to a post, thence north 14 degrees east 208 perches to a white walnut on the bank of the Ohio, thence up the river 202 perches to a white walnut, thence crossing the river obliquely and up the south side of the Allegheny 762 perches to a spanish oak, the corner of Croghan's claim, thence south 60 degrees east 249 perches to a sugar tree, south 85 degrees east 192 perches to a sugar tree, thence by vacant land south 18 degrees east 236 perches to a white oak, thence south 40 degrees west 150 perches to a white oak, thence west by claim of Samuel Sample 192 perches to a hickory, thence south 65 degrees west 74 perches to a red oak, on the bank of the Monongahela, thence obliquely across the river, south 78 degrees west 308 perches to the beginning, at the spanish oak.

As these hickories, white oaks, sugar trees, and spanish oaks have nearly all disappeared, and even if still standing, would not be readily recognized, we have procured a more modern and intelligible account of this survey.

The spanish oak, the place of beginning, stood near the south bank of the Monongahela river, just in the middle of McKee street. The manor line is there the eastern line of the Gregg property. The hickory corner, south from the spanish oak, stood not far from the Buck tavern on the Brownsville road. The white walnut on the Ohio, stood a short distance above the Saw-mill run, where the Washington and Steubenville roads unite. The white walnut from which the line starts across the river, stood near the old glass house, erected by James O'Hara and Isaac Craig, and now owned by Frederick Lorenz. The spanish oak, on the Allegheny river, stood near the line between Croghan's-ville and Springfield farm. From that point the manor line passes along the western side of the Springfield farm, crosses the Fourth street road five or six hundred yards east of the Colony, makes a corner near Mrs. Murray's tavern and strikes the Monongahela three or four hundred feet above the mouth of the Two Mile run.

Curious questions for speculation are presented by this matter of the "Manor of Pittsburgh." By surveying it off and separating it from the country around, the proprietary manifested his determination to reserve it from sale and hold it as private property while the land in the vicinity was offered for sale. The occurrence of our revolution and the conduct of the proprietary rendered it necessary for the Commonwealth to pass the act divesting the proprietary of all interest, in the territory without the various manors, but leaving his title in the manors undisturbed. This action of the Legislature, no doubt, induced the proprietaries, John Penn, jr. and John Penn, to divide and sell the manor at an earlier day than they would have done, had they retained all the land in the State which was unsold. Now the questions: what would have been the population of the country around and its condition had the proprietaries continued to hold it as private property? Could such a monopoly be tolerated here? and how long?

In October 1770, George Washington arrived here on his way to the Kenhawa. We permit him to speak for himself as to what he saw here, by an extract from his journal:

"October 17th.—Dr. Craik and myself, with Capt. Crawford and others, arrived at Fort Pitt, distant from the crossing forty-three and a half measured miles. In riding this distance we passed over a great deal of exceedingly fine land, chiefly white oak, especially from Sewickley creek to Turtle creek, but the whole broken; resembling, as I think the whole lands in this country do, the Loudoun lands. We lodged in what is called the town, distant about three hundred yards from the fort, at one Semple's,* who keeps a very good house of public entertainment. The houses, which are built of logs, and ranged in streets, are on the Monongahela, and I suppose may be about twenty in number, and inhabited by Indian traders. The fort is built on the point between the rivers Allegheny and Monongahela, but not so near the pitch of it as Fort Duquesne stood. It is five sided and regular, two of which near the land are of brick; the others stockade. A moat encompasses it. The garrison consists of two companies of Royal Irish, commanded by Captain Edmondson.

"18th.—Dined in the fort with Colonel Croghan and the officers of the garrison; supped there also, meeting with great civility from the gentlemen, and engaged to dine with Colonel Croghan the next day at his seat, about four miles up the Allegheny.†

* This was the house of Samuel Semple, situated at the corner of Water and Ferry streets, where the Virginia House now stands. It was a two story, double hewn log house. We have been informed that it was built by Colonel George Morgan about 1764, and was the first shingle roofed house in Pittsburgh. The half of the lower story next to Ferry street was divided into two rooms, while the portion to the right of the hall entering from Water street was all in one room, and in it stood the first billiard table we ever saw. No doubt the officers of the two Royal Irish companies, and gentlemen residing and visiting here, spent many a pleasant hour in Mr. Semple's "very good house of public entertainment."

† Colonel Croghan's seat was, according to our recollection, on the east side of the Allegheny river, nearly opposite to where Mr. McCandless is now residing. To be more precise, it was on the lot which is on our right when we first reach the Allegheny, when going from Lawrenceville up towards Sharpsburgh.

"19th.—Received a message from Colonel Croghan, that the White Mingo and other chiefs of the Six Nations had something to say to me, and desiring that I would be at his house about eleven, where they were to meet me. I went up and received a speech, with a string of wampum, from the White Mingo,* to the following effect:

"'That as I was a person whom some of them remember to have seen when I was sent on an embassy to the French, and most of them had heard of, they were come to bid me welcome to this country, and desire that the people of Virginia would consider them as friends and brothers, linked together in one chain; that I would inform the governor that it was their wish to live in peace and harmony with the white people, and that though there had been some unhappy differences between them and the people on our frontiers, they were all made up, and they hoped forgotten; and concluded with saying that their brothers of Virginia did not come among them and trade as the inhabitants of other provinces did, from whence they were afraid that we did not look upon them with so friendly an eye as they could wish.'

"To this I answered, after thanking them for their friendly welcome, 'that all the injuries and affronts that had passed on either side, were now totally forgotten, and that I was sure nothing was more wished and desired by the people of Virginia, than to live in

* *White Mingo* was a chief of the Six Nations, of the Senecas. He was present at the conference held here in April and May 1768. In a draft of a survey of thirteen hundred and fifty-two acres and allowance, made for George Croghan, on 27th of June 1769, White Mingo's castle is laid down on the west side of the Allegheny river, nearly two miles above Wainwright's Island.

the strictest friendship with them; that the Virginians were a people not so much engaged in trade as the Pennsylvanians, which was the reason of their not being so much among them, but that it was possible they might for the time to come have stricter connexions with them, and that I would acquaint the government with their desires.'

"After we dined at Colonel Croghan's we returned to Pittsburgh, Colonel Croghan with us, who intended to accompany us part of the way down the river, having engaged an Indian called the Pheasant, and one Joseph Nicholson, an interpreter, to attend us the whole voyage, also a young Indian warrior.

"20th.—We embarked in a large canoe, with sufficient store of provisions and necessaries, and the following persons besides Dr. Craik and myself, to wit, Captain Crawford, Joseph Nicholson, Robert Bell, William Harrison, Charles Morgan and Daniel Rendon, a boy of Captain Crawford's, and the Indians, who were in a canoe by themselves. From Fort Pitt we sent our horses and boys back to Captain Crawford's, with orders to meet us there again on the 14th day of November. Colonel Croghan, Lieutenant Hamilton and Magee set out with us. At two we dined at Mr. Magee's,* and encamped ten miles below, and four above Logstown. We passed several large islands which appeared to be very good, as the bottoms also did on each side of the river alternately; the hills on one side being opposite to the bottoms on the other,

* This name is, no doubt, misspelt. The person meant was certainly Alexander McKee. James McKee, a man of scrupulous veracity, has often mentioned to us the visit of Washington to his brother. He resided a short distance from the mouth of Chartier's Creek.

which seem generally to be about three or four hundred yards wide, and so *vice versa*.

It happens singularly enough, that the very first description of the point on which Pittsburgh stands was from the pen of Washington, and the very first statement, which exists, of the number of houses here, is from the same pen. He estimates the number of houses at this place, out of the fort, of course, at about twenty. We have, no doubt, that the number, was more likely to be under than over his estimate. But suppose there were twenty and that there were six persons to a house; Pittsburgh then contained exclusive of the garrison one hundred and twenty persons, men, women and children.

In October, 1772, orders were received by Major Edmondson, the commanding officer here, from Gen. Gage, the commander-in-chief of the British forces in North America, to abandon Fort Pitt. In carrying out this order Major Edmonson sold the pickets, stones, bricks, timber and iron, in the walls and buildings of the fort and redoubts, for the sum of fifty pounds, New York currency. Fort Pitt was then abandoned and a corporal and three men were left, to take care of the boats and batteaux intended to keep up the communication with the Illinois country.

Thus it appears, that Fort Pitt, which had cost the Government about £60,000 sterling, and which was designed to secure forever British empire on the Ohio, was within thirteen years ordered to be abandoned. Such is the short sightedness of our wisest statesmen that even William Pitt could not foresee, the early abandonment of the formidable work which bore his name.

The fort was not destroyed, though abandoned as a military post by the British Government. During the ensuing year it was re-occupied and repaired by Dr. John Connelly, under orders from Lord Dunmore, Governor of Virginia, and during our revolutionary war, it was constantly occupied first by Virginia troops, under Captain John Neville, and subsequently by Continental troops under General Hand, Colonel Broadhead and General Wm. Irvine.

CHAPTER VI.

The year 1774 one of much movement here; controversy between Pennsylvania and Virginia about their boundary line; meetings here and at Hanna's town in favor of resistance to British encroachments; conference here with Guyasutha and other Indian chiefs 6th of July, 1776; character of Guyasutha, services, his speech, John Neville's reply, his rejoinder.

The year 1774 was a time of excitement and movement here. In that year, for the last time citizens of these States engaged in war with the Indians as subjects of Great Britain, and under the command of British officers. In that year Lord Dunmore passed through this place on his way down the Ohio, to co-operate with General Lewis, of Virginia, in an attack upon the Ohio Indians. In that year the massacre of Logan's family took place at Baker's Bottom, and in the same year the eloquent speech, commonly known as Logan's speech, was delivered to Lord Dunmore by Colonel John Gibson, at the camp near to Chilicothe.

About the same time the controversy between Pennsylvania and Virginia, about their boundary line, which commenced as early as 1752, seemed to have come to maturity and was on the very verge of gliding into civil war. Virginia relied upon a charter granted by James the First, which was broad enough in its term to cover nearly one half this continent, and this liberal grant they relied upon, although the Company to which it was made had been dissolved by a judgment on a writ of *Quo Warranto*, and although the lands had reverted to the crown.

Pennsylvania, or rather the Penns claimed under a charter from Charles 2nd, in 1681, which assigns the Delaware river as the eastern boundary and then says, "*said lands to extend westward five degrees in longitude, to be computed from the said eastern bounds.*"

Under this charter the Penns contended that Pennsylvania extended several miles west of Fort Pitt; while on the other hand it was contended that Virginia embraced not only this place but all the country east of us to the Laurel Hill.

Early in 1774, Dr. John Connolly, a Pennsylvanian, by birth, but a partisan and friend of Lord Dunmore, came here from Virginia, with authority from that nobleman, took possession of the Fort, calling it *Fort Dunmore*, and issued his proclamation calling the militia together on the 25th January, 1774; for so doing, *Arthur St. Clair*, a magistrate of Westmoreland county, Pennsylvania, issued a warrant against him and had him committed to jail at Hanna's town, which was then the seat of justice, for all this country.

Connolly was soon released, by entering bail for his appearance. He then went to Staunton and was sworn in as a Justice of the Peace, of Augusta county, Virginia, in which, it was alleged, the country around Pittsburgh was embraced. Towards the latter part of March, he returned to this place, with both civil and military authority, to put the laws of Virginia in force. About the 5th of April, the Court assembled at Hanna's town, the seat of Justice for Westmoreland county, Pennsylvania. Soon after, Connolly, with about one hundred and fifty men, all armed and with colors flying, appeared there; placed sentinels at the door of the court house, who refused to admit the magistrates, unless with the consent of their commander. A meeting then took place between Connolly and the magistrates, in which the former stated that he had come there in fulfilment of his promise to the Sheriff; but denied the authority of the Court, and declared that the magistrates had no right to hold a Court. He added, however, that to prevent confusion, he agreed that the magistrates might act as a Court in all matters which might be submitted to them by the acquiescence of the people, until he should receive instructions to the contrary. To this the magistrates replied, that their authority rested on the legislative authority of Pennsylvania; that it had been regularly exercised; that they would continue to exercise it in the same regular manner, and that they would do all in their power to preserve the public tranquility. They added, in conclusion, an assurance that the province of Pennsylvania would use every exertion to accommodate differences, by fixing a temporary boundary until the true one could be ascertained.

"On the eight of April, the Justices, Æneas Mackay, Devereux Smith and Andrew M'Farlane, returned from the Court to Pittsburgh, where they resided, and on the next day they were arrested by Connolly's Sheriff, and on refusing to give bail, were sent off under guard to Staunton, in Virginia. After travelling one day together, Mr. Mackay got permission to go by way of Williamsburgh to see Lord Dunmore; and after some conversation with him, his Lordship wrote to the Sheriff requesting him to permit the prisoners to return home; saying, "I will be answerable for their appearance, in case it be required." Mackay immediately proceeded to Staunton; and in a letter dated at that place, on the 5th of May, he informed Governor Penn that he and his fellow prisoners were to set out on their homeward journey, forthwith. On the 19th day of April, intelligence of the arrest of the Justices reached the Governor; and on the 21st at the meeting of the Council, it was determined to send two Commissioners to Virginia, to represent to the government there, the ill consequences which may ensue if an immediate stop be not put to the disorders which then existed in the west, and to consult upon the most proper means for establishing peace and good order in that quarter.

"James Tilghman and Andrew Allen were appointed, with instructions, first, to request the Governor of Virginia to unite with the proprietaries of Pennsylvania to petition His Majesty in Council, to appoint Commissioners to run the boundary line; the expense to be equally borne by the two Colonies; second, to use every exertion to induce the Governor to agree to some *temporary* line; but in no event to assent to any line which would give Virginia jurisdiction of the country on the east side of the Monongahela river.

"The Commissioners arrived at Williamsburgh on the 19th May, and on the 21st had an oral conference with the Governor; in which he expressed his willingness to join in an application to the King, to appoint Commissioners to settle the boundary; but also declared, that Virginia would defray no part of the expense. As to the temporary line, he desired the Commissioners to make their propositions in writing.

"In compliance with this request, they, on the 23d, addressed him a letter containing the following proposition:—"That a survey be taken by Surveyors, to be appointed by the two Governments, with as much accuracy as may serve the present purpose, of the *courses of the Delaware*, from the mouth of Christiana creek, or near it, where Mason and Dixon's line intersects the Delaware, to that part of said river which lies in the latitude of Fort Pitt, and as much farther as may be needful for the present purpose. That the line of Mason and Dixon be extended to the distance of five degress of longitude from the Delaware; and that from the end of said five degrees, a line or lines, corresponding to the courses of the Delaware, be run to the river Ohio, as nearly as may be, at the distance of five degrees from said river in every part." And that the extension of Mason and Dixon's line, and the line or lines corresponding to the courses of the Delaware, be taken as the line of jurisdiction, until the boundary can be run and settled by Royal authority.

"Lord Dunmore, in his reply, dated 24th May, contended that the western boundary could not be of "such an inconvenient and difficult to be ascertained shape," as it would be if made to correspond to the courses of the Delaware. He thought it should be a meridian line, at the distance of five degrees from the Delaware, in the forty-second degree of latitude.

"He then, after some arguments which it is unnecessary to recite, remarked, that unless the Commissioners could propose some plan that favored as much the sentiments of the government of Virginia as of Pennsylvania, he saw that no accommodation could be entered into previous to the King's decision. The Commissioners, in their reply of the 26th, say, that for the purpose of producing harmony and peace, "we shall be willing to recede from our Charter bounds, so far as to make the river Monongahela, from the line of Mason and Dixon, the western boundary of jurisdiction, which would at once settle our present dispute, without the great trouble and expense of running lines, or the inconvenience of keeping the jurisdiction in suspense."

"On the same day, Lord Dunmore replied in a long letter, manifesting throughout a most uncourteous and rude spirit. The following are the most material passages, showing, as they do, that further correspondence with him was utterly useless:—

"'And what were your proposals to reconcile these difficulties? Why, in your first, you propose that every thing shall be given up to Pennsylvania; and in your second, that Virginia shall be content, without having any thing given up to it; at least, I can find nothing given up by your proposal of the Monongahela, &c. What else then can I conclude, but that no *real* intention is meant to avoid the great and reciprocal inconveniences of a doubtful boundary," &c. Further on he says,—'Your resolution, with respect to Fort Pitt, (*the jurisdiction over which place, I must tell you, at all events, will not be relinquished by this Government*, without His Majesty's orders,) puts an entire stop to further treaty.' "

" On the 27th, the Commissioners, in a brief reply, state, that the determination of his Lordship not to relinquish Fort Pitt, puts a period to the treaty."

" After a careful perusal of this correspondence, and an attentive consideration of Lord Dunmore's conduct in 1774 and 1775, the conclusion is forced upon the mind, that he was a very weak and arbitrary man, or else that the suspicion, then entertained, that he wished to promote ill will and hostility between Pennsylvanians and Virginians, as well as between the Indians and whites, was well founded. During the whole of this correspondence, this place was called Fort Pitt; the new name of Fort Dunmore was never mentioned. The Commissioners, in their first letter, gave it the old name, and Dunmore did the same in his letters to them; although he had before recognized the new name bestowed by Connolly."

" This negotiation having thus failed, Connolly continued to domineer with a high-hand at Fort Pitt. In a letter from Æneas Mackay to Governor Penn, dated June, we find the following strong and emphatic language :—" The deplorable state of affairs in this part of your government, is truly distressing. We are robbed, insulted and dragooned by Connolly and his militia, in this place and its environs."

" To form an adequate conception of the condition of the inhabitants in this place, at that time, we must take into view, not only the oppressive conduct of Connolly, but also bear in mind that the war of the Revolution was rapidly approaching, and that hostilities between the Indians and Virginians, were actually raging at that time. The Indians, it is true, were understood to say that they would not touch the Pennsylvanians; but still they must have felt much of the embarrassment arising out of the Indian war. So great was the anxiety and distress of the adherents of the proprietary, that they at one time thought of leaving this place, and removing to Kittaning, which lay in another manor. Another project was, to raise a stockade around the town of Pittsburgh, being that part of our city which lies between Water and Second streets, and Market and Ferry streets. Neither project was carried into execution, and I merely refer to them as signs of the times, and as evidences of the state of feeling then prevailing here.

"On the 8th September, the Earl of Dartmouth, one of the Secretaries of State, wrote a letter to Lord Dunmore, containing some items of intelligence, in relation to this place, which are of interest as forming a part of the history of Fort Pitt, and of the controversy. After stating that the Governor of Pennsylvania had attributed the hostility of the Indians, to the unprovoked attacks upon them by the Virginians, and had also alleged that a party of Virginians had attacked and wounded some Indians, who, at the risk of their lives, had escorted some traders to Pittsburgh, he proceeds to say:—'My intelligence, through a variety of other channels, confirms these facts.' He further adds, that he is informed, that 'one Connolly, using your Lordship's name, and pleading your authority, has presumed to re-establish the Fort at Pittsburgh, which had been demolished by the King's express order.' He then concludes by stating, that he gives this information so that 'the facts asserted, if not true, may be contradicted by his Lordship's authority; but if true, which he cannot suppose, such steps may be taken as the King's dignity and justice shall dictate.'

"The publication of this letter should have exonerated the British ministry from all suspicion of countenancing the scheme attributed to Dunmore or Connolly, of exciting ill blood and war between the Indians and whites.

"On the 17th of September, Lord Dunmore being at this place preparing for his expedition against the Indians, issued a proclamation dated at *Fort Dunmore*, reciting that, 'Whereas, the ancient claim laid to this country by the Colony of Virginia, founded upon reason, upon pre-occupancy, and the general acquiescence of all persons, together with the instructions I have lately received, to take this country under my administration; and the evident injustice manifestly offered to His Majesty, by the immediate strides taken by the proprietors of Pennsylvania, in prosecution of their *wild* claim, demand immediate remedy.' He then calls on all His Majesty's subjects *West of Laurel Hill*, to pay due respect to that proclamation, prohibiting the execution of any act of authority on behalf of the province of Pennsylvania, at their peril; but, on the contrary, that due regard and entire obedience be paid to the laws of His Majesty's Colony of Virginia, &c.

"On the 12th of October, Governor Penn issued another proclamation, which is of too great length to be inserted here. In reply, however, to that portion of Lord Dunmore's proclamation, which speaks of the 'general acquiescence of all persons' in the claim of Virginia, he mentions that, 'in an act passed at the very last session of Parliament, for the government of Quebec, the western extent of the Charter to Penn is fully recognized; said province being described as being bounded by the northern and western bounds of Pennsylvania. Wherefore there is reason to infer, that any instructions to the Governor of Virginia, to take that country under his administration, must be founded on some misrepresentation respecting the western extent of Pennsylvania.' It concludes by calling on all persons west of Laurel Hill, to retain the settlements made under that province, and to pay due obedience to the laws of that province; and by charging all magistrates to proceed as usual in the administration of justice.

"On November 24th, Connolly sent out a warrant for a Mr. Scott to appear and answer for a number of offences, charged to have been committed while acting under authority from Pennsylvania. Mr. Scott refused to pay any attention to this warrant; and on the same day a number of armed men came to his house and carried him to Fort Burd, now Brownsville, where he was required either to enter into recognisance with two sureties, to appear at the next Court to be held at Pittsburgh for the county of Augusta, December 20th, 1775, or at any future day when the Court should be held there; or else be committed to prison. Mr. Scott gave the required bail; but I have not been able to ascertain the final disposition of his case; though, I presume, the prosecution was abandoned under the subsequent recommendation of the Delegates in Congress, from these two States.

"On the twenty-fourth of November, a party of armed men under command of Connolly, went to Hanna's town, and released two prisoners confined in the jail under execution.

"In January, 1775, information being given to the Executive Council, that William Crawford, the President Judge of Westmoreland county, had joined the Virginians in opposing the jurisdiction of Pennsylvania; the Council advised the Governor to supersede him in his office as Judge; which was done forthwith.

"On the 7th of February, another party of armed men went to Hanna's town, broke open the jail, and released three prisoners. Benjamin Harrison, a son-in-law of Crawford, commanded this party, Connolly having some days before started for Williamsburg. In April and May, three of the Pennsylvania magistrates were arrested and held in custody for performing the duties of their office.

"The power of Lord Dunmore and his agent, Connolly, was, however, fast drawing to a close. On the 8th of June, the former abandoned his palace in Williamsburg, and took refuge on board the Fowey man-of-war, where soon after he was joined by Connolly, who was then busily engaged in planning an attack upon the western frontier.

"The continued collisions and disorder at Pittsburgh could not fail to attract the attention of all the patriotic citizens of the two States, and on the 25th of July, 1775, the Delegates in Congress, including among others, Thomas Jefferson, Patrick Henry, and Benjamin Franklin, united in a circular, urging the people in the disputed region, to mutual forbearance. In that circular was the following language: 'We recommend it to you, that all bodies of armed men, kept up by *either party*, be dismissed; and that all those on either side, who are in confinement, or on bail, for taking part in the contest be discharged.'

"There were no armed men maintained by the Pennsylvanians; so that the expression about "either party," was probably only used to avoid the appearance of invidiousness; and Connolly and his men had taken effectual measures for the release of Virginians from confinement.

"On the 7th of August, the following resolution was adopted by the Virginia Provincial Convention, which had assembled at Williamsburg, on the first of the month:

"*Resolved*, That Captain John Neville be directed to march with his company of one hundred men, and take possession of Fort Pitt, and that said company be in the pay of this Colony from the time of their marching."

"The arrival of Captain Neville at Fort Pitt seems to have been entirely unexpected to the Pennsylvanians, and to have created quite a considerable excitement. Commissioners appointed by Congress, were then here to hold a treaty with the Indians, and Mr. St. Clair in a letter to John Penn, dated 17th September, has the following remarks: 'The treaty is not yet opened, as the Indians are not yet come in; but there are accounts of their being on the way, and well disposed. We have, however, been surprised by a manœuvre of the people of Virginia, that may have a tendency to alter this favorable disposition.'

" 'About one hundred armed men marched from Winchester, and took possession of the Fort on the 11th instant, which has so much disturbed the Delegates from the Congress, that they have thoughts of moving some place else to hold the treaty.'

" 'This step has already, as might be expected, served to exasperate the dispute between the inhabitants of the country, and entirely destroyed the prospect of a cessation of our grievances, from the salutary and conciliating advice of the Delegates in their circular letter.' "

" There is, perhaps, some difficulty in reconciling the conduct of the Virginia Convention, in ordering Captain Neville to Fort Pitt, with the recommendation of the Virginia and Pennsylvania Delegates in Congress, that 'all bodies of armed men in pay, of either party,' should be discharged. No doubt, however, this only referred to bodies of armed men, kept up by the Virginians or Pennsylvanians in the disputed region. Mr. St. Clair seems always to have been very watchful of the interests of Pennsylvania during the controversy; and no doubt, the surprise expressed by him was unaffected; and yet there were strong reasons why Fort Pitt should be promptly occupied by troops in the confidence of the Whigs of the Revolution. The war for independence had commenced by the actions at Lexington and Bunker Hill; and Connolly, a bold, able and enterprising man, was busy arranging some scheme of operations, in which Fort Pitt would be an important and controlling position. It would seem, therefore, to have been nothing more than an act of ordinary prudence and foresight to send here some officer, in whose firmness, fidelity and discretion, implicit confidence could be placed.

"Captain Neville was then about forty-three or forty-four, about the same age as Washington.

"He was a man of very frank and hearty address, of sound judgment, of much firmness and decision of character, and probably, in all respects, as well suited to the emergency for which he was selected, as any individual who could have been named, and who would have undertaken the duty.

"That he acted with great prudence and impartiality, may be inferred from the fact, that none of the evils, predicted by St. Clair, occurred. A more full notice of his life and services will be given hereafter.

"On the 22d day of November, 1775, Connolly, and two of his associates, were arrested at Fredericktown, Maryland. His connection with the British General Gage, and Lord Dunmore, and the whole of his plans for invading the western frontier with British troops and Indians, and taking possession of Fort Pitt, were fully exposed. He was, therefore, confined, and subsequently, by order of Congress, for greater security, sent to Philadelphia. His arrest and confinement probably broke up the whole scheme which he had prepared, and in which he was to be the controlling spirit. Connolly, after the Revolution, resided in Canada; where he enjoyed the confidence and liberality of the English Government.

To bring the account of this controversy, which has already occupied so much space to a close, we mention that under the kinder feelings produced by united resistance to Great Britain, movements were made early in 1779, to bring the question to an amicable settlement. For this purpose George Bryan, John Ewing and David Rittenhouse, on the part of Pennsylvania, and Dr. James Madison, late Bishop of the Protestant Episcopal Church, and Robert Andrews, on the part of Virginia, were appointed Commissioners to agree upon a boundary. These gentlemen met at Baltimore on the 31st of August, 1779, and entered into the following agreement:

"'We (naming the Commissioners) do hereby mutually, in behalf of our respective States, ratify and confirm the following agreement, viz: To extend Mason and Dixon's line due west five degrees of longitude, to be computed from the river Delaware, for the southern boundary of Pennsylvania, and that a meridian, drawn from the western extremity thereof, to the northern limit of said State, be the western boundary of said State forever.'

This agreement was confirmed and ratified by the Legislature of Virginia, upon certain conditions, on the 23d of June, 1780, and by the General Assembly of Pennsylvania, on the 23d of September, 1780.

It now only remained to mark the lines upon the ground, so that the citizens should know to what authorities they owed allegiance and obedience, and to whom to look for protection.

"For this desirable purpose, each State selected the best and most suitable men within its reach; so that their work when completed, would merit and secure entire confidence in its accuracy.

"The Commissioners on the part of Pennsylvania were, David Rittenhouse, John Lukens, John Ewing and Captain Hutchins; and those on the part of Virginia were, Andrew Ellicott, (who then resided in Maryland,) Bishop Madison, Robert Andrews, and T.

J*

Page. These gentlemen performed the duty assigned them, in the summer and fall of 1784.

"The southern boundary of the State being thus extended to its western extremity, it only remained to run a meridian line from that point to the Ohio river, to close the controversy with Virginia. This task was committed to Messrs. Rittenhouse and Porter, from Pennsylvania, and Andrew Ellicot and Joseph Neville, from Virginia; who entered upon their work in May, 1785, and on the 23d of August, united in the following report:

"'We, the subscribers, Commissioners, appointed by the State of Pennsylvania and Virginia, to ascertain the boundary between said States, do certify, that we have carried on a meridian line from the south-west corner of Pennsylvania, northward to the river Ohio; and marked it by cutting a wide vista over all the principal hills, intersected by the said line, and by falling or deadening a line of trees, generally, through all the lower grounds. And we have likewise placed stones, marked on the east side P, and on the west side V, on the most of the principal hills, and where the lines strikes the Ohio; which stones are accurately placed in the true meridian, bounding the States aforesaid.'

"Persons traveling on the Pittsburgh and Steubenville turnpike road, may see one of the stones a short distance west of Paris, and about thirty miles west of Pittsburgh.

"Virginia having on the first of March, 1784, ceded to the United States all her territory north of the Ohio river, had no special interest in extending the boundary of Pennsylvania farther north. The boundary was extended to Lake Erie the ensuing year, by Messrs. Porter and McClean.

We have thought it best to carry forward our brief history of this controversy to its conclusion, although in doing so, we have been compelled to violate the chronological order of events. We have preferred disposing of that subject at once, without interrupting the course of the narrative.

At the very time when the United Colonies commenced their great struggle against the arbitrary schemes of Great Britain, the inhabitants of this section of country, were not only involved in hostilities with the Indian tribes, but were almost on the verge of civil war among themselves. Under such circumstances, it would scarcely be expected that they would be at leisure and disposed to enter into the contest against the mother country, upon a mere abstract question, unaccompanied by any immediate, palpable acts of oppression. Yet we find that upon the 16th of May, 1775, only four weeks after the battle of Lexington, meetings were held at this place, and at Hanna's town, and resolutions *unanimously* passed in entire consonance with the whig feeling of the other portions of the country.

These proceedings cannot fail to be interesting to our readers, and we therefore embrace them in our work. The meeting at Hanna's town was, no doubt, composed entirely of Pennsylvanians. Arthur St. Clair mentions in one of his letters that he was present at it, and took part in the proceedings. The meeting here, though *Augusta* county, Virginia, is mentioned, was not composed exclusively of Virginians. Devereux Smith, a devoted adherent of John Penn, and several others were present.

Of those who were engaged in the two meetings, Arthur St. Clair was subsequently a Major General in the revolutionary army, and John Gibson, William Crawford and John Neville, commanded Virginia regiments in the same service.

AUGUSTA COUNTY (VIRGINIA) COMMITTEE.

"At a meeting of the inhabitants of that part of Augusta county that lies on the west side of the Laurel Hill, at Pittsburgh, the 16th day of May, 1775, the following gentlemen were chosen a committee for the said district, viz: George Croghan, John Campbell, Edward Ward, Thomas Smallman, John Cannon, John McCullough, William Gee, George Valandigham, John Gibson, Dorsey Penticost, Edward Cook, William Crawford, Devereux Smith, John Anderson, David Rodgers, Jacob Vanmetre, Henry Enoch, James Ennis, George Willson, William Vance, David Shepherd, William Elliot, Richmond Willis, Samuel Sample, John Ormsby, Richard McMaher, John Neville and John Swearingen.

"The foregoing gentlemen met in committee, and resolved that John Campbell, John Ormsby, Edward Ward, Thomas Smallman, Samuel Sample, John Anderson, and Devereux Smith, or any four of them, be a Standing Committee, and have full power to meet at such times as they shall judge necessary, and in case of any emergency, to call the committee of this district together, and shall be vested with the same power and authority as the other standing committee and committees or correspondence are in the other counties within this colony.

"*Resolved unanimously*, That the cordial and most grateful thanks of this committee are a tribute due to John Harvie, Esquire, our worthy representative in the late Colonial Convention held at Richmond, for his faithful discharge of that important trust reposed in him; and to John Neville, Esquire, our worthy delegate, whom nothing but sickness prevented from representing us in that respectable assembly.

"*Resolved unanimously*, That this committee have the highest sense of the spirited behavior of their brethren in New England, and do most cordially approve of their opposing the invaders of American rights and privileges to the utmost extreme, and that each member of this committee, respectively, will animate and encourage their neighborhood to follow the brave example.

"The imminent danger that threatens America in general, from ministerial and parliamentary denunciations of our ruin, and is now carrying into execution by open acts of unprovoked hostilities in our sister colony of Massachusetts, as well as the danger to be apprehended to this colony in particular from a domestic enemy, said to be prompted by the wicked minions of power to execute our ruin, added to the menaces of an Indian war, likewise said to be in contemplation, thereby think to engage our attention, and divert it from that still more interesting object of liberty and freedom, that deeply, and with so much justice hath called forth the attention of all America; for the prevention of all, or any of those impending evils, it is

"*Resolved*, That the recommendation of the Richmond Convention, of the 20th of last March, relative to the embodying, arming, and disciplining the militia, be immediately carried into execution with the greatest diligence in this country, by the officers appointed for that end; and that the recommendation of the said Convention to the several committees of this colony, to collect from their constituents, in such manner as shall be most agreeable to them, so much money as shall be sufficient to purchase half a pound of gunpowder, and one pound of lead, flints, and cartridge paper, for every tithable person in their county, be likewise carried into execution.

"This committee, therefore, out of the deepest sense of the expediency of this measure, most earnestly entreat that every member of this committee do collect from each tithable person in their several districts the sums of two shillings and six pence, which we deem no more than sufficient for the above purpose, and give proper receipts to all such as pay the same into their hands; and the sum so collected to be paid into the hands of Mr. John Campbell, who is to give proper security to this committee, or their successors, for the due and faithful application of the money so deposited with him for the above purpose, by or with the advice of this committee, or their successors; and this committee, as your representatives, and who are most ardently laboring for your preservation, call on you, our constituents, our friends, brethren, and fellow-sufferers, in the name of God, of every thing you hold sacred or valuable, for the sake of your wives, children, and unborn generations, that you will, every one of you, in your several stations, to the utmost of your power, assist in levying such sum, by not only paying yourselves, but by assisting those who are not at present in a condition to do so. We heartily lament the case of all such as have not this sum at command in this day of necessity; to all such we recommend to tender security to such as Providence has enabled to lend them so much; and this committee do pledge their faith and fortunes to you, their constituents, that we shall, without fee or reward, use our best endeavors to procure, with the money so collected, the ammunition our present exigencies have made so exceedingly necessary.

"As this committee has reason to believe there is a quantity of ammunition destined for this place for the purpose of government, and as this country, on the west side of the Laurel Hill, is greatly distressed for want of ammunition, and deprived of the means of procuring it, by reason of its situation, as easy as the lower counties of this colony, they do earnestly request the committees of Frederick, Augusta, and Hampshire, that they will not suffer the ammunition to pass through their counties for the purposes of government, but will secure it for the use of this destitute country, and immediately inform this committee of their having done so.

"*Resolved*, That this committee do approve of the resolution of the committee of the other part of this county, relative to the cultivating a friendship with the Indians; and if any person shall be so depraved as to take the life of any Indian that may come to us in a friendly manner, we will, as one man, use our utmost endeavors to bring such offender to condign punishment.

"*Ordered*, That the standing committee be directed

to secure such arms and ammunition as are not employed in actual service, or private property, and that they get the same repaired, and deliver them to such Captains of Independent Companies as may make application for the same, and taking such Captain's receipt for the arms so delivered.

"*Resolved*, That the sum of fifteen pounds, current money, be raised by subscription, and that the same be transmitted to Robert Carter Nicholas, Esq., for the use of the deputies sent from this colony to the general Congress. Which sum of money was immediately paid by the committee then present.

"Mr. John Campbell reported, from the select committee for considering the grievances and instructions to the delegates, which he read in his place, and handed it to the clerk's table, where it was again read, and is as follows:

TO JOHN HARVIE AND GEORGE ROOTES, ESQUIRES.

"GENTLEMEN: You being chosen to represent the people on the west side of the Laurel Hill in the colonial Congress for the ensuing year, we, the committee for the people aforesaid, desire you will lay the grievances hereafter mentioned before the Congress at their first meeting, as we conceive it highly necessary they should be redressed, to put us on a footing with the rest of our brethren in the colony.

"1st. That many of the inhabitants in this part of the county have expended large sums of money, and supplied the soldiers in the last Indian war with provisions and other necessaries, many of whom have expended all they had; and though, at the same time, we bear a grateful remembrance of the good intentions of the late colonial Congress, so feeling and generously expressed in their resolves, yet the unhappy situation we are reduced to by the payment of those supplies being delayed, involves this new and flourishing country in extreme poverty.

"2d. That the maintaining a garrison at this place, when there is no other method used for supplying them with provisions, but by impressing from the inhabitants of the country, ought to be considered.

"3d. That this country, joining the Indian territory and the province of Quebec, (which by its late change of constitution is rendered inimical to liberty,) lies exposed to the inroads of the savages and the militia of that province; and should the ministry or their emissaries be able to stir up either of them against the colonies, this county will be in need of support to enable them to provide against, and withstand any attempt that may be made on their civil and religious liberties.

"4th. That for want of freeholders we cannot get legal grand jurors, which are necessary for the well government of the country.

"5th. That the unsettled boundary between this colony and the province of Pennsylvania, is the occasion of many disputes.

"6th. That the collecting the duty on skins and furs, for which a commission hath lately been sent up here, will banish the Indian trade from this place and colony.

"Which report being agreed to,

"*Resolved unanimously*, That a fair copy be drawn off and delivered to our delegates as their instructions.

"*Ordered*, That the foregoing proceedings be certified by the clerk of this committee, and published in the Virginia Gazette.

"By order of the committee.

"JAMES BERWICK, *Clerk*.

MEETING OF THE INHABITANTS OF WESTMORELAND COUNTY, PA.

"At a general meeting of the inhabitants of the county of Westmoreland, held at Hanna's town the 16th day of May, 1775, for taking into consideration the very alarming situation of the country, occasioned by the dispute with Great Britain:

"*Resolved unanimously*, That the Parliament of Great Britain, by several late acts, have declared the inhabitants of the Massachusetts Bay to be in rebellion, and the ministry, by endeavoring to enforce those acts, have attempted to reduce the said inhabitants to a more wretched state of slavery than ever before existed in any state or country. Not content with violating their constitutional and chartered privileges, they would strip them of the rights of humanity, exposing their lives to the wanton and unpunishable sport of a licentious soldiery, and depriving them of the very means of subsistence.

Resolved unanimously, That there is no reason to doubt but the same system of tyranny and oppression will (should it meet with success in Massachusetts Bay) be extended to other parts of America: it is therefore become the indispensable duty of every American, of every man who has any public virtue or love for his country, or any bowels for posterity, by every means which God has put in his power, to resist and oppose the execution of it; that for us we will be ready to oppose it with our lives and fortunes. And the better to enable us to accomplish it, we will immediately form ourselves into a military body, to consist of companies to be made up out of the several townships under the following association, which is declared to be the Association of Westmoreland County:

"Possessed with the most unshaken loyalty and fidelity to His Majesty, King George the Third, whom we acknowledge to be our lawful and rightful King, and who we wish may be the beloved sovereign of a free and happy people throughout the whole British Empire; we declare to the world, that we do not mean by this Association to deviate from that loyalty which we hold it our bounden duty to observe; but, animated with the love of liberty, it is no less our duty to maintain and defend our just rights (which, with sorrow, we have seen of late wantonly violated in many instances by a wicked Ministry and a corrupted Parliament) and transmit them entire to our posterity, for which we do agree and associate together:

"1st. To arm and form ourselves into a regiment or regiments, and choose officers to command us in such proportions as shall be thought necessary.

"2d. We will, with alacrity, endeavor to make ourselves masters of the manual exercise, and such evolutions as may be necessary to enable us to act in a body with concert; and to that end we will meet at such times and places as shall be appointed either for the companies or the regiment, by the officers commanding each when chosen.

"3d. That should our country be invaded by a foreign enemy, or should troops be sent from Great Britain to enforce the late arbitrary acts of its Parliament, we will cheerfully submit to military discipline, and to the utmost of our power resist and oppose them, or either of them, and will coincide with any plan that may be formed for the defence of America in general, or Pennsylvania in particular.

"4th. That we do not wish or desire any innovation, but only that things may be restored to, and go on in the same way as before the era of the Stamp Act, when Boston grew great, and America was happy. As a proof of this disposition, we will quietly submit to the laws by which we have been accustomed to be governed before that period, and will, in our several or associate capacities, be ready when called on to assist the civil magistrate to carry the same in execution.

"5th. That when the British Parliament shall have repealed their late obnoxious statutes, and shall recede from their claim to tax us, and make laws for us in every instance; or some general plan of union and reconciliation has been formed and accepted by America, this our Association shall be dissolved; but till then it shall remain in full force; and to the observation of it, we bind ourselves by every thing dear and sacred amongst men.

"No licensed murder! no famine introduced by law!

"*Resolved*, That on Wednesday, the twenty-fourth instant, the township meet to accede to the said Association, and choose their officers."

Two days after the Declaration of Independence a meeting was held at this place, which though not productive of any important results, is worthy of notice on account of the principal actor in it, on the part of the Indians and his emphatic tone. This person was *Guyasutha*, a leader of the Seneca tribe of the Six Nations. A most distinguished character indeed, in all the movements here, from the time of Washington's first visit until after the close of our revolution. He was one of the Indians who accompanied Washington from Logstown to Le Bœuf. He was then young and not very prominent. He was present, and a leading character in the conference with Colonel Bradstreet, near Lake Erie, in 1764, and a few weeks later at the conference with Bouquet on the Muskingum. He was a leading character in the conference held at this place in April and May, 1768. He was the leader in the attack upon and burning of Hanna's town in 1782. In 1770, while Washington was descending the Ohio river, he was visited by an Indian whom he recognized as one of his companions in 1754. It was Guyasutha. His name, too, has been so variously spelt that it is sometimes difficult to trace him in different notices. *Guyasutha*, *Guyasootha*, *Kiasutha*, *Kaishuta*, *Guyasudy*, and General Richard Butler, who understood some of the Indian dialects spelt it *Kiasola*. He survived all the troubles of the French war, of the war sometimes called Pontiac's and sometimes Guyasutha's, and of our Revolution, the most fatal of all to the power and glory of the Six Nations. Finally he died in our neighborhood within the memory of many now living, and left his name to the beautiful plain on the Allegheny river, where his remains now rest. The writer of these annals well recollects him, when in his latter days he had become as striking an emblem of the decayed condition of the Six Nations, as in the prime of life he had been of their power and glory. When we contrast his language in July, 1776, with his fallen condition twenty years later, a feeling of regret and melancholy unconsciously steals over us at the decline of a heroic people.

At a meeting held at Fort Pitt, July 6th, 1776, present Kiashuta, who had just returned from Niagara, Captain Pipe, a Delaware chief; Shade, a Shawanese chief, and several other Shawanese and Delawares, also Major Trent, Major Ward, Captain Neville and his officers.

Kiashuta then produced a belt of wampum, which was to be sent from the Six Nations to the Shawanese, Delawares, Wyandots and other Western Indians, acquainting them that the Six Nations were determined to take no part in the war between Great Britian and America, and desiring them to do the same. He was ordered by the Six Nations to send the belt through the Indian country.

He then spoke to the whites present as follows:—

"*Brothers*, we will not suffer either English or "Americans to pass through our country. Should "either attempt it, we shall forewarn them three times, "and should they persist they must abide the conse- "quences. I am appointed by the Six Nations to take "care of this country; that is of the Indians on the "other side of the Ohio, (meaning, no doubt, *the Alle-* "*gheny*,) and I desire you will not think of an expedi- "tion against Detroit, for I repeat, we will not suffer "an army to pass through our country."

He then made short addresses to the Delawares and Shawanese.

Captain Neville then said: "*Brother Kiashuta,* I "am much obliged to you, for your good speech. You "may depend we shall not attempt to march an army "through your country, without first acquainting you "with it, unless we hear of a British army coming this "course; in such case we must make all possible haste "to march and endeavor to stop them."

To which Kiashuta replied. "There is not the least "danger of that, as they (the Six Nations) would make "it their business to prevent either an English or an "American army passing through their country."

CHAPTER VII.

Colonel George Morgan appointed Indian Agent at Pittsburgh; four Commissioners for the middle department of United States, appointed to hold treaties with the Indians; meet here; Indians slow assembling; apprehensions of a general war with the Indians; prospects more cheering; Six Nations, Delawares, Shawanese and Mohicans to the number of six hundred and forty-four assemble here, and give the strongest assurances of friendship; arrival of fourteen boat builders, from Philadelphia; bitter hostility of the people to the Indians; provisions scarce and dear; Girty, Elliot and McKee escape; letter from Governor of Louisiana to Col. Morgan, six months on its way, no person in Congress could read it; General McIntosh in command; Fort McIntosh built; expedition against Ohio Indians; Fort Laurens built, besieged, abandoned; curious due bill; Col. Broadhead succeeds Gen. McIntosh; his expedition up the Allegheny; depreciation of paper money; attempts to regulate prices; Broadhead expedition to Coshocton; his correspondence from October 1780 till October 1781.

In April 1776, Col. George Morgan was appointed by Congress, Indian agent for the middle department of the United States, and his head quarters fixed at Pittsburgh. From his journal and letters, we get occasional, notices of transactions here.

Congress perceived at an early day of the struggle for independence, the importance of securing the friendship of the Indians or, at least, their neutrality, and appointed Commissioners to hold treaties with them at different agencies. For the middle department Thomas Walker, John Harvey, John Montgomery and Jasper Yates were appointed. They met at this place in July, 1776, but were not able to assemble the different tribes until October. In the meantime they were busily engaged in holding communications with the different tribes, and persuading them to meet together at this place. Some of the more distant tribes were influenced by Hamilton, the British Governor at Detroit, and these tribes had some influence with the Shawanese and Delawares. At one time in September, the commissioners, had come to the conclusion founded on the best testimony they could obtain, that a general Indian war was inevitable, and they issued an order for assembling, all the militia that could be spared, at Fort Pitt for its defence. On the 8th of November Col. Morgan in a letter to John Hancock, president of Congress said, "I have the happiness to inform you that the cloud which threatened to break over us is likely to disperse. The Six Nations, with the Munsies, Delawares, Shawanese and Mohicons who have been assembled here with their principal chiefs and warriors, to the number of six hundred and forty-four, have given the strongest assurance of their determination, to preserve inviolate the peace and neutrality with the United States."

The winter of 1776–7 was spent in comparative quiet, in Fort Pitt, Major Neville was still in command there with his company of one hundred men.

On the 23d of February, 1777, fourteen boat carpenters and sawyers arrived at Fort Pitt from Philaphia, and were set to work on the Monongahela, fourteen miles above the fort, near a saw mill. They built thirty large batteaux, forty feet long, nine feet wide, and thirty two inches deep. They were intended to transport troops in case it became necessary to invade the Indian country.

A bitter feeling of hostility existed against the Indians in the minds of the whites, especially of the Virginians. Col. Morgan, in a letter dated March 15th, 1777, gives the following account of the state of things here. "Parties have, even been assembled to massacre our known friends at their hunting camps, as well as messengers on business to me; and I have esteemed it necessary to let those messengers sleep in my own chamber for security."

Small parties of Mingoes and other outlaw Indians continued to harass and murder the whites; especially the Virginians, against whom they had more cause of complaint than any others.

In January 1778, provisions became very scarce and flour rose to sixteen dollars a barrel.

On the 28th of March, 1778, Simon Girty, Alexander McKee and Mathew Elliot made their escape from Pittsburgh, and ever after were active agents of the British government, and exercised much influence with the Indians, against the United States.

In the spring of 1778, the Commissioners for Indian affairs, ordered the building of six large boats for the defence of the navigation between the military posts on the Ohio. Each boat was to carry a four pound cannon, and to be constructed so as to be useful either in attack or defence.

"In April of this year Col. Morgan addressed a letter to Don Bernardo Galvez, Governor of Louisiana, from which we gather two facts quite worthy of notice. The first is that the Governor's letter to Col. Morgan, dated at New Orleans, on the 9th of August, 1777, did not reach this place till the 24th of February, 1778, more than six months after it was written. The other is that the Colonel not understanding the Spanish language sent the letter to Congress by express, but, "unfortunately," says the Colonel, "not a member of that body understands it, nor has any person yet been found, capable and worthy of trust, to translate it."

Fort Pitt seems to have risen in importance in the estimation of Congress, and demanded a more imposing force for its defence than the command of Major Neville. General Lachlan McIntosh, with portions of the 8th Regiment of Pennsylvania and 13th of Virginia, were ordered here.

A formidable incursion into the Indian country was planned for the summer of 1778. Fifteen hundred men were to assemble at the mouth of the Kenhawa and as many more to drop down from Fort Pitt. The united forces were then to enter the Indian territory to destroy their towns and crops. The former body never assembled. So that General McIntosh prepared to march from this place directly into the territory of the hostile Indians, by the way of the Big Beaver, nearly on the same route that Col. Bouquet had pursued fourteen years earlier.

Preparatory to this expedition, Fort McIntosh was built where Beaver town now stands. It was a regular stockaded work, with four bastions and defended by six pieces of cannon. Before proceeding on this expedition it was thought prudent to convene the Delaware Indians at Pittsburgh, and obtain their consent to the passing of the troops, through their territory. This was accordingly done on the 17th September, 1778, by Thomas Lewis and Andrew Lewis, commissioners on the part of the United States. In October Gen. McIntosh assembled one thousand men, at the newly erected fort, at the mouth of Beaver, and commenced this expedition, which seems to have been unproductive of any good effect. The season was so far advanced that the army only proceeded about seventy miles west of Fort McIntosh and halted on the west bank of the Tuskarawas river, a little below the mouth of Sandy creek. Here they built a fort on an elevated piece of ground and named it Fort Laurens. Col. John Gibson was left in the fort with one hundred and fifty men, and the army returned to Fort Pitt. In the month of January, 1779, the Shawanese and Wyandots collected a large body of warriors, invested the fort and cut off all intercourse with it. It was so closely watched that the necessary supplies of wood and water could only be obtained at great hazard. During the investment a number of the garrison were killed and the others suffered a good deal from the scarcity of provisions; and finally the ill advised post was abandoned in the ensuing summer.

In January, 1779, provisions became very scarce and dear. The principal portion of the flour, meat, &c. had to be brought from the Eastern side of the mountains, on horseback. Bacon, at Pittsburgh, was a dollar a pound. Many other articles rose in proportion.

The following is a specimen of a due bill, drawn at Fort Laurens:

"I do certify that I am indebted to the bearer, "Captain Johnny, seven bucks and one doe, for the "use of the States, this 12th of April, 1779. Signed "Samuel Sample, Assistant Quarter Master. The "above is due to him for pork, for the use of the gar-"rison at Fort Laurens.

"Signed, JOHN GIBSON, Colonel."

In March, 1779, Colonel Broadhead was in command at Fort Pitt. Washington had then in view an expedition under Broadhead, up the Allegheny river, and even against Fort Niagara, to co-operate with an army under Gen. Sullivan, who was to attack the hostile portion of the Six Nations, by the North branch of the Susquehannah. The idea of attempting a co-operation was, however, soon abandoned for the following reasons as stated by Washington himself:

"The difficulty of providing supplies in time, and a "want of satisfactory information of the country up "the Allegheny."

On the 11th of August, however, Col. Broadhead left Fort Pitt, with six hundred men, rank and file, including militia and volunteers, having one month's provisions, all of which except the live cattle, was transported by water, under the escort of one hundred men, to the mouth of Mahoning. There the provisions, &c. were transferred from the boats to the pack horses. The army then marched to Buckaloons, an Indian village at the mouth of Broken Straw creek, a tributary of the Allegheny. Here a breastwork of trees was thrown up and forty men left to guard the provisions, &c. while the army advanced further to another Seneca town called *Yohroonwago*, probably about the same place, where five years after a grant was made to that worthy and wise Indian chief *Cornplanter*. The troops remained there three days destroying the town and corn-fields. The quantity of corn and other vegetable destroyed, Col. Brodhead supposes, exceeded five hundred acres, and they took about three thousand dollars worth of plunder. The whole number of houses in the towns was about one hundred and thirty. The old towns of Conowago, Buckaloons, and another town on French creek about twenty miles above the mouth which they passed on their return were also burnt. Many of the houses were large and calculated to accomodate three or four families each. Not a man or beast fell into the enemy's hands during the march. The army reached Fort Pitt on its return on the 14th day of September.

The depreciation of the paper currency or continental money had, in 1779, become a very serious burden to the people and all over the country, great ingenuity was exercised to discover a remedy. Embargoes, commercial restrictions, tender laws, and limitations of prices were all tried, but in vain. Prices still sank. "I had money enough some time ago," said an anonymous writer, "to buy a hogshead of sugar. I sold it "again and got a great deal more money than it cost "me; yet when I went into the market again, the "money would only get me a tierce. I sold that too, "at a great profit; yet the money received would only "buy a barrel. I have now more money than ever, "yet I am not so rich as when I had less."

To prevent this continual depreciation of the value of the paper money every expedient, except the proper one, was resorted to. Prices wholesale and retail were fixed. Rents were fixed, persons asking more than the settled price, as well as those giving more were censured. But no plan of reducing excessive issues was thought of, or at least none was adopted.

Pittsburgh, like the other and older portions of the union, was infected with the same kind of political quackery. The following are extracts from the proceedings of a meeting of the officers of the army at this place on the 5th of October 1779:

PITTSBURGH, October 5, 1779.

The officers of the line and staff in the western department, having long beheld with concern the growing evils produced by the avaricious and grasping trader, now commonly known and distinguished by the disgraceful epithet of speculator, find themselves under the necessity of forming and adopting a system of regulations, similar to those formed and adopted by their brother officers, and the main army. And in doing this—

We, the officers of the western department, beg leave to declare that our motives are pure and disinterested. We have no sinister views. Our happiness is to see our country happy; our pride to give her peace and safety; and our glory is to render her independent. In this we have happily succeeded, and were it not for the encouragement held out to our hardened, obstinate and inveterate enemy, by the depreciation of our money—in a great degree, if not wholly occasioned by the wicked arts of the disaffected, and the mean tricks of speculators, the olive branch would long ere this have happily expanded its influence over this bleeding land: nor should we now have seen our towns in flames; nor heard of ravished, virtuous, insulted matrons, nor of British bayonets being pointed at the breasts of our patriots. Similar causes will ever produce similar effects; to prevent the latter, the former must be removed. Mischiefs of such enormity, can no longer be winked at, or dispensed with. The soldier and the citizen, who have sacrificed their all; who have fought, and bled, and conquered; who have humbled the arrogant and haughty Briton, as well as the fierce and barbarous savage, cannot now tamely submit to see their well-earned laurels unwove, and all their great and good deeds blasted, overturned, and undone, by caterpillars of states, and muckworms of royalty; such are the insects that are preying on the vitals of America, and who are living and fattening on the core of her credit; and therefore we are determined, with the blessings of our God, and the approbation of our Commandant, to effectually remove and smother them, so that they shall no longer feed on the fair and tender blossom of freedom, nor hereafter be a pest to our posterity.

The civil laws have been found inadequate to the removal of these growing evils. Therefore, to stop the rapid progress of such despoilers of their country, as well as to support the credit of our currency, and give it a fixed and permanent value, we have at last found it absolutely necessary to call a meeting of officers of the line and staff, when after some deliberation a committee was moved for, which met with unanimous concurrence; a motion was then made for the nomination of a chairman, which was also agreed to, and

Colonel John Gibson, of the ninth Virginia regiment, was appointed. The committee accordingly met on Tuesday the 5th October, and proceeded to business; and as the prices of every article were daily, rapidly, and shamefully increasing; and some time must necessarily elapse, before the necessary papers, town regulations, and traders invoices could be procured, so that a reasonable and living profit might be allowed them, on the regulated sale of their goods.

Therefore resolved, That a select committee be appointed to collect all papers, and get what information they can possibly obtain, relative to the regulations which may have taken place down the country, and by them endeavor to ascertain the price of goods as they ought to sell at this place, and lay them, with what other matters they may conceive necessary, before the committee at the next meeting.

Resolved, That two gentlemen of the committee, viz: Captain Tannihill, and Captain Fridlay,* be deputed to wait on the traders of Pittsburgh, and acquaint them that the sale of their goods were prohibited and forbid by the committee, till the regulations could be formed with accuracy, and transmitted them, under the pain and penalty of being held up as inimical to their country, as well as forfeiting the countenance, protection and trade of the army, wherupon the committee adjourned.

Wednesday the 6th of October, the committee having met, and the select committee having made their reports, the following resolutions were agreed to, viz:

Resolved, That at the present enormous prices, un-

* This, no doubt, should be Findlay, Captain John Findlay, son-in-law of David Duncan.

less dire and absolute necessity compels, to buy shall be deemed as criminal as to sell, and should the traders refuse to sell at the regulated prices agreed on and fixed by this committee,

Resolved, That the Commandant of the western department be waited upon by a committee, and earnestly requested for the good of the community as well as the army, that said traders be immediately ordered to withdraw themselves and property from this post, being fully determined to have a reasonable trade or no trade, and live upon our rations and what our country can afford us; and should it be necessary, clothe ourselves with the produce of the forests, rather than live upon the virtuous part of the community, to gratify our sanguinary enemies, and enrich rapacity; and as it is the unanimous opinion of this committee, that the specious designing speculator is a monster of a deeper dye, and more malignant nature than the savage Mingo in the wilderness, whose mischiefs are partial, while those occasioned by the speculator, have become universal. The trade of a Mingo is blood, and they are in alliance with Britons. But speculating monsters, who are deemed and treated as citizens of America, and partake of her benefits, swoop all before them; tear up our credit by the root; travel like a pestilence; and carry destruction to every corner of the continent. And in a time of public danger, like the present, when the subjects of a free state can have but one interest, and ought to have but one wish and one sentiment.

Resolved, That any person whatever, holding a commission, place or employment under the United States, who shall directly or indirectly be concerned in trade or speculation of any kind, shall not be kept company with, or even spoken to by any person in the public service, that is on the footing of a gentleman, excepting at such time when necessary duty may require: and those who countenance a speculator shall be deemed by the committee as accessary, and held up to the world in the same colours, and be treated with the same degree of scorn and contempt.

The invoices of the traders being produced to the committee, they were carefully perused and maturely considered, and after some debate thereon, the committee at last unanimously determined, that from the exorbitant prices affixed to the greatest part of the different articles contained therein, no regulations could be made on invoices: Therefore,

Resolved, That said traders be not permitted to sell any part of said merchandize specified in said invoices, at any post or garrison, on this side the Allegheny mountains.

And this committee particularly considers the conduct of such traders as injurious, by their engrossing and forestalling large quantities of grain, thereby enhancing and raising the price thereof: in order to prevent the evil consequences, that must naturally flow therefrom, as well as to prohibit trade in general, till a reasonable trade can be obtained, and traders become satisfied with a moderate profit.

Resolved, That a guard be placed over the stores of the traders of Pittsburgh, and that they be not permitted to sell to any person on any account whatever, and that circular letters with the resolutions of this committee, be transmitted to the principal gentlemen of the different counties on this side the Allegheny mountains, requesting their approbation, assistance, and concurrence therein.

And this committee wishing to deal tenderly with all, to avoid, (as much as in their power) injuring any, and to act on such principles as may convince all mankind of their impartiality, as well as to prevent future adventurers from making use of the plea of ignorance.

Resolved, That until such times as traders will conform to the regulations entered into and published by the virtuous part of the community at Philadelphia, Boston, and the generality of the principal trading towns on the continent, no goods whatever shall be purchased, or offered for sale, at any post or garrison, on this side the Allegheny mountains; and that all trading adventurers, who wish for the countenance, protection and trade of the army, are hereby required by this Committee to obtain a permit as well as certificate, specifying the regulated prices, at the time of purchase, from the Secretary of the Committee, previous to the opening of their goods for sale, and they shall also confine themselves to such profits on their sales, as were formerly allowed at this place. And provided trading adventurers will comply with the regulations and restrictions.

Resolved, That they shall be treated with the respect due to worthy citizens, and friends to their country, and shall meet with every indulgence the commandant at this post or the committee can possibly grant them, and all those of different complexions, whatever appellation they may choose to assume, whether monopolizers, forestallers, engrossers, or speculators are hereby cautioned and advised not to cross the Allegheny mountain, as this Committee cannot answer for the conduct of an insulted public, nor for the resentment of the army.

From the time of the meeting above referred to, we have no account of transactions here for several months. Colonel Brodhead appears to have been a man of ardent temperament and anxious to distinguish himself and serve his country. He had in contemplation, an expedition down the Ohio and Mississippi against Natchez; but Washington thought the force he could raise for that purpose would probably be insufficient, and besides thought that the information as to the situation of that post was not such as would justify so distant an expedition, from which return would be so difficult and hazardous in case of failure. The Colonel also had in view a winter expedition against Detroit, but Washington again objected, that there were neither men nor supplies sufficient.

Washington's letter containing these objections was dated on the 4th of January, 1780, and it happened that before a force leaving Fort Pitt, after that date, could have reached Natchez, that post as well as Baton Rouge, with six hundred and fifty British troops, with military stores and other property, were taken by a party of Spaniards, under the command of Don Galvez, Governor of Louisiana.

In the summer Colonel Brodhead made a campaign to Coshocton.

The place of rendezvous was Wheeling, where about eight hundred regulars and militia collected. From Wheeling, they made a rapid march by the nearest route to the Muskingum. When the army had reached the river, a little below Salem, the lowest Moravian town, Col. Brodhead sent an express to the missionary of the place, the Rev. John Heckewelder, informing him of his arrival in the neighborhood with his army, requesting a small supply of provisions, and a visit from him in his camp. The christian Indians sent the supply of provisions, and Mr. Heckewelder repaired to Colonel Brodhead's camp. Colonel Brodhead then said, "that being on an expedition against the hostile Indians, at or near the forks of the river, he was anxious to know before he proceeded any further, whether any of the christian Indians were out hunting, or on business in the direction he was going." Being answered in the negative, he declared that, "nothing would give him greater pain, than to hear that any one of the Moravian Indians had been molested by his troops; as these Indians had conducted themselves from the commencement of the war, in a manner that did them honor."

While, however, he was assuring Mr. Heckewelder that the christian Indians had nothing to fear, an officer came with great speed from one quarter of the camp, and reported that a particular division of the militia "were preparing to break off for the purpose of destroying the Moravian settlements up the river, and he feared they could not be restrained from so doing." Colonel Brodhead and Colonel Shepherd of Wheeling, immediately took such measures as prevented it.

The army then proceeded until within a few miles of Coshocton, when an Indian prisoner was taken. Soon after, two more Indians were discovered and fired upon, but notwithstanding one of them was wounded, both made their escape.

Colonel Brodhead, knowing that these two Indians

would endeavor to give immediate notice of the approach of the army, ordered a rapid march, in order to reach the town before them, and take it by surprise. This was done in the midst of a heavy fall of rain, and the plan succeeded. The army reached the place in three divisions,—the right and left wings approached the river a little above and below the town, while the centre marched directly upon it. The whole number of the Indians in the village, on the east side of the river, together with ten or twelve from a little village some distance above, were made prisoners, without firing a single shot. The river having risen to a great height, owing to the recent fall of rain, the army could not cross it. Owing to this, the villages on the west side of the river escaped destruction.

Among the prisoners, sixteen warriors were pointed out by Pekillon, a friendly Delaware chief, who was with the army of Colonel Brodhead. A little after dark, a council of war was held, to determine on the fate of the warriors. They were doomed to death. They were then bound, taken a little distance below town, despatched with tomahawks and spears, and scalped.

Early the next morning an Indian presented himself on the opposite bank of the river, and asked for the "Big Captain." Colonel Brodhead presented himself, and asked the Indian what he wanted? The Indian replied, "I want peace." "Send over some of your chiefs," said Brodhead. "May be you kill." He was answered, "They shall not be killed." One of the chiefs, a well looking man, came over the river and entered into conversation with General Brodhead in the street; but while engaged in conversation, a cowardly wretch, by the name of Wetzel, belonging to the army, came up behind him, with a tomahawk concealed in the bosom of his hunting shirt, and struck him a blow on the back of his head. He fell and instantly expired.

About mid-day the army commenced its retreat from Coshocton. Colonel Brodhead committed the care of the prisoners to the militia. They were about twenty in number. After marching about a mile, the men commenced killing them, and did not cease until the whole were murdered and scalped, except a few women and children, who were spared and taken to Fort Pitt.

CHAPTER VIII.

Extracts from correspondence of Colonel Brodhead, 1780 and 1781; General William Irvine, appointed to command here, arrives; general order issued upon receipt of news of Cornwallis' surrender; notice of General Irvine and his opinion against the position of Fort Pitt; letter from him to General Washington.

We have the correspondence of Colonel Brodhead, from the 17th October, 1780, till 28th of October, 1781, from which we make extracts as follows, to exhibit the state of things here during that time:

"To General Washington,—*October* 17*th*, 1780.—"I have sent out parties to take cattle and grain from "the inhabitants, and expect to get a considerable "supply of flour as the mills begin to grind. But the "inhabitants disappoint us of beef, by driving their "cattle into the mountains; we have neither bread "nor meat at present, but expect a small supply im- "mediately."

"To THE GOVERNOR OF PENNSYLVANIA,—*November* "*2d*, 1780.—Forty Delaware Indians came in to join "us in an expedition against the hostile Indians. But "as a party of about forty men from Hanna's town "attempted to destroy them, and were only prevented "by a guard of regular soldiers, it may not be easy to "call them out again.

"I hear, this moment, that Thomas Smallman has "made a secret and clandestine purchase of an Island "in the Ohio, two miles below this post, commonly "called McKee's Island. The deed, I am told, is "signed by two Delaware chiefs."

"To COL. EPHRAIM BLAINE,—*November 3d*, 1780.— "It is clear to every body, that a sufficient supply of "meat for half the present consumption cannot be had "here, even for money. Flour may be had on this "side the mountains; but too much salt cannot be "sent, as it will procure meat when money cannot. "Unless you can furnish us with a quantity of meat "from below the mountains, I shall have the mortifica- "tion to remain on the defensive another campaign, "*which above all things I abhor and detest.*"

"To REV. D. ZEISBERGER,—*December 2d*, 1780.— "Proposes that he should send fifteen or twenty best "hunters to Little Kenhawa, to kill buffalo, elks and "bears, to be salted down in canoes made for that "purpose."

"To Hon. Richard Peters.—*Fort Pitt*, December "7th, 1780.—For a long time past I have two parties "commanded by field officers, in the country, to im- "press cattle, but their success has been so small, that "the troops have frequently been without meat for "several days together. * * * * *

"I learn more and more of the disaffection of many "of the inhabitants on this side of the mountains. "The King of Great Britain's health is often drunk in "companies, and I believe those wish to see the regu- "lar troops removed as a favorable opportunity to "submit to British government."

"To Col. E. Blaine.—*Fort Pitt*, December 16th, 1780.—Dear Sir: The troops have not tasted meat at this post for six days past, and I hear of none that we can purchase, or procure, by our compulsory means; indeed there is very little meat to be had on this side the mountain at any rate. I hope some means are devised for supplying this department, if not, I shall be under the disagreeable necessity of risking my men in most dangerous situations to kill wild meat, or march them to the interior part of the country, for it will scarcely be expected that they will be content to live on bread and water only.

"I am impatient to hear from you, and am, &c.,

"D. B."

"To Joseph Reed, President of the Executive Council of Pennsylvania.—*Fort Pitt*, January 22d, 1781.—I have the pleasure to enclose a list of bonds, notes, &c., late the property of a tory Ross, who was formerly an agent at this place for the King of Britain's contractors, and deserted from his parole. I am informed that his estate is worth near ten thousand pounds in specie, and that it will inure to the benefit of our State.

"Mr. William Wilson a few days ago wrote me that he had undertaken to furnish my troops with an hundred head of cattle upon private contract and with private money. This account, as there was no other prospect of obtaining meat, and the troops were suffering for want of it, whilst we were scarcely supplied with flour, was flattering, and cheered the drooping spirits of both officers and men. But as meat could not be purchased on account of the great scarcity on this side the mountains, Mr. Wilson immediately proceeded to the South branch of Pawtomack, to perform the contract, and now I have the mortification to be informed by his brother who is just arrived from Old Town, that a prohibitory law of the State of Virginia will prevent his getting the cattle he may have purchased for consumption here. I sincerely wish there was not occasion to trouble you with a further tale of misfortunes. But as the United States in general, and our State in particular, are immediately interested in retaining in this district all the grain that has been raised in it, it might appear inimical in me were I to remain silent respecting certain instructions lately sent by Governor Jefferson for the purchase of 200,000 rations on this side the mountains for the use of the troops under Colonel Clarke, for which purpose he has already advanced 300,000* pounds, and promised to furnish on the first notice, any further sum that may be necessary to complete the payment of that purchase. Because this contract, together with the

* This is, no doubt, Continental money.

consumption of multitudes of emigrants arrived and expected in this district, (chiefly to avoid military duty and taxes,) will scarcely leave a pound of flour for the regular or other troops which it may be necessary to employ either offensively or defensively against the enemy, for the defence of this part of the frontier settlements.

"It seems the State of Virginia is now preparing to acquire more extensive territory, by sending a great body of men under Colonel (whom they intend to raise to the rank of Brigadier) Clarke, to attempt the reduction of Detroit. I have hitherto been encouraged to flatter myself, that I should sooner or later be enabled to reduce that place. But it seems the United States cannot furnish either troops or resources for the purpose, but the State of Virginia can.

"The Indian Captains appointed by the British commandant at Detroit are clothed in the most elegant manner, and have many valuable presents made them. The captains I have appointed by authority of Congress, are naked and receive nothing but a little whiskey, for which they are reviled by the Indians in general, so that unless some kind of system is introduced I must expect to see all Indians in favor of Britain in despite of every address in my power. I fear I have trespassed on your patience, but you'l please to excuse me, I have never kept a thing a secret from you which you ought to know, or were interested in, your patriotism and candor, as well as your station in life commanding most perfect respect and warmest wishes whilst I have the honor to be, &c. D. B.

"P. S. I have wrote to Governor Jefferson respecting his instructions to his Commissary, and assured him that I should not consider myself at liberty to suffer the transportation of provisions out of this district, until I received instructions from the proper authority."

"To his Excellency General Washington,—*Fort Pitt*, February 18th, 1781.—Dear General: Since my last the half Indian Bawbee, by the concurrence of a serjeant belonging to the late Captain Heths' company, made his escape, and persuaded a fifer of the ninth Virginia regiment to desert to the enemy. The Delaware chiefs at Coochocking seized the deserter and sent him back, and he is confined in irons, but cannot be tried until your Excellency is pleased to order a General Court Martial."

"To Joseph Reed, Esq.,—*Fort Pitt*, February, 23d, 1781.—I have just received instructions from the commander-in-chief to detach my field pieces, howitzers and train, also a part of my small force under Colonel Clarke, who I am told is to drive all before him, by his supposed unbounded influence in the western country. * * * * * *

"The Maryland corps being ordered to Richmond, in Virginia, my force will not exceed two hundred men, many of which, were soldiers plenty, I would not wish to have."

The officer who commanded the troops, sent to join General Clarke, was Captain Isaac Craig. He proceeded to the Falls; but the Kentuckians on whom Clarke greatly relied, disappointed him, and Captain Craig, with his command, returned to Fort Pitt.

"To Col. Joseph Beeler, (Circular,)—*Fort Pitt*, March 4th, 1781.—I have just received letters by Capt. Montour, stating that the Delawares of Coochocking, with very few exceptions, have declared in favor of the British, and that some of them have already come against our settlements."

"To HIS EXCELLENCY GENERAL WASHINGTON,—*Fort Pitt*, March 10th, 1781.—The troops under my command have been at half allowance of meat ever since the 20th of December, and frequently both before and since, has been without any for several days together."

In August, 1781, Col. Brodhead became involved in a very angry controversy with some of his officers, Col. Gibson at their head. His situation was really unpleasant. In a letter to Washington, dated 19th August, he says: "Thus by the clamor of some disaffected persons and others, I find myself in the most disagreeable situation I ever experienced."

"To CAPTAIN JOHN CLARKE, commanding at Fort McIntosh,—*Fort Pitt*, August 24th, 1781.—I have this moment received information that the enemy are coming against us in great force and particularly against your post. You will, therefore, put your post in the best state of defence, &c. * * * *

"The men who carry this letter are to proceed immediately to Wheeling with my letter; but are to call at places where they can alarm the people."

On the same day a circular letter was addressed to the county Lieutenants, assuring them that the enemy was approaching and calling on them to order out the militia to defend the frontier.

The information received by Col. Brodhead was perhaps correct. In a letter from Washington to General Clarke, dated 25th April, 1781, he says: "A few days ago I received a piece of intelligence from New York,

M*

which it may be material for you to know. It is that Colonel Connolly, who formerly lived upon the Ohio, who was taken prisoner in 1775, and lately exchanged, is to proceed to Quebec as soon as the season will permit, with as many refugees as he can collect at New York; that he is to join Sir John Johnson, in Canada, and that they are to proceed with their combined forces by the way of Birch Island and Lake Ontario to Venango. It is, also, said that Connolly carries blank commissions, which are to be given to persons already in the country, and that there are several hundred persons now in the neighborhood of Fort Pitt, who are to join him. As this corresponds with a suspicion which Col. Brodhead entertains, I have written to him to take measures to secure or remove every suspected person."

Connolly was a daring, enterprising and sanguine man, he had been a good deal in this country, and believed, whether correctly or incorrectly, we cannot say, that there were many tories here. He had even written to Col. John Gibson, hoping to conciliate him. In this letter he urges the Colonel to "avoid an over zealous exertion of what is now *ridiculously* called a *patriotic spirit*," and tells him to "act as a good subject, and expect the *rewards* due to your services." Possibly the over sanguine temperament of Connolly may have misled him as to the feelings of many persons here. Certainly we know nothing against Col. Gibson to justify any suspicion of his integrity. Perhaps Col. Brodhead may have entertained doubts of his patriotism during their controversy, but he did not venture to express such doubts in his letters; and Washington manifested his confidence in Gibson by deciding in his favor and giving him the command while Colonel Brodhead was under trial.

While upon this subject I may as well state that Gen. Wm. Irvine, who commanded here in 1782, in a letter to Washington, written in 1788, gives the following statement :

" The following account I have from a Chief of the Seneca tribe, as well as from a white man named Mathews, a Virginian, who says he was taken prisoner by the Indians at Kanawha in 1777. He has lived with the Indians since that time. As far as I could judge, he appeared to be well acquainted with this part of country. I employed him as interpreter. He stated that from the upper end of Jadaque* Lake that it was not more than nine miles along the path or road to Lake Erie, and that there was formerly a wagon road between the two Lakes.

"The Indian related that he was about fourteen years old, when the French went first to establish a post at Fort Pitt; that he accompanied an uncle who was chief warrior, on that occasion, who attended the French; that the head of Lake *Jadaque* was the spot where the detachment embarked; that they fell down to Fort Duquesne without any obstruction, in large canoes, with all their artillery, stores, provision, &c. He added, that French Creek was made the medium of communication afterwards—why, he could not tell, but always wondered at it, as he expressed himself, knowing the other to be so much better. The Seneca related many things to corroborate and convince me of his truth. He stated, that he was constantly employ-

* Now spelt Chautauque.

ed by the British during the late war, and he had the rank of captain, and that he commanded the party which was defeated on the Allegheny by Colonel Brodhead; that in the year 1782 a detachment composed of three hundred British, and five hundred Indians, was formed and actually embarked in canoes on Lake Jadaque, with twelve pieces of artillery, with an avowed intention of attacking Fort Pitt. This expedition he says, was laid aside, in consequence of the reported repairs and strength of Fort Pitt, carried by a spy from the neighborhood of the fort.

"They then contented themselves with the usual mode of warfare, by sending small parties on the frontier, one of whom burned 'Hanna's town.' I remember very well, that in August, 1782, we picked up at Fort Pitt, a number of canoes, which had drifted down the river; and I received repeated accounts in June and July, from a Canadian who deserted to me, as well as from some friendly Indians, of this armament; but I never knew before then, where they had assembled."

"COL. BRODHEAD TO GEN. WASHINGTON,—*August 29th*, 1781.—The Maryland corps was stationed at a post on the frontier of Westmoreland county, and have in a body deserted and crossed the mountains. Indeed, I am afraid the other corps will soon follow, if their sufferings are not attended to."

"TO THE SAME,—*September 6th*, 1781.—Col. Gibson still continues to counteract me, and the officers who favored his claim reject my orders, others refuse his, and things are in the utmost confusion."

The unfortunate dissensions prevailing at Fort Pitt, rendered it necessary to send some other person to take the command. General William Irvine, an Irishman by birth, and a Pennsylvanian by adoption, was selected by Congress, and ordered to proceed immediately to this point. We cannot ascertain precisely when he arrived here. It must, however, have been as early as the 6th November, 1781, on which day the following order was issued:

"FORT PITT, November 6th, 1781.

"Parole—*General.* Countersign—*Joy.*

"General Irvine has the pleasure to congratulate "the troops upon the great and glorious news. Lord "Cornwallis, with the troops under his command, sur- "rendered prisoners of war on the 19th of October "last, to the allied armies of America and France, "under the immediate command of his Excellency "General Washington. The prisoners amount to up- "wards of five thousand regular troops, near two "thousand tories, and as many negroes, besides a num- "ber of merchants and other followers.

"Thirteen pieces of artillery will be fired this day "at 10 o'clock, in the Fort, at which time the troops "will be under arms, with their colors displayed. The "Commissaries will issue a gill of whiskey extraordi- "nary to the non-commissioned officers and privates, "upon this joyful occasion.

"Accurate regimental returns will be made to-mor- "row morning at nine o'clock, of the officers, drums "and fifes, and privates, accounting for every man, "where he is, how employed and how long so employ- "ed."

We think it highly probable, that General Irvine arrived at Fort Pitt, very shortly before the above general order was issued, and brought the news with him. The last clause of the order seems intended to draw forth full information of the condition of troops, among whom he had just arrived.

General Irvine was a well informed gentleman, had been educated for a physician, seems to have been a ready writer, and from his letters, while here, we can get frequent glances at the condition of things here. We mean, therefore, to draw liberally upon his correspondence, and give below large extracts. By the first of these extracts, it will be seen that the writer regarded the site of Fort Pitt as very indefensible. Certainly there could not be one less capable of resisting a force provided with artillery. As to the post near the mouth of Chartier's creek, pointed out to him by Hutchins, it is difficult to decide whether it was McKee's Rocks or the lofty hill back of Jas. McKee's old mansion house, and westward of the mouth of the creek. The statement that "it is inaccessible on three sides," would apply best to the rocks, but it certainly could not be said that there is no commanding ground within three thousand yards. The hill back of Mr. Kee's old mansion, is not distant three thousand yards, and certainly commands the "Rocks"—as also do the hills across the Ohio.

This situation at the mount of Chartier's creek, has attracted much attention at different times. The Ohio Company, before Washington's first visit here, had selected it as the site for a town. Col. Hutchins, and afterwards Gen. Irvine approved it as the location for a military post; and now a public spirited Coal and Railroad Company have selected it as the terminus of the first rail road, with steam motive power, in this region; and as the great station for the distribution of the products of their mines. But we proceed to the letters.

Extract of a letter from Gen. William Irvine to Gen. Washington, dated Fort Pitt, December, 1781:

"SIR:—At the time Congress directed me to repair to this place, I took for granted your Excellency would have information thereof, through different channels, and knowing how particularly you were at that moment engaged, I did not think proper to give unnecessary trouble. This, I flatter myself, will excuse me with your Excellency, for not writing sooner.

"Previous to my arrival, Col. Gibson had received your letter directing him to take the command, which was acquiesced in by Col. Brodhead, and things went on in the usual channel, except the dispute occasioned Col. Gibson's intended expedition against Sandusky being laid aside; and perhaps it also prevented many other necessary arrangements.

"The examination of witnesses against Col. Brodhead is still going on, and I am told will continue some weeks. Agreeable to my orders from Congress, to retain no more officers here than sufficient for the men, I have made the following arrangements. Re-formed the remains of the late 8th Pennsylvania Regiment into two Companies, and call them a detachment from the Pennsylvania Line, to be commanded by Lieut. Col. Bayard.

"Baron Steuben had some time ago directed Col. Gibson to re-form his regiment also into two companies, retaining with him the staff of the regiment, and to send all the supernumerary officers into Virginia. The re-formation was so made, but the officers were so distressed for want of clothing and other necessaries, that they were not able to proceed. However, they are now making exertions, and I hope will soon set out.

"I have ordered the supernumerary officers of the Pennsylvania line to repair forthwith to their proper regiments in the line. The whole of the troops (infantry) here are thrown into two companies. I have been trying to economize, but every thing is in so wretched a state that there is very little in my power. I never saw troops cut so truly deplorable a figure. Indeed, when I arrived, no man would believe, from their appearance, that they were soldiers,—nay, it would be difficult to determine whether they were *white men*, and though they do not yet come up to my wishes, they are some better.

"As it does not rest with me to decide on the impropriety of any person's conduct, shall only make a few general observations. The consumption of public stores, in my opinion, has been enormous, particularly military stores, and I fear the reasons given for it will not be justifiable, viz: that the militia would all fly if they had not powder and lead given them, not only when in service, but to keep at their houses. It is true, the County Lieutenants and others, who are called responsible men, have promised to be accountable. But, I am certain, not an ounce can ever be again collected. I find that near 2000 lbs. of lead, and 4000 lbs. of powder have been issued to the militia, since the dispute began between Cols. Brodhead and Gibson, chiefly by orders of the former; besides arms, accoutrements, &c., and not a man called into actual service. The Magazine is nearly exhausted; there not being as much remaining as was issued since the first of last September.

"I presume your Excellency has been informed by the Governor of Virginia, or by Gen. Clarke, of the failure of his expedition. But least this should not be the case, I will relate all the particulars that have come to my knowledge.

"Captain Craig, with the detachment of artillery, returned here on the 20th inst. He got up with great difficulty, and much fatigue to the men, being forty days on the way, occasioned by the lowness of the water. He was obliged to throw away his gun-carriages, but brought his pieces and best stores safe. He left Gen. Clarke at the Rapids, and says the General was not able to prosecute his intended plan of operations for want of men; being able to collect in the whole only about 750 men. The buffalo meat was all rotten, and he adds the General is apprehensive of a visit from Detroit, and is not without fears the settlement will be obliged to break up, unless reinforcements soon arrive from Virginia. The Indians have been so numerous in that country, that the inhabitants have been obliged to keep close, and the General could not venture out to fight them.

A Colonel Lochry, of Westmoreland county, Pa., with about 100 men in all, composed of volunteers, and a company raised by Pennsylvania, for the defence of that county, started to join Gen. Clarke, who, it is said, ordered him to unite with him (Clarke) at the mouth of the Miami, up which river it was previously designed to proceed; but the General having changed his plan, left a small party at the Miami with directions to Lochrey to follow him to the mouth of the Falls. Sundry accounts agree that this party, and all of Lochrey's troops to a man were waylaid by the Indians and British, (for it is said they had artillery,) and all killed or taken, not a man escaping, either to join Gen. Clarke, or to return home. When Captain Craig left the General he would not be persuaded but that Lochry with his party had returned home. These misfortunes throw the people of this country into the greatest consternation, and almost despair, particularly Westmoreland county, Lochry's party being all the best men of their frontier. At present they talk of flying early in the spring to the eastern side of the mountains, and are daily flocking to me to inquire what support they may expect. I think there is too much reason to fear that Gen. Clarke's and Col. Gibson's expeditions failing, will greatly encourage the savages to fall on the country with double fury, and perhaps the British from Detroit to visit this post; which, instead of being in a tolerable state of defence, is, in fact, but a heap of ruins. I need not inform your Excellency that it is at best but a bad situation for defence. I have been viewing the country in this vicinity, and find no place equal for a post to the mouth of Chartier's Creek, about four miles down the river. Capt. Hutchins pointed that place out to me before I left Philadelphia, and says there is no place equal to it any where within forty miles of Fort Pitt. I think it best calculated on many accounts. First, the ground is such that works may be constructed to contain any number of men, from 50 to 1000. It is by nature almost inaccessible on three sides, and on the fourth no commanding ground within 3000 yards. Secondly, as it would effectually cover the settlement on Chartier's Creek, the necessity for keeping a post at Fort McIntosh would of course cease. In case of making that the main post, Fort Pitt should be demolished, except the north bastion, on which a strong block-house should be erected. A small party in it would as effectually keep up a communication with the settlements on the Monongahela, as the whole garrison now does, for the necessary detachments to McIntosh, Wheeling, &c., so divide the troops that no one place can be held without a large body of troops indeed. I do not like Fort McIntosh being kept a post in the present situation of things. If the enemy from Detroit should undertake to make us a visit, it would be an excellent place for them to take by surprise, from whence they could send out Indians and other partizans, and lay the whole country waste before we could dislodge them."

This destruction of Lochry's or rather Laughery's party of one hundred and seven men, took place near the mouth of a creek in the State of Indiana, a short distance below the mouth of the great Miami, and which still bears his name.

Subsequently to the writing of the above letter, it seems that Gen. Irvine must have left Fort Pitt and gone eastward; for on the 8th day of March, 1782, an order and instructions were issued by Gen. Washington directing him to proceed without delay to Fort Pitt. Gen. Irvine appears to have complied promptly, and on the 30th of March, 1782, wrote the following letter to Gen. Washington:

FORT PITT, March 30th, 1782.

SIR:—I arrived here the 25th of March; at that time things were in greater confusion than can well be conceived. The country people were to all appearance in a fit of phrenzy; about three hundred had just returned from the Moravian towns, where they found about ninety men, women and children, all of whom they put to death, 'tis said after cool deliberation and considering the matter for three days. The whole were collected into their church, and died while singing hymns. On their return, a party came and attacked a few Delaware Indians who have yet remained with us on a small Island close by this garrison ; killed two who had captain's commissions in our service, and several others, the remainder effected their escape into the Fort, except two who ran into the woods and have not since been heard of. There was an officers' guard on the Island at the same time ; but he either did not do his duty, or his men connived at the thing—which, I am not able to ascertain. This last outrage was committed the day before I arrived. Nothing of this nature has been attempted since. A number of wrong-headed men had conceived an opinion that Col. Gibson was a friend to Indians, and that he must be kil'ed also. These transactions, added to the then mutinous disposition of the regular troops, had nearly brought on the loss of the whole country. I am confident, if this post was evacuated, the bounds of Canada would be extended to the Laurel Hill in a few weeks. I have the pleasure, however, to inform your excellency that things now wear a more favorable aspect. The troops are again reduced to obedience ; and I have had a meeting, or convention, of the county Lieutenants and several field officers, with whom I have made arrangements for defending their frontier, and who promise to exert themselves in drawing out the militia, agreeable to the law, on my requisitions.

Civil authority is by no means properly established in this country ; which I doubt not, proceeds in some degree from inattention in the executive of Virginia and

Pennsylvania not running the boundary line—which is at present an excuse for neglect of duty of all kinds for at least twenty miles on each side the line. More evils will arise from this than people are aware of. There is a prospect on foot here for emigrating and setting up a new State. A certain J—— is at the head of this party; he is ambitious, restless, and some say disaffected; most people, however, agree, he is open to corruption. He has been in England since the beginning of the present war. Should these people actually emigrate, they must be entirely cut off, or immediately take protection from the British, which I fear is the real design of some of the party, though I think a great majority have no other views than to acquire lands.

As I apprehended taking cognizance of the matters would come best from the civil departments, I have written to the governors of Virginia and Pennsylvania on the subject, which I should not have done till I had first acquainted your excellency thereof, but for this consideration, viz: that the 25th of May is the day appointed for the emigrants to rendezvous; consequently a representation from you would be too late, in case the States should think proper to take measures to prevent them.

CHAPTER IX.

State of things here in May, 1782; letter from Gen. Irvine to Gen. Lincoln, Secretary of War; same to Wm. Moore, Esq., President of Executive Council of Pennsylvania; to Gen. Washington; Peace between the U. States and Great Britain; the Penns conclude to sell their lands in the Manor of Pittsburgh; first sale to Craig and Bayard, January, 1784; Town of Pittsburgh laid out in May and June, 1784; Second Treaty of Fort Stanwix; lands in the bounds of this State north of the Ohio and west of the Allegheny ceded to this Commonwealth; arrival of Arthur Lee here; extract from his journal; low estimate of this place; cost of Fort Pitt; account of the work and improvements in the Fort; Distillery in Pittsburgh; Salt works on Big Beaver, 1786; Pittsburgh Gazette established July, 1786; Description of Pittsburgh from 1st number of the Gazette; further notices from subsequent number of Gazette; September, 1786, mail route to Pittsburgh established, once in two weeks; market house and market days established; Presbyterian Congregation of Pittsburgh incorporated by Legislature; the May Flower, the boat with the first emigrants to Marietta, arrived here 3d of April, 1788.

On the 2d of May, 1782, Gen. Irvine wrote the following letter to General Lincoln, Secretary of War. Pittsburgh was then in a very distracted condition indeed. She had just escaped from the controversy between Pennsylvania and Virginia. The partisans of Connolly on one side, and those of Pennsylvania on the other, were still there, and the bitterness of feeling between them, probably, not entirely, allayed. The British and Indians in Canada and western New York, still entertained hopes of retaking the place, and were, perhaps, at that very time making arrangements to attack it. Finally the struggle between Col. Gibson and his friends on one side and Col. Brodhead and his adherents on the other, in which, perhaps, the old feeling between the two States, may have entered, still continued. Major Ward was, we suppose, the same man who was taken prisoner here by Contrecœur in 1754, and seems to have been a pretty bold speculator, and not very particular about the title. Certainly, in this case, he had no shadow of title to any ground within the Manor.

The dissensions between Brodhead and Gibson, had no doubt, led to great relaxation of discipline among the troops, and all the energy of Irvine was needed to restore discipline.

Fort Pitt, May 2d, 1781.

Sir: I do myself the honor to inclose you Lt. Col. Weibert's report to me of the situation and circumstances of this Post, the ground, houses round it, &c., in which he has not discovered any thing but what I was before well acquainted with. But as the officer who preceded me in command, had great contention respecting his occupying some houses, particularly Maj. Ward's, who brought a civil action against him; several others brought civil suits. This same Ward *claims* what was formerly called the King's Orchard, which lies immediately joining, and encircles the bastions of the Fort. This I have inclosed with a slight fence, and use it as a pasture for the public and officers' horses. This man is teasing me to promise him a certain rent, which I cannot with propriety do.

As to the houses, I have not yet pulled any of them down, but mean in case of any intelligence of the approach of an enemy, to set fire to them. Ward's is an old wooden building, which was formerly a redoubt, but has been carried from the place it formerly stood on, and was built house fashion ; it is not worth much, though he sets a high value on it. Irwin's house was also a redoubt, but it is now environed by the other houses of the town of Pittsburgh. 'Tis certain that if it is meant to occupy this place any length of time, as would appear to be the intention by the Commander-in-Chief, and your orders to me, these houses and several other obstructions should be instantly removed. In case of emergency, I will not hesitate a moment to do it, but these people think it hard to have it done, as long as they are not apprehensive of danger. I assure you, sir, this is a very troublesome command—sufficiently so, without being obliged to quarrel with the inhabitants. I could wish you would take these points into consideration, and instruct me respecting them.

If any troops should be sent to this quarter, or any exertions made, some few tents, at least bell tents, would be necessary. I did not make any demand of this article from the Quarter Master General, as I at that time thought them unnecessary for garrison duty. The few troops here are the most licentious men, and worst behaved I ever saw, owing, I presume, in a great measure, to their not being hitherto kept under any subordination, or tolerable degree of discipline. I will try what effect a few prompt and exemplary punishments will have. Two are now under sentence, and shall be executed to-morrow. They not only disobeyed their officer who commanded at Fort McIntosh, but actually struck him ; and it is supposed would have killed him, had he not been rescued by two other soldiers.

I believe no person has obtained a legal right for the Orchard ; it is part of what is called a Proprietary

Manor, the property of Mr. Penn; but when Lord Dunmore took it into his head to extend Virginia to this place, Ward and others might probably have obtained grants from him. As it is now well known to be the in the State of Pennsylvania, I suppose his grants are not worth a farthing.

Be this as it may, I have no right to determine anything respecting the claimants of private property, as twenty others claim it as well as Ward.

I have the honor to be, &c.,

To the Hon. Maj. Gen. Lincoln, Secretary of War.

The following letter to William Moore, Esq., the Chief Magistrate of this State, contains some information as to the state of affairs here, about the time it was written:

FORT PITT, May 9th, 1782.

SIR: Since my letter of the third instant, to your Excellency, Mr. Pentecost and Mr. Cannon have been with me; they and every intelligent person whom I have conversed with on the subject, are of opinion that it will be almost impossible even to obtain a just account of the conduct of the militia at Muskingum. No man can give any account except some of the party themselves; if, therefore, an inquiry should appear serious, they are not obliged, nor will they give evidence; for this and other reasons, I am of opinion further inquiry into the matter will not only be fruitless, but in the end may be attended with disagreeable consequences.

A volunteer expedition is talked of against Sandusky, which, if well conducted, may be of great service to the country; if they behave well on this occasion, it may also in some measure atone for the barbarity they are charged with at Muskingum. They have consulted me, and I shall give every countenance in my power, if their numbers, arrangements, &c., promise a prospect of success.

Another kind of expedition is much talked of, which is to emigrate and set up a new State. The matter is carried so far as to advertise a day of general rendezvous, the 25th inst. A certain Mr. Jackson is said to be at the head of this party. He has a form of constitution written by himself, for the new government. I am well informed he is now on the east side of the mountains, trying to purchase or otherwise provide artillery and stores. A number of people, I really believe, have serious thoughts of this matter, but I am led to think they will not be able, at this time, to put their plan into execution. Should they be so mad as to attempt it, I think they will either be cut to pieces, or they will be obliged to take protection from and join the British. Perhaps some have this in view, though a great majority are, I think, well-meaning people, who have at present no other view than to acquire large tracts of land.

As I thought a knowledge of these intentions might be useful to the Executives of Pennsylvania and Virginia, the emigrants being now subjects of both States, I have written to the Governor of Virginia on the subject also.

Mr. Jackson has been in England since the commencement of the present war. Some people think he is too trifling a being to be worthy of notice. Be this as it may, he has now many followers, and it is, I think, highly probable that men of more influence than he are privately at work. Jackson, it is said, was once in affluent circumstances, is now indigent, and was always open to corruption. I have no personal knowledge of the man, and have this character of him in too general terms to be able to assert it as genuine.

No considerable damage has been done by the savages since my arrival here last; the whole of killed and captured, I have any account of amount, to six souls. I think they must be either preparing for a great stroke, or are apprehensive of a visit from us.

I have the honor to be, &c.,

His Excellency, Wm. Moore, Esq., President of the Executive Council of Pennsylvania.

The volunteer expedition here spoken of was that under Colonel William Crawford, which turned out so unfortunately, in his defeat and subsequent cruel sacrifice by the Indians. The atrocity of the Moravian affair, in this case, met a retaliation equally atrocious. The annexed letter gives some account of the result of Crawford's expedition, and as it is a matter belonging to general history and has been largely noticed, we shall enter into no farther detail about it.

LETTER TO GENERAL WASHINGTON.

Fort Pitt, July 11th, 1782.

SIR: Dr. Knight (a surgeon I sent with Col. Crawford,) returned on the 4th instant to this place; he brings an account of the melancholy fate of poor Crawford. The day after the main body retreated, the Colonel, Doctor, and nine others, were overtaken about thirty miles from the field of action, by a body of Indians, to whom they surrendered, were taken back to Sandusky, where they all, except the Doctor, were put to death; the unfortunate Colonel, in particular, was burned and tortured in every manner they could invent. The Doctor, after being a spectator of this distressing scene, was sent to the Shawanese town under guard of one Indian, where he was told he would share the same fate next day; but fortunately found an opportunity of demolishing the fellow, and making his escape. The Doctor adds that a certain Simon Girty, who was formerly in our service and deserted with McKee, is now said to have a commission in the British service, was present at torturing Col. Crawford; and that he (the Doctor) was informed by an Indian that a British Captain commands at Sandusky, that he believes he was present also, but is not certain; but says he saw a person there who was dressed and appeared like a British officer. He also says the Colonel begged of Girty to shoot him, but he paid no regard to the request. A certain Shlover has also come in yesterday, who was under sentence at the Shawanese town; he says a Mr. Wm. Harrison, son-in-law to Col. Crawford, was quartered and burned. Both he and the Doctor say they were assured by several Indians whom they formerly knew, that not a single soul should in future escape torture, and gave as a reason for this conduct the Moravian affair. A number of people informed me that Col. Crawford ought to be considered as a Continental Officer, and are of opinion retaliation should take place. These, however, are such facts as I can get. Dr. Knight is a man of undoubted veracity.

This account has struck the people of this country with a strange mixture of fear and resentment. Their solicitations for making another excursion are increasing daily, and they are actually beginning to prepare for it. I have honor to be, &c.,

To His Excellency General Washington.

From the date of the above letter until the beginning of the year 1784, we at no time obtain a single distinct view of proceedings at this place. On the 30th of November, 1782, sixteen months subsequent to the date of the above letter, preliminary articles of peace between the United States and Great Britain were signed at Paris. From the period when the news of that event was received here, military movements and preparation would cease, and business would probably stagnate for a time. In the fall of 1783, the proprietaries, John Penn, jr., and John Penn, concluded to sell the lands within the Manor of Pittsburgh. The first sale was made in January, 1784, to *Isaac Craig and Stephen Bayard*, of all the ground between Fort Pitt and the Allegheny river, "supposed to contain about three acres." Subsequently, however, to the date of that agreement, the proprietaries concluded to lay out a town at the junction of the rivers, so as to embrace within its limits the three acres agreed to be sold, as well as all the ground covered by the Fort. We presume, the purchasers of the three acres assented to this division of the ground, as they afterwards received a deed describing the ground, not by the acre, but by the metes and bounds fixed by the plan of the town, except that the lots on the Monongahela were described as extending to the river, instead of being limited by Water street, as the plan exhibits them.

The laying out of the town was completed by Thos. Vickroy, of Bedford county, in June, and approved by Tench Francis, the attorney of the proprietors, on the 30th September, 1784. Sales immediately commenced, many applications for lots were made, as soon as the survey was completed and before it had been traced on paper.

In a pocket memorandum book of Major Craig I find some notes and copies of letters which throw some little light on affairs here about the time of laying out the town.

In a letter dated Pittsburgh, July 25th, 1784, he says: "Immediately after my return from Philadel- "phia to this place, I called on *Major Marbury*, who "still continued to command here and handed him the "Quarter Master General and Secretary of War's "orders for part of the buildings and five hundred "pounds of Iron, the former part of the order he said "he would comply with, the latter he could not; be- "cause he had disposed of the iron in purchase of "provisions and in payment of wagon hire. Lieut. "Lucket has, since, succeeded Major Marbury, and "seems reluctant to give me possession of a building, "so I have provided a house for the reception of the "goods when they arrive, and have a party employed "in the preparation of timber for the cisterns, pumps, "&c., for the Distillery. I am convinced that our "best plan will be to erect a wind-mill at the junction "of the rivers instead of a horse mill. It would do "all our grinding for the distillery and at other times "do work for the inhabitants. At the point there is "almost always a breeze up or down the rivers; while "water-mills here scarcely work more than six months "in the year."

What an emphatic commentary do the above remarks afford upon the unappreciable importance to this country of the introduction of the steam engine!! Certainly neither water nor wind mills could ever have accomplished what the steam engine has already done; much less what it is destined hereafter to do for the valley of the Mississippi.

In another letter dated July 29th, 1784, Major "Craig says: "I have made some progress in a sub-"scription for a post rider, and believe I shall succeed; "it would be of great advantage to this country." In the letter he reiterates his opinion in favor of a wind-mill. The subscription paper fell short.

Within a month after the approval of the survey an event occurred which doubtless contributed to the progress of the young town at the head of the Ohio. When Pittsburgh was surveyed, and down to the 21st day of October, 1784, the country north of the Ohio and west of the Allegheny river, including our thriving sister city, were still owned and occupied by the natives. On that day a treaty was concluded with the Six Nations at Fort Stanwix, now Rome, New York, by which their title was extinguished to all that region of country. This extinguishment of the Indian title though an important matter, was not one whose influence would be immediately felt. The Indians still continued to rove through that country, and even ten years later fired their rifles and hurled their tomahawks at the venturous white men who rashly settled there.

In December, 1784, Arthur Lee, a Virginian by birth, a brother of Francis Lightfoot Lee and of Richard Bland Lee, both signers of the Declaration of Independence, and himself, along with Dr. Franklin and Silas Deane, Commissioners to France and the bearers of the first letter of Credence ever issued by Congress, arrived here. He had just been at Fort Stanwix, in

New York, holding the treaty at that place. Having not very long before visited France and Spain he would probably not be very much pleased with the appearance of a town inhabited "almost entirely" by Indian traders and Scotch and Irish; we will, however, let him speak for himself.

December 17th. We embarked on the Monongahela, and soon entered the Ohio, on our way to Fort McIntosh. The Ohio is a continuation of the Monongahela and Allegheny. They enter it at right angles. This appears plainly when you have passed the mouth of the Allegheny. Upon looking back you see at some distance, directly up the Monongahela, but the point of the two banks only that form the mouth of the Allegheny is visible, none of its water. Yet it has often been said that the Ohio was a continuation of the Allegheny.

Four miles down the river brings you to Montour's Island; which is six miles long, and about half a mile broad on an average, and contains about two thousand acres of very good land, the greater part of it never overflowed. The assembly of Pennsylvania gave Gen. Irwin a right of pre-emption to this land. They were moved to do it by an old and influential Presbyterian member, who with great gravity assured them he knew the Island and that it contained about one hundred and fifty acres. The property of it is contested between Gen. Irwin, Col. Neville, and Col. Simms of Alexandria. The next place is Loggstown, which was formerly a settlement on both sides of the Ohio, and the place where the treaty of Lancaster was confirmed by the western Indians. From Loggstown to the mouth of Beaver Creek, is — miles, and from thence to Fort McIntosh, one mile. This fort is built of well hewn logs, with four bastions; its figure an irregular square, the face to the river being longer than the side to the land. It is about equal to a square of fifty yards, is well built, and strong against musketry; but the opposite side of the river commands it entirely, and a single piece of artillery from thence would reduce it. This fort was built by us during the war, and is not therefore noted in Hutchins' map. The place was formerly a large Indian settlement, and French trading place. There are peach trees still remaining. It is a beautiful plain, extending about two miles along the river, and one to the hills; surrounded on the east by Beaver Creek, and on the west by a small run, which meanders through a most excellent piece of meadow ground, full of shell-bark hickory, black-walnut, and oak. About one mile and a half up the Beaver Creek, there enters a small, but perennial stream, very fit for a mill-seat; so that the possession of the land from there to the western stream, would include a fine meadow, a mill-seat, a beautiful plain for small grain, and rich, well-timbered uplands. It falls just within the western boundary of Pennsylvania; and is reserved by the state out of the sale of the land, as a precious morsel for some favorite of the legislature. The Ohio here is about four hundred yards wide. The Monongahela at Fort Pitt is about two hundred and eighty wide. The Allegheny, about two hundred. The former frequently overflows, and falls much sooner than the latter, owing to its rapidity and extent. The banks of the Monongahela on the west, or opposite side to Pittsburgh, are steep close to the water, and about two hundred yards high. About a third of the way from the top is a vein of coal, above one of the rocks. The coal is burnt in the town, and considered very good. The property of this and of the town is in the Penns. They have lotted out the face of the hill at thirty pounds a lot, to dig coal as far in as the perpendicular falling from the summit of the bank. Fort Pitt is regularly built, cost the Crown £600, and is commanded by cannon from the opposite bank of the Monongahela, and from a hill above the town called Grant's Hill, from the catastrophe which befel Gen. Grant at that place. He was advancing with some Highland regiments and Virginia light-infantry before the army under Gen. Forbes, took his station upon this hill, and had the folly to order his drums to beat and his bag-pipes to play, in expectation of frightening the French and Indian garrison of the then Fort Du Quesne, to surrender. But the commandant sending a part of the Indians in his rear, sallied out upon him, killed all the Highlanders, and made him prisoner. The Virginia troops, under Col. Lewis, being more upon their guard, mostly escaped.

Pittsburgh is inhabited almost entirely by Scots and Irish, who live in paltry log-houses, and are as dirty as in the north of Ireland, or even Scotland. There is a great deal of small trade carried on; the goods being brought at the vast expense of forty-five shillings per cwt., from Philadelphia and Baltimore. They take in the shops, money, wheat, flour and skins. There are in the town four attorneys, two doctors, and not a priest of any persuasion, nor church, nor chapel; so that they are likely to be damned, without *the benefit of clergy*. The rivers encroach fast on the town; and to such a degree, that, as a gentleman told me, the

Allegheny had within thirty years of *his* memory, carried away one hundred yards. The place, *I believe*, will never be very considerable."

Possibly at the time Arthur Lee spoke thus contemptuously of this place, there may have been still some soreness in relation to the termination of the controversy about the boundary line. Certainly his opinion as to the future destiny of this place was not well considered. It was then but little more than thirty years since the first attempt at settlement here during twenty-five of which, at least, the place was the subject of contention between foreign nations and American States. Could he now revisit this point he would probably be surprised to see the change already produced here and would not be very much gratified by the comparison of Pittsburgh with Richmond.

There is an error, probably typographical, in the estimate of the cost of Fort Pitt; Judge Brackenridge, in an article which we shall soon notice, fixes the cost at *sixty thousand* pounds; which, we think, could not be very far wrong. The fort was an extensive work, there was within its ramparts, one range of brick quarters for the officers, and another range of hewn log houses, probably for the soldiers, besides blockhouses in two or three of the bastions, the curtain of the north-western rampart was casemated, the two faces of the work towards the country *revetted*, that is supported on the outside by a substantial brick wall, thick enough to resist the pressure of the earth, and high enough to be used as a ball alley, and the parade ground was paved with hard burnt brick.

It seems, there were then two doctors and four lawyers here, but no clergyman. The writer of these sketches has in his possession a letter from the late Professor Robert Patterson, of Philadelphia, dated October 6th, 1780, in which he says, "my brother Joseph (the late Rev. Jos. Patterson,) is located on the head waters of Racoon, which is, I believe, near Fort Pitt." Reverend John McMillan was, also, at Cannonsburg some years previous.

The town being now laid out and the proprietors prepared to make titles to the lots; it might be expected the town would begin to expand by degrees, and some kind of manufactories be established. About that time Isaac Craig and Stephen Bayard, who were already engaged in the mercantile business, formed a partnership with Turnbull, Marmie & Co., of Philadelphia, and in addition to their original object added a distillery here, a saw-mill up the Allegheny, and Salt-works some where on Big Beaver.

We cannot ascertain exactly when the distillery went into operation; the closest reference to it, however, which we have found, is in a letter from Turnbull, Marmie & Co., to Craig, Bayard & Co., dated, "Philadelphia, October 28th, 1784," saying: "We are very anxious to hear that the stills have reached you in good order, and that you will be able to set them going this fall."

Those were not temperance days. A letter from the Salt-works, to Craig & Bayard, says: "I am greatly in want of three barrels of whiskey and a barrel of rum. For want of them, my neighbor gets all the skins and furs."

In 1786, on the 29th of July, another manufacture was established here, one well calculated to correct the evil influences of the distillery, we mean the making of newspapers. On the day above mentioned, John Scull and Joseph Hall, issued the first number of the Pittsburgh Gazette, the first newspaper ever printed west of the Allegheny mountains.

In the first number of the Gazette, there appeared a very graphic description of Pittsburgh and its vicinity from the pen of the late Judge Brackenridge, which we think well worthy of republication in our book.

FROM BRACKENRIDGE'S "GAZETTE PUBLICATIONS."

It was in the spring of the year 1781, that leaving the city of Philadelphia I crossed the Allegheny mountain, and took my residence in the town of Pittsburgh:

> "If town it might be call'd, that town was none,
> "Distinguishable by house or street———."

But in fact a few old buildings, under the walls of a garrison, which stood at the junction of the two rivers. Nevertheless it appeared to me as what would one day be a town of note, and in the mean time might be pushed forward by the usual means that raise such places. Two or three years had elapsed, and some progress had been made in improvement, when a Gazette was established at this place for the western country, and one of my earliest contributions was the following, intended to give some reputation to the town, with a view to induce emigration to this particular spot, whether it contributed in any degree to this object, I do not know, nor is it material. It will serve to give some idea of what the town was at an early period, and the state of society at that time, July 26, 1786.

ON THE SITUATION OF THE TOWN OF PITTSBURGH, AND THE STATE OF SOCIETY AT THAT PLACE.

The Allegheny river running from the north-east, and the Monongahela from the south-west, meet at the angle of about 33 degrees, and form the Ohio. This is said to signify, in some of the Indian languages, bloody; so that the Ohio river may be translated the River of Blood. The French have called it La Belle Riviere, that is the Beautiful and Fair River, but this is not intended by them as having any relation to the name Ohio.

It may have received the name of Ohio about the beginning of the present century, when the Six Nations made war upon their fellow savages in these territories and subjected several tribes.

The word Monongahela is said to signify, in some of the Indian languages the *Falling-in-Banks*, that is, the stream of the Falling-in, or Mouldering Banks.

At the distance of about four or five hundred yards from the head of the Ohio is a small island, lying to the north-west side of the river, at the distance of about 70 yards from the shore. It is covered with wood, and at the lowest part, is a lofty hill famous for the number of wild turkies which inhabit it. The island is not more in length than one quarter of a mile, and in breadth about 100 yards. A small space on the upper end is cleared and overgrown with grass. The savages had cleared it during the late war, a party of them attached to the United States having placed their wigwams and raised corn there. The Ohio, at the distance of about one mile from its source, winds round the lower end of the island and disappears. I call the confluence of the Allegheny and Monongahela the source of the Ohio.

It is pleasant to observe the conflict of these two waters where they meet: when of an equal height the contest is equal, and a small rippling appears from the point of land at their junction to the distance of about five hundred yards. When the Allegheny is master, as the term is, the current keeps its course a great way into the Monongahela, before it is overcome, and falls into the bed of tne Ohio. The Monongahela in like manner having the mastery, bears away the Allegheny and with its muddy waters discolors the chrystal current of that river. This happens frequently, inasmuch as these two rivers, coming from different climates of the country, are seldom swoln at the same time. The flood of the Allegheny rises perhaps the highest. I have observed it to have been at least 30 feet above the level, by the impression of the ice on the branches of trees which overhang the river, and had been cut at the breaking up of the winter, when the snow and frost melting towards the north-east throw themselves down with amazing rapidity and violence in a mighty deluge. The current of the Allegheny is in general more rapid than that of the Monongahe'a, and though not broader or of greater depth, yet, from this circumstance throws forward a greater quantity of water in the same space of time. In this river, at the distance of about one mile above the town of Pittsburgh is a beautiful little island, which, if there are river gods and nymphs, they may be supposed to haunt. At the upper end of the island and towards the western shore is a small ripple, as it is called, where the water, bubbling as if it sprung from the pebbles of a fountain, gives vivacity and an air of cheerfulness to the scene.

The fish of the Allegheny are harder and firmer than those of the Monongahela or Ohio, owing, as is supposed, to the greater coldness and purity of the water. The fish in general of those rivers are good. They are, the pike, weighing frequently 15 or 20 pounds, the perch much larger than any I have ever seen in the bay of Chesapeake, which is the only tide from whence I have ever seen perch; there is also the sturgeon and many more kinds of fish.

It is a high amusement to those who are fond of fishing, to angle in those waters, more especially at the time of a gentle flood, when the frequent nibbles of the large and small fishes entertain the expectation, and sometimes gratify it by a bite; and when those of the larger size are taken, it is neçessary to play them a considerable time before it can be judged safe to draw them in. I have seen a canoe half loaded in a morning by some of those most expert in the employment, but you will see in a spring evening the banks of the rivers lined with men fishing at intervals from one another. This, with the streams gently gliding, the woods, at a distance, green, and the shadows lengthening towards the town, forms a delightful scene. Fond of the water, I have been sometimes highly pleased in going with a select party, in a small barge, up or down the rivers, and landing at a cool spring, to enjoy the verdant turf, amidst the shady bowers of ashwood, sugar-tree or oak, planted by the hand of nature, not art.

It may be said by some who will read this description which I have given, or may be about to give, that it is minute and useless, inasmuch as they are observations of things well known. But let it be considered that it is not intended for the people of this country, but for those at a distance, who may not yet be acquainted with the natural situation of the town of Pittsburgh, or having heard of it, may wish to be more particularly informed. Who knows what families of fortune it may induce to emigrate to this place?

There is a rock known by the name of McKee's rock, at the distance of about three miles below the head of the Ohio. It is end of a promontory, where the river bends to the north-west, and where, by the rushing of the floods, the earth has been cut away during several ages, so that now the huge overhanging rocks appear, hollowed beneath, so as to form a dome of majesty and grandeur, near one hundred feet in height. Here are the names of French and British officers engraved, who in the former times, in parties of pleasure, had visited this place. The town of Pittsburgh, at the head of the Ohio, is scarcely visible from hence, by means of an intervening Island, the lower end of which is nearly opposite the rocks. Just below them at the bending of the river is a deep eddy water, which has been sounded by a line of thirty fathoms, and no bottom found. Above them is a beautiful extent of bottom, containing five or six hundred acres, and the ground rising to the inland country with an easy ascent, so as to form an extensive landscape. As you ascend the river from these rocks to the town of Pittsburgh, you pass by on your right hand the mouth of a brook known by the name of the Saw-mill run. This empties itself about half a mile below the town, and is overlooked by a building on its banks, on the point of a hill which fronts the east, and is first struck by the beam of the rising sun. At a small distance from its mouth is a saw-mill, about 20 perches below the situation of an old mill built by the British, the remains of some parts of which are yet seen.

At the head of the Ohio stands the town of Pittsburgh, on an angular piece of ground, the two rivers forming the two sides of the angle. Just at the point, stood, when I first came to this country, a tree, leaning against which I have often overlooked the wave, or committing my garments to its shade have bathed in the transparent tide. How have I regretted its undeserved fate when the early winter's flood, tore it from the roots and left the bank bare.

On this point stood the old French fort known by the name of Fort Duquesne, which was evacuated and blown up by the French in the campaign of the British under Gen. Forbes. The appearance of the ditch and mound, with the salient angles and bastions still remains, so as to prevent that perfect level of the ground which otherwise would exist. It has been long overgrown with the finest verdure, and depastured on by cattle; but since the town has been laid out it has been enclosed, and buildings are erected.

Just above these works is the present garrison, built by Gen. Stanwix, and is said to have cost the crown of Britain £60,000. Be that as it may, it has been a work of great labor and of little use—for, situated on a plain, it is commanded by heights and rising grounds on every side, and some at less than the distance of a mile. The fortification is regular, constructed according to the rules of art, and about three years ago, put into good repair by Gen. Irwin who commanded at this post. It has the advantage of an excellent magazine, built of stone; but the time is come, and it is hoped will not again return, when the use of this garrison is at an end. There is a line of posts below it on the Ohio river, to the distance of three hundred miles. The savages come to this place for trade, not for war, and any future contest that we may have with them, will be on the heads of the more northern rivers that fall into the Mississippi.

The bank of the Allegheny river, on the north-west side of the town of Pittsburgh, is planted with an orchard of apple trees, with some pear trees intermixed. These were brought, it is said, and planted by a British officer who commanded at this place early on the first occupation of it by the crown of England. He has deserved the thanks of those who have since enjoyed it, as the fruit is excellent, and the trees bear in abundance every year. Near the garrison on the Allegheny bank, were formerly what were called the king's artillery gardens, delightful spots, cultivated highly to usefulness and pleasure, the soil favoring the growth of plants and flowers, equal with any on the globe. Over this ground the ancient herbs and plants springing up underneath the foot, it is delightful still to walk, covered with the orchard shade.

On the margin of this river once stood a row of houses, elegant and neat, and not unworthy of the European taste, but have been swept away in the course of time, some for the purpose of forming an opening to the river from the garrison, that the artillery might incommode the enemy approaching and deprived of shelter; some torn away by the fury of the rising river, indignant of too near a pressure on its banks. These buildings were the receptacles of the ancient Indian trade, which, coming from the westward, centred in this quarter: but of these buildings, like decayed monuments of grandeur, no trace remains. Those who, twenty years ago, saw them flourish, can only say, here they stood.

From the verdant walk on the margin of this beautiful river, you have a view of an island about a mile above, round which the river twines with a resplendent brightness; gliding on the eastern bank, it would wish to keep a straight direction, once supposed to be its course: but thrown beneath, it modestly submits and falls towards the town. When the poet comes with his enchanting song to pour his magic numbers on this scene, this little island may aspire to live with those in the Ægean sea, where the song of Homer drew the image of delight, or where the Cam or Isis embracing in their bosoms gems like these, are sung by Milton, father of the modern bards.

On the west side of the Allegheny river, and opposite the orchard, is a level of three thousand acres, reserved by the state to be laid out in lots for the purpose of a town. A small stream at right angles to the river passes through it. On this ground it is supposed a town may stand; but on all hands it is excluded from the praise of being a situation so convenient as on the side of the river, where the present town is placed; yet it is a most delightful grove of oak, cherry and walnut trees: but we return and take a view of the Monongahela on the southern side of the town.

This bank is closely set with buildings for the distance of near half a mile, and behind this range the town chiefly lies, falling back on the plains between the two rivers. To the eastward is Grant's hill, a beautiful rising ground, discovering marks of ancient cultivation ; the forest having long ago withdrawn, and shown the head and brow beset with green and flowers. From this hill two chrystal fountains issue, which in the heat of summer continue with a limpid current to refresh the taste. It is pleasant to celebrate a festival on the summit of this ground. In the year 1781 a bower had been erected, covered with green shrubs. The sons and daughters of the day assembling, joined in the festivity, viewing the rivers at a distance, and listening to the music of the military on the plain beneath them. When the moonlight rising from the east, had softened into gray, the prospect, a lofty pile of wood enflamed, with pyramidal rising, illuminated both the rivers and the town, which far around reflected brightness. Approaching in the appearance of a river god, a swain begirt with weeds natural to these streams, and crowned with leaves of the sugar tree, hailed us, and gave prophetic hints of the grandeur of our future empire. His words I remember not, but it seemed to me for a moment, that the mystic agency of deities well known in Greece and Rome, was not a fable ; but that powers unseen haunt the woods and rivers, who take part in the affairs of mortals, and are pleased with the celebration of events that spring from great achievements and from virtue.

This is the hill, and from whence it takes its name, where in the war which terminated in the year 1763. Grant advancing with about 800 Caledonians or Highland Scotch troops, beat a reveille a little after sunrise to the French garrison, who accompanied with a num- of savages, sallied out and flanking him unseen from the bottom on the left and right then covered with wood, ascended the hill, tomahawked and cut his troops to pieces, and made Grant himself prisoner. Bones and weapons are yet found on the hill, the bones white with the weather, the weapons covered with rust.

On the summit of this hill is a mound of earth, supposed to be a catacomb or ancient burying place of the savages. There can be no doubt of this, as on the opening some of the like tumuli or hills of earth, bones are found. In places where stones are plenty, these mounds are raised of stones, and skeletons are found in them. To the north-east of Grant's hill, there is one still higher at the distance of about a quarter of a mile, which is called the Quarry hill, from the excellent stone quarry that has been opened in it. From this hill there is an easy descent the whole way to the town, and an excellent smooth road, so that the stones can be easily procured to erect any building at Pittsburgh. From the Quarry-hill you have a view of four or five miles of the Allegheny river, along which lies a fine bottom, and in high cultivation, with different inclosures and farm-houses; the river winding through the whole prospect.

This hill would seem to stand as that whereon a strong redoubt might be placed, to command the commerce of the Allegheny river, while directly opposite on the Monongahela side, to the south-east stands a hill of the same height and appearance, known by the name of Ayres' hill, so called from a British engineer of that name, who gave his opinion in favor of this ground as that whereon the fort ought to be constructed, as being the highest ground, and which must command the rivers, and the plain with the inferior rising grounds on which the town is built. The hill has been cultivated on the summit by a Highland regiment, who built upon it, though the buildings are now gone, and the brow of the hill is still covered with wood.

From Ayres' hill issue several fountains, falling chiefly towards the north, into a small brook, which increasing, encircles the foot of the hill, and takes its course through several beautiful little meads into the Monongahela river. On this brook, before it takes its turn to the Monongahela, in a delightful little valley, and in the neighborhood of some plum-trees, the natives of the country, was the ancient residence of a certain Anthony Thompson, the vestiges of whose habitation still remain; an extent of ground cleared by him lies to the north, accustomed to long cultivation, and now thrown out a common. The best brick may be made from this ground, the fine loam and sand of which the soil consists, and the water just at hand, highly favoring the object.

As you ascend from this valley, through which a main leading road passes from the country, you see the Monongahela, and approaching Grant's hill on the right, you have the point of view from whence the town is seen to the best advantage. It is hid from you until by the winding of the road you begin to turn the point of the hill; you then see house by house on the Monongahela side opening to your view, until you are in front of the main town, in a direct line to the confluence of the rivers. Then the buildings on the Allegheny show themselves with the plain extending to the right, which had been concealed. You have in the mean time a view of the rising grounds beyond the rivers, crowned with lofty woods. I was once greatly struck in a summer morning, viewing from the ground the early vapor rising from the river. It hung midway between the foot and summit of the hill, so that the green above, had the appearance of an island in the clouds.

It may be here observed, that at the junction of these two rivers until eight o'clock of summer mornings, a light fog is usually incumbent: but it is of a salutary nature, inasmuch as it consists of vapor not exhaled from stagnant water, but which the sun of the preceding day had extracted from trees and flowers, and in the evening had sent back in dew, so that rising with a second sun in fog, and becoming of aromatic quality, it is experienced to be healthful.

The town of Pittsburgh, as at present built, stands chiefly on what is called the third bank; that is the third rising of the ground above the Allegheny water. For there is the first bank, which confines the river at the present time; and about three hundred feet removed is a second like the falling of a garden; then a third, at the distance of about three hundred yards; and lastly, a fourth bank, all of easy inclination, and parallel with the Allegheny river. These banks would seem in successive periods to have the margin of the river which gradually has changed its course, and has been thrown from one decent to another, to the present bed where it lies. In digging wells the kind of stones are found which we observe in the Allegheny current, worn smooth by the attrition of the water. Shells also intermixed with these are thrown out. Nature therefore, or the river, seems to have formed the bed of this town as a garden with level walks, and fallings of the ground. Hence the advantage of descending gardens on these banks, which art elsewhere endeavors, with the greatest industry to form. Nor is the soil less happy than the situation. The mould is light and rich. The finest gardens in the known world may be formed here.

The town consists at present of about an hundred dwelling houses, with buildings appurtenant. More are daily added, and for some time past it has improved with an equal but continual pace. The inhabitants, children, men and women, are about fifteen hundred;* this number doubling almost every year from the accession of people from abroad, and from those born in the town. As I pass along, I may remark that this new country is in general highly prolific; whether it is that the vegetable air, if I may so express it, constantly perfumed with aromatic flavor, and impregnated with salts drawn from the fresh soil, is more favorable to the production of men and other animals than decayed grounds.

There is not a more delightful spot under heaven to spend any of the summer months than at this place. I am astonished that there should be such repairing to the Warm Springs in Virginia, a place pent up between the hills where the sun pours its beams concentrated as in a burning glass, and not a breath of air stirs; where the eye can wander scarcely half a furlong, while here we have the breezes of the river, coming from the Mississippi and the ocean; the gales that fan the woods, and are sent from the refreshing lakes to the northward; in the meantime the prospect of extensive hills and dales, whence the fragrant air brings odors of a thousand flowers and plants, or of the corn and grain

* This estimate of the population here is a most extravagant one, being about fifteen to a house; which is incredible. We will have occasion to refer to this matter of houses and population again.

of husbandmen, upon its balmy wings. Here we have the town and country together. How pleasant it is in a summer evening, to walk out upon these grounds, the smooth green surface of the earth, and the woodland shade softening the late fervid beams of the sun; how pleasant by a chrystal fountain is a tea party under one of those hills, with the rivers and the plains beneath.

Nor is the winter season enjoyed with less festivity than in more populous and cultivated towns. The buildings warm; fuel abundant, consisting of the finest coal from the neighboring hills, or of ash, hickory or oak, brought down in rafts by the rivers. In the mean time the climate is less severe at this place than on the other side of the mountain, lying deep in the bosom of the wood; sheltered on the north-east, by the bending of the Allegheny heights, and on the south-west, warmed by the tepid winds from the bay of Mexico, and the great southern ocean.

In the fall of the year and during the winter season, there is usually a great concourse of strangers at this place, from the different States, about to descend the river to the westward, or to make excursions into the uninhabited and adjoining country. These, with the inhabitants of the town spend the evening in parties at the different houses, or at public balls, where they are surprised to find an elegant assembly of ladies, not to be surpassed in beauty and accomplishments perhaps by any on the continent.

It must appear like enchantment to a stranger, who after travelling an hundred miles from the settlements, across a dreary mountain, and through the adjoining country, where in many places the spurs of the mountain still continue, and cultivation does not always show itself, to see, all at once, and almost on the verge of the inhabited globe, a town with smoking chimneys, halls lighted up with splendor, ladies and gentlemen assembled, various music, and the mazes of the dance. He may suppose it to be the effect of magic, or that he is come into a new world where there is all the refinement of the former, and more benevolence of heart."

In subsequent numbers of the same paper, on the 19th and 26th of August, 1786, it is stated that there was one clergyman of the Calvinistic faith, (Samuel Barr,) settled here, and one German Lutheran *occasionally* preached here.

It is also stated that "a church of squared timber, and moderate dimensions is on the way to be built." This church stood within the ground now covered by the First Presbyterian Church, and was suffered to stand until the brick building was reared around it.

There were then here, two physicians, Dr. Bedford was one of them; and two lawyers, Brackenridge, and perhaps John Woods or James Ross.

The price of carriage from Philadelphia, was sixpence for each pound weight. The writer of the article makes this prediction. "However improved the "conveyance may be, and by whatever channel, the "importation of heavy articles will still be expensive. "The manufacture of them will therefore become more "an object here than elsewhere.

When the Pittsburgh Gazette was first issued, there was no mail to this place; all correspondence was carried on by special express, or casual travellers. In the

Pittsburgh Gazette of September 30th, 1788, we find the following extract of a letter dated "Philadelphia, "September 14th, 1786. Mr. Brison has returned "from New York, with orders to establish a post from "this place to Pittsburgh, and one from Virginia to "Bedford. The two to meet at Bedford."

On the 1st of March, 1787, a meeting of the inhabitants of Pittsburgh was held, and Messrs. Hugh Ross, Stephen Bayard and Rev. Samuel Barr, appointed a committe to report a plan for building a market house, and establishing market days. The meeting was also invited to meet again in the public square, on the ensuing Saturday, to hear the report of the committee. The market house was erected on the gronnd now vacant, corner of Market and Second Streets.

On the 29th of September, 1787, an act was passed by the Legislature of Pennsylvania, incorporating the Presbyterian Congregation of the town of Pittsburgh, and among the Trustees we find the name of their pastor, Samuel Barr, who, of course, must have been here previous to that time. So that the ground of Arthur Lee's reproach, that "there was no priest of any persuasion here," was soon wiped away.

At that same session of the Legislature, an act was also passed for the establishment of an Academy, or Public School, at Pittsburgh.

This same year, 1787, also gave birth to two other most noble and importannt measures, which, no doubt, contributed greatly to our prosperity, as well as to the growth and happiness of the whole country. We mean the Constitution of the United States, and the glorious Ordinance for the government of the North Western Territory. The former, by giving the country a firm, national government, gave assurance and tranquillity, and the latter by placing near us a free, thriving and industrious population, secured to our infant manufactories, a large body of valuable customers.

On the 3d of April, 1788, the *May Flower*, the first boat with New England emigrants for the mouth of the Muskingum, arrived here from Simrall's Ferry, where West Newton now stands. This was the beginning of that emigration which filled the great Territory with a civilized population, which has converted the wilderness into a garden, and made the valleys to bloom as a rose.

Dr. Hildreth, of Marietta, gives the following account of the starting of the May Flower from Robb's town, now better known as West Newton, and of the passage down the *Youghhiogany* river.

"After laying in a stock of provisions, they pushed " out merrily into the 'Yoh,' as it was familiarly called " by all the borderers of that region, and floated rapid-" ly along, sometimes grazing on the shallows, and at " other times grounding on the sand-bars. By dint of " rowing and pushing, they made out to get on; espe-" cially after falling into the larger current of the Mo-" nongahela, and reached Pittsburgh on Sunday even-" ing. They were now at the junction of these two noble " streams, the Allegheny and the Monongahela, and " saw the waters of the charming Ohio, the object of " all their toils, and were apparently at the end of their " journey. Near the point of land where the Ohio takes " its name, they landed their uncouth and unwieldy " water-craft, making it fast to a stake on the bank. It " was late in the afternoon, and the men went up into " the town to purchase some articles needed to make " the families comfortable on the downward voyage.

"Pittsburgh then contained four or five hundred in-"habitants, several retail stores, and a small garrison "of troops was kept in old Fort Pitt. To our travel-"lers who had lately seen nothing but trees and rocks, "with here and there a solitary hut, it seemed to be "quite a large town. The houses were chiefly built of "logs, but now and then one had assumed the appear-"ance of neatness and comfort."

CHAPTER IX.

Allegheny County established; Indians troublesome; Harmar's campaign, and defeat; Alarm at Pittsburgh; Letter of Major Craig, explaining occurrences here; Great change here since 1791; Indian murders within a few miles; Commencement of the building of a new fort; Major Craig contracts for forty-two boats to transport troops down the Ohio; May 11th, 1792, Fifty boats ready, will transport three thousand troops; May 18th, 1792, Capt. Hughes with his detachment, first occupants of the new Fort; Named Fort Fayette; Nov. 30th, Army of Gen. Wayne assembled at Legionville on the Ohio; Severe discipline at that place; Laconic note from Captain John Finley; Celebration of Washington's birth-day; May 3d, 1793, Army embarked at Legionville and descended the Ohio; Correspondence between citizens of Pittsburgh and Gen. Wayne; Trial of Brady; Anecdote of Guyasutha; Navigation of the Ohio no worse above Wheeling than below; Line of mail boats established from Wheeling to Limestone, now *Maysville*; Western Insurrection—different accounts of it; Alexander Hamilton's Report; Judge Wilkinson's Notes; John Neville's services and character; Presley Neville; Abraham Kirkpatrick; Isaac Craig; Extract of letter from Alexander Hamilton to Major Craig. David Lenox; Presley Neville, Isaac Craig and two others taken by the Insurgents and escape.

Our town was, up to the summer of 1788, in Westmoreland County, and our citizens had to go more than thirty miles to attend court; but on the 24th of September, 1788, an act of Legislature was passed, erecting the new county of Allegheny out of parts of Washington and Westmoreland. By this act the courts were to be held in Pittsburgh, until certain trustees named therein should erect suitable buildings on the reserved tract opposite Pittsburgh, where Allegheny City now stands. But, by an act passed the next Spring, the trustees were authorized to purchase lots in Pittsburgh, for Court-house and Jail.

On the western side of the Allegheny river, just opposite to Pittsburgh, now stands the city of Allegheny, connected with Pittsburgh by three substantial bridges, and an aqueduct also serving as a bridge. That place was laid out by the order of the sovereign authority of Pennsylvania, in the year 1789. It is an exact square of one hundred lots, with a large public square. The lots each sixty feet by two hundred and forty. The out-lots are numerous, and extend up the Allegheny and down the Ohio altogether about six and one fourth miles.

Postages at	Pittsburgh,	year ending	Oct. 1st, 1790,	$110 99
"	Richmond,	"	"	2,191 25
"	Pittsburgh,	"	June 30, 1850,	39,569 71
"	Richmond,	"	"	27,007 24

The Indians, stimulated probably by British traders, were troublesome in 1790, and the President, believing that offensive measures were the only means of protecting the citizens from their incursions, planned an expedition against the hostile tribes on the Scioto and Wabash, to be under the command of General Harmar, an officer of considerable experience.

The army under this officer to proceed from Fort

Washington to the Scioto river. Gen. Harmar marched with about fourteen hundred troops, militia and regulars, on the 30th September, 1790, and after destroying several towns on the Scioto, and meeting a pretty severe repulse, and losing several valuable officers and one hundred and fifty men, returned again to Fort Washington. The result of this expedition of Gen. Harmar, seems to have greatly encouraged the hostile tribes of Indians. Their incursions were extended even to the vicinity of our city. The following letter, written at this place, details occurrences which took place here less than sixty years ago, and exhibits a very marked contrast with the present condition of affairs. The writer of this letter, Major Isaac Craig, was Deputy Quarter Master General and Military Store Keeper; as such he had a very extensive correspondence with the Secretary of War, the Quarter Master General, and the commandants of the different military stations, in the West. Of this correspondence we have eight bound volumes, and a mass of loose letters, and will probably have frequent occasion to refer to them, in the prosecution of our work. The Store House at that time was an old log building, much decayed, in the bounds of Fort Pitt, but entirely unguarded or otherwise protected.

FORT PITT, MARCH 25, 1791.

"SIR:—In consequence of a number of people killed and several taken prisoners by the Indians, in the vicinity of this place, within a few days past, and frequent reports of large parties of savages being on our frontier, the people of this town have made repeated applications for arms and ammunition to me, which I have hitherto refused; but in a town meeting held yesterday, it was resolved that the principal men of the town should wait on me, and request a loan of a hundred muskets, with bayonets and cartouch boxes, and they should enter into an obligation to re-deliver said arms, &c. in good order, to me in two months, or sooner if demanded by me, in consequence of any order of the commanding officer, or Secretary of War; but in case of my refusal to comply with their requisition, it was resolved to break open the stores and take such a number as they might think proper. Accordingly, ten of the most respectable characters of the town waited on me this day, and made the above demand; and they told me they were determined to take them in case of my refusal—that nothing but the necessity of putting the town in a state of defence, and their desire to guard the public stores, could have induced them to such a determination. I repeated my instructions to the gentlemen, and told them I must be guilty of a breach of orders, by issuing the smallest article without proper authority, and that their properest step would be to send an express to the Secretary of War, requesting an order on me for such articles as they thought necessary. They agreed with me that it was proper to send an express, but that there was not an hour to be lost in arming the inhabitants of the town. I had then no alternative but either to see the store houses broken open, and perhaps part of the stores destroyed, or to deliver one hundred muskets, and make these gentlemen accountable, and obtain a guard for the protection of the stores. I have chosen the latter, and taken an obligation signed by ten of the most respectable characters, by which they are accountable for 100 muskets, bayonets and cartouch boxes—obliged to re-deliver them in two months from this date, or sooner, if demanded—furnish such a guard for the stores as I may think necessary, and also to make application by express for your approbation of this transaction. I hope, Sir, it will appear to you, that of two evils, one of which was unavoidable, I have made choice of the least. I shall be very unhappy in your disapprobation of my conduct in this transaction.

I am, Sir, your obedient humble servant.

ISAAC CRAIG.

Hon. Major General Knox, Secretary of War, Philadelphia."

In reply to this letter the Secretary of War wrote as follows. "The issuing of the arms seems to have been justified by the occasion. No doubt will arise but they will be considered as part of the two hundred muskets, for which I gave the Governor an order on the 31st of last month."

A subsequent letter from Major Craig states that they had been so received.

What a change have sixty years produced in the situation of our city and of the whole country! The wilderness of 1791 is now succceeded by cultivated fields, the Indian war-path has given way to rail-roads and canals, and the lurking Shawanese, Wyandots and Delawares are removed hundreds of miles away, and their places supplied by millions of active, enterprising and industrious pale faces. We may mourn the fate of the red men, but surely, when the Almighty created this earth, and placed a man and woman upon it, he designed that it should be inhabited by a people more numerous, than could possibly be supported with the habits of the Indian.

In a letter dated March 31st, 1781, Major Craig has the following remark; "Your (Gen. Knox's) ob- "servations on the murder of the Indians at Beaver "Creek,* are already confirmed. Several persons with- "in a few miles of this place have lately fallen victims "to the revenge of those Indians who escaped on Bea- "ver Creek."

Another letter to the Secretary of War, dated May 19th, 1791, says; "We have frequent accounts of "murders being committed on our frontiers by the In- "dians. Several parties of them have penetrated ten, "fifteen and twenty miles into the country."

Same to same, Oct. 6th, 1791. "Messrs. Turnbull "and Marmie continue to pull down and sell the ma- "terials of the Fort. Small parties of Indians are still "thought to be in our neighborhood."

Extract of a letter from Gen. Knox to Major Craig, dated December 16th, 1791. "I request you immediately to procure materials for a block-house and picketted fort to be erected in such part of Pittsburgh, as shall be the best position, to cover the town as well as the public stores which shall be forwarded from time to time. As you have been an artillery officer during the late war, I request you to act as an engineer. I give you a sketch of the work generally, which you must adapt to the nature of the ground. It is possible that some private property may be interfered with by the position you take, but an appraisement must take place according to law and the result sent to me."

* This refers to the killing of some Delaware Indians by Samuel Brady, near the block-house which formerly stood near the lower end of New Brighton. Brady was afterwards tried at this place and acquitted, as will be seen hereafter.

Extract of a letter from Major Craig to Gen. Knox, dated 29th December, 1791. "I am making every "possible exertion for the erection of a work to defend "this town and the public stores. Accounts from fort "Franklin, as well as your orders, urge the necessity "of prompt attention to the defence of this place. By "next post, I shall inclose you a sketch of the ground "and the work, that I have judged necessary; it will "be erected on eight lots, Nos. 55, 56, 57, 58, 91, 92, "93 and 94; they belong to John Penn, jr. and John "Penn; Anthony Butler, Esq., of Philadelphia, is "their agent, the prices were fixed when the town was "laid out. It is not intended to cover the whole of "the lots with the work, but the portion not covered "will be suitable for gardens, for the garrison.

"I take the liberty of inclosing to you two letters "from fort Franklin, and extracts of other letters of "same date, (December 26th,) by which it appears, "that that garrison is in imminent danger, and that "the fidelity of the northern Indians is not to be de-"pended upon.

"I am mounting four six pounders on ship carriages, "for the block-houses; but there are no round shot "nor grape shot for that caliber here, the last being "sent to fort Washington."

Same to same, January 12th, 1792. "As there is "no six pound shot here, I have taken the liberty to "engage four hundred at Turnbull & Marmie's Fur-"nace,* which is now in blast. Reports by the way

* We have taken some pains to ascertain the time when this furnace, the first west of the mountains, was erected, and where it was located, and have ascertained that it was situated on Jacob's creek, fifteen miles from the mouth, and that it went into blast on the 1st of November, 1790.

"of fort Franklin say, that in the late action (St. "Clair's Defeat, November 4th, 1791,) the Indians "had three hundred killed and many wounded, that "there were eight hundred Canadians and several "British officers in the action. I shall take the liberty "of communicating to the inhabitants of Pittsburgh, "your assurance of such ample and generous means "of defence. I believe with you, that Cornplanter is "sincere; but would not a work at Presquile, on the "Lake, give greater confidence to him and his adher-"ents."

In the eleventh volume of the "American Museum," is given the following list of mechanics in this place, in 1792:

"1 Clock and Watch Maker, 2 Coopers, 1 Skin Dresser and Breeches maker, 2 Tanners and Curriers, 4 Cabinet-makers, 2 Hatters, 2 Weavers, 5 Black-smiths, 5 Shoemakers, 3 Saddlers, 1 Malster and Brewer, 2 Tinners, 3 Wheelwrights, 1 Stocking-weaver, 1 Rope-maker, 2 White-smiths. Total 36 Mechanics. The number of families was said to be 130."

Major Craig to General Knox, dated 11th March, 1792. "I have contracted for forty-two boats, viz: "32 of 50 feet each, 4 of 60 feet and 6 of 55, they "are to be one fourth wider than those purchased last "year, viz: fifteen feet, to be also stronger and better "finished. Delivered here with five oars to each. "Price per foot, 8*s.* and 9*d.*—$1,17 per foot."

Same to Capt. Jonathan Cass, Fort Franklin, dated April 7th, 1792. "The Indians crossed the river be-"low Wheeling on the 4th instant and killed nine per-"sons near that place."

Same to Gen. Knox, May 11th, 1792. "The fifty

"boats now ready, will transport three thousand men, "they are the best that ever came here, and, I believe, "the cheapest."

Same to same, May 18th, 1792. "Capt. Hughes, "with his detachment, has occupied the barracks in "the new fort since the 1st instant. Two of the six-"pounders are very well mounted in the second story "of one of the block-houses. The others will be "mounted in a few days. The work, if you have no "objections, I will name *Fort La Fayette*." The Secretary approved this name.

Same to Gen. Knox, dated 15th June, 1792. "Gen. "Wayne arrived here yesterday."

The following letter from the publisher and proprietor of the Pittsburgh Gazette, seems worthy of preservation, as an evidence of the difficulties which he had to encounter, six years after he had commenced the publication of that paper:

"Monday Morning, July 1st, 1792.

"*Dear Sir:* John Wright's pack-horses, by whom I receive my paper from Chambersburgh, has returned without bringing me any—owing to none being finished. As I am entirely out, and do not know what to do, I take the liberty of applying to you for some you have in the public stores, (and of which I have had some,) as a loan, or an exchange, for the kind herein enclosed—and as this kind is smaller, I will make an adequate allowance—or if you could wait two or three weeks, I will return you paper of a superior quality for any purpose, as I have sent to Philadelphia, by Mr. Brackenridge, for a large quantity, and John Wright's pack-horses return immediately for Chambersburgh, and will bring me up some—as I conceive you will not want the paper as soon as I can replace it, I flatter myself you will let me have three reams, and as soon as I receive mine it shall be returned, or if you choose to take the inclosed in exchange, it shall be immediately sent you—if you can oblige me with the paper it will do any time this day, and I shall consider myself as under a very particular obligation.

"I am, dear sir, your most obedient servant,

"JOHN SCULL.

"Major Isaac Craig."

Major Craig to Samuel Hodgdon, Q. M. General, November 9th, 1792. "This morning a detachment "of the troops and the artificers, with the necessary "tools for building, set off for the winter ground *be-* "*low** *Logstown*, on the Ohio; in a few days the whole "army will follow."

Same to Gen. Knox, 30th November, 1792. "This "morning, at an early hour, the artillery, infantry and "rifle corps, except a small garrison left in fort Fay- "ette, embarked and descended the Ohio to *Legionville*, "the cavalry crossed the Allegheny at the same time "and will reach the winter ground as soon as the

* In another letter written on the same day to General Knox, Major Craig speaks of the encampment being, "*near* Logstown;" and still in another letter to the same, dated 16th November, he says: "the troops have descended the river to their winter ground *at* Logstown."

From all these expressions it seems manifest that the understanding sixty years ago, was that Logstown was on the same side of the Ohio river, where, we know, Legionville was, that is the north side. Had Logstown been on the opposite side of the river, the three words "below," "near" and "at" would not have all been thus used, and the proper words "opposite" or "nearly opposite," entirely omitted. This understanding of the matter is entirely in agreement with all the old authorities; Croghan excepted. Logstown, I am satisfied, stood on the bank of the Ohio, immediately above the run below which it is well known Legionville stood.

"boats. As soon as the troops had embarked, the "General (Wayne) went on board his barge, under a "salute from a militia artillery corps of this place, "and all have, no doubt, before this time, reached their "winter quarters."

We have heard Gen. Wayne censured for severity of discipline while he was at Pittsburgh; especially in the execution of Sergeant Trotter. The following extract of a letter from Gen. Wayne to the Secretary of War, dated July 20th, 1792, shows a very bad feeling among the troops, and would seem to require some strong remedy.

"Major Ashton's detachment arrived here on Monday. Lieutenant Campbell with Stoke's dragoons, "and Faulkner's riflemen on Tuesday. Not less than "fifty of Ashton's detachment and seven dragoons "deserted on the way from Carlisle to this place."

Legionville was the place selected by Gen. Wayne, for the discipline of his men; there he prepared them for that campaign against the Indians, which terminated so successfully.

The troops remained at Legionville until the 30th of April, 1793, and during all that time were subject to constant and severe drill and exercise. Sham fights were frequently resorted to, and neither life nor the lash was spared. The following is a note found among the papers of Major Craig; the writer was a soldier of the Revolution, Captain John Finley, and at that time Assistant Quarter Master. The note is laconic and a very significant allusion to the discipline of "Mad Anthony."

"Major Craig, please send down some whip cord for "cats,—they have no cats to whip men with.

"Legionville, Feb. 22d, 1793. JNO. FINLEY."

On the very next day, perhaps at the very time the above note was written, the following display was taking place at Legionville:

LEGIONVILLE, February 24th.

The 22d instant, being the anniversary birth day of the PRESIDENT of the United States, Major General Wayne, commander-in-chief of the American army, issued the following orders for a general review in honor of the day. The Legionary corps consisting of cavalry, artillery infantry, and corps of riflemen.

"Head-Quarters, Legionville, Feb. 20, 1793.

"The Legion will be reviewed the day after to-morrow, at 10 o'clock, A. M., when every soldier capable of doing duty, must appear as a soldier ought to do, and for which the respective officers will be accountable.

"The cavalry, artillery, and infantry will march in two columns; the right platoon in front of the right, and the left platoon in front of the left. The artillery and cavalry equally divided in front and rear of each column. The guards for the redoubts No. 1 and 2, will form the van and rear guards of the right column. Those of No. 3 and 4 will be the van and rear-guards of the left column. When the columns display, the cavalry, artillery, van and rear-guards attached to the right column will form on the right, those attached to the left column will form on the left. The right wing of rifle corps will march in open files, forming a column of flankers to the right—the left wing of rifle corps will march in the same order, forming a column of flankers on the left, and will form to the left. The signal for marching will be a gun from the park of artillery."

The legion were drawn up on their usual parade, and took up the line of march as directed in the orders for the day, strongly flanked by the rifle companies, and gained a commanding eminence some distance in front of the grand cantonment, drew up in form, and preserved the utmost regularity throughout the whole of their manœuvres. Each officer and soldier appearing in perfect military dress.

Considerable time took place in going through the various evolutions and firings, highly pleasing to every spectator.

The legion formed in two columns as before, with the artillery and ammunition wagons in the centre, continuing their march to the left, previous to which, a considerable number of infantry and rifle-men were detached, with orders to possess certain strong grounds, in front of the line of march, when, on the approach of the columns, a brisk engagement took place, and soon became general, and bearing with it much the appearance of a real action for upwards of 20 minutes, owing to the incessant peals of cannon and musquetry.

The columns having formed a hollow square, the cavalry in the centre, whence they sallied forth, and with the light troops made a brisk charge and terminated the engagement, which was obstinately maintained in every direction.

The firings having ceased, the legion regained the grand parade, and having formed the line in front discharged three times with their usual regularity. The artillery were then advanced in front of the line and commenced the federal salute of three times fifteen shells from howitzers, highly delightful to behold in their ranges, and explosions in the air, each re-echoing the day so estimable in the remembrance of each patriot citizen and soldier.

About three o'clock in the afternoon the legion returned to their cantonment in the same manner they marched off in the morning, and on being drawn up on their accustomed parade the commander-in-chief passed in review and received the salute of the line. The troops being dismissed, the General gave all the officers off duty the polite invitation of dining with him, at which agreeable interview hospitality presided, and brotherly love pervaded the whole. The dinner being ended, the following patriotic toasts were given:

1. The PRESIDENT, and the day—May he see many happy returns of it.

2. May our meeting with the savages produce conviction to the world, that the American Legion are the only troops proper to oppose them.

3. The American Fair—May the legion at all times merit their smiles.

4. The memory of those heroes who fell in defence of American liberty.

5. The American Legislatures—May their laws be founded in wisdom, and obeyed with promptitude.

6. The non-commissioned officers and privates of the late army and of the present legion.

7. The nation of France—May her arms be triumphant and her liberty permanent.

8. Our friend and brother La Fayette—May a generous nation forgive his errors (if any) and receive him to her bosom.

9. The land we live in—May America prove a secure asylum to the unfortunate.

Thus ended the day with the utmost hilarity and

good order throughout the whole army, and in the evening brilliant fire works were exhibited in the artillery park. A SPECTATOR.

While Gen. Wayne was at Legionville, he was visited by several chiefs of the Six Nations, amongst others that prominent character Kiashuta, and by that worthy, upright and sensible man Cornplanter. The latter afterwards went on a peace seeking mission to the hostile Indians, but in vain. They were too much elated by their triumphs over Harmar and St. Clair, or too much under the influence of British traders. While Cornplanter was on his mission, three of his people near the Genesee were unprovokedly attacked by the whites, one killed, another severely wounded. Upon hearing this news, Cornplanter exclaimed, "It is hard "when I and my people are trying to make peace for "the whites, that we should receive such a reward."

Major Craig to Gen. Knox, May 3d, 1793. "On "the 30th ultimo, Major Gen. Wayne, with the troops "under his command at Legionville, embarked in good "order and set off for Fort Washington; the troops "were in high spirits. The boats being well fitted for "transportation made a fine appearance. As the river "was considerably swelled by the late rains, it is pro-"bable the troops will reach Fort Washington in six "days."

A few days before the General left Legionville, he was at Pittsburgh, when the following correspondence took place:

Major General Anthony Wayne, Commander-in-Chief of the army of the United States.

The inhabitants of Pittsburgh, embrace the occasion of your visit to this this town from your winter quarters at Legionville, to express their respect for you personally, which is impressed upon them, from an experience of your just attention to the rights of the citizens while your army lay at this place, and from their observation of your unremitted exertions to preserve, improve and prepare the troops under your command for the service for which they were intended.

We have sanguine hopes, notwithstanding the misfortunes of the two last campaigns, that with soldiers in such health, subordination and discipline, the exultation of a savage enemy might be reduced, and their minds brought to a temper, of treating on proper principles, and preserving that treaty with some fidelity, from a recollection of what they had been made to suffer, the only principle by which, in present circumstances, they can be governed. But as there never was an Indian treaty without a peace, where goods are to be distributed, we expect one at present; and there can be no peace durable unless founded in affection or fear, and as there can be neither of these in the present case, we expect war, in a short time, again; and when it comes, as come it will, we shall be happy to see so vigilant and able an officer, with an army of his own forming, once more to do what ought to be done now, and by chastising first, lay the foundation of a more permanent peace with the enemy.

By directions of the inhabitants,

JOHN GIBSON, Chairman.

The personal respect, and the approbation of my conduct, so very politely and obligingly expressed by the inhabitants of Pittsburgh, have made an indelible impression of esteem and gratitude in my breast, that can only end with life.

A permanent peace with the hostile Indians appears to be the sincere wish and desire of government, and very sanguine expectations are entertained of its taking place in the course of the summer, through the mediation of the commissioners, appointed for that purpose.

If after every effort shall be made by them, it shall then be found, that peace is unattainable, but by the sacrifice of national character and honor, it is to be hoped, that the citizens of the United States of America, will have but one mind, as to the vigor with which the war shall be pursued.

In that event, I shall hope to be powerfully reinforced by the brave and virtuous frontier volunteers, with whose aid, I fondly trust, we shall produce a conviction to the minds of the savages, of our superiority in the field, which will soon lead the way to a permanent peace, so much the wish and desire of all good men.

With these hopes and impressions, I have the honor to be, with sincere respect and esteem for the inhabitants of Pittsburgh,

Your and their most devoted
And obliged humble servant,
ANTHONY WAYNE.

The Honorable General John Gibson, Chairman.

The following we find in a Philadelphia paper.

"PITTSBURGH, MAY 4, 1793.

"Lieutenant Col. John Clark, commandant of the 4th Sub-Legion, is to command the different posts on this frontier—His head quarters will be at this place."

"PITTSBURGH, MAY 25, 1793.

"On Monday last, the 20th of this month, a Court of Oyer and Terminer and Goal Delivery, and of Nisi Prius, for the county of Allegheny, was held at this place by the Chief-Justice and Judge Yeates.

"The only criminal business that came before the Judges was the trial of Capt. Samuel Brady, who, when the Judges were last here, had been indicted for murder, in killing certain Indians near the mouth of Beaver Creek, in the spring of the year 1791.

"It was proved to the satisfaction of the court, that notwithstanding the treaties of Fort Stanwix, M'Intosh, Muskingum, and Miami, which established peace between the Indians and the people of the United States, and obliged the Indians to surrender all who should commit any murder on our frontiers—certain banditti of them had from time to time infested the western frontier, stolen horses, taken boats, and murdered our citizens; that recently, before the killing of the Indians, for which Brady was now tried, several people from Ohio county, particularly Boggs, Paul Riley's family, and Mrs. Vanbuskirke, had been put to death; that to pursue the Indians who had committed these murders, and to recover some property stolen, a party of volunteers from Ohio county, of which Brady was one, crossed the Ohio, and led by the trail of the Indians towards the place where the killing happened, fired and killed those for whose death Brady was tried. It was proved by the oath of Keyashuta, an Indian chief, that the Delawares had long before let go the chain, that they, the Shawanese, Chippewas, Ottawas, Wyandots, and some renegade Mingoes, were in the battle against Gen. Harmar, 1790. It was also proved that the attack and firing of Capt. Kirkwood's house was by Delawares, that some of the instances of murder and rapine above mentioned were by Delawares, that the persons killed were Delawares and had in their possession some of the property just before taken from Ohio county, manifested an intention of proceeding to commit other murders on our citizens, and, when fired on by those who attacked them, and whom they had just discovered, were in the act of seizing their guns: and, moreover, the relation of John Hamilton, a trader on the spot, satisfied the court of the malignant and hostile temper of those very Indians.

"The Chief Justice, in a charge distinguished not less by learning than humanity, explained the laws of war, and the right of putting enemies to death, urged the impropriety of killing those who might with safety be taken prisoners, and the baseness of killing women; lamented that any acts of outrage, by our citizens should occasion retaliation on themselves; but stating that in his opinion, the Indians killed were hostile, directed, if the jury concurred in his opinion, of which he had no doubt, they should acquit the prisoner without leaving the bar. The jury did so, and the court ordered Captain Brady to be discharged on payment of fees."

In relation to the testimony of Guyasutha, in this case, the late James Ross, Esq. who was Brady's counsel, told a characteristic story. The testimony of that Indian was so very strong in favor of the defendant, that even his counsel was abashed. After the trial was over, he spoke to Guyasutha, and rather expressed his surprise at the decided tone of his testimony: upon which that Chief clapped his hand upon his breast and exclaimed, "*Am I not the friend of Brady?*" It seems obvious that he considered himself as much bound to swear for his friend, as he would be to fight in his defence.

The following extracts of letters show that the question about the navigation of the Ohio, above and below Wheeling, was started many years ago.

Major Craig to Gen. Knox, 14th June, 1793.

"The navigation of the Ohio is not materially better "from Wheeling than from Pittsburgh in a dry season, "and our best Ohio pilots say they find nearly the "same difficulty, until they pass the rapids below Lit-"tle Kanawa; indeed, we have found that more acci-"dents have happened to boats, and more loss sustain-"ed below Wheeling, than above."

This statement was fully confirmed by letters from Col. John Gibson, and Major George McCully, both well acquainted with the river and long accustomed to navigate it. They both pronounce Letart's Falls the worst place on the river, and Captina Bar as bad as any place above Wheeling.

Same to Jas O'Hara, Q. M. Gen. Seps. 30th, 1793.

A contagious fever having raged in Philadelphia for a considerable time, and still continuing, the Secretary of War being apprehensive a part of the clothing might be infected with the contagion, directed me to have them opened and aired at this post. I have, accordingly, had such packages as were pointed out to me by Mr. Hodgdon, opened, well aired and re-packed. This operation has caused a great deal of disagreeable feeling, and has given much uneasiness to the inhabitants, who feared it might introduce the disease here. From my own experience, however, and from that of Charles and Emanuel Conrad, who have for three weeks been constantly employed with the woolen goods. I think there is scarce a probability of their being infected."

On the 22d of April, 1794, the first act was passed incorporating the town of Pittsburgh into a Borough. The bounds of the borough were as follows. Beginning at the Point, or confluence of the rivers Monongahela and Allegheny, and running up the beach of the Monongahela three courses and distances given, to Short street, thirty-nine perches, to Grant Street two hundred and seven perches ; mouth of Suke's Run forty-nine perches, then north thirty degrees east, one hundred and fifty perches to a post in Andrew Watson's field, thence north nineteen degrees west one hundred and fifty perches to the Allegheny river, thence down the same three hundred and fifteen perches to the point of beginning.

Now that we have Telegraph Lines, and Rail-road Cars, that travel almost with the speed of the wind, we are disposed to wonder at the patience of our immediate ancestors, who were greatly rejoiced when a Post Office was established here, and a mail promised once in two weeks from Philadelphia. This was accomplished sixty-five years ago; but a mail from Limestone and Fort Washington was a still later desideratum. No regular intercourse could be carried on from Pittsburgh to Kentucky, or to the military posts along the river, by a route through the territory north of the Ohio. None but a strong and well armed party could hope to escape unharmed through that country, while the Shawanese and Wyandots were hostile. All communication to Limestone, or to Wayne's army at Fort Washington, must be sent by transient travelers, or by expresses through Western Virginia and Northern

Kentucky. Such means of correspondence between an army and its government, were entirely too uncertain to be depended upon: so that, in July, 1794, a line of mail boats was established to run from Wheeling to Limestone and back, once in every two weeks. From Wheeling to Pittsburgh and back, the mails were to be carried on horseback. The mail boats were twenty-four feet long, built like a whale boat, and steered with a rudder. They were manned by a steersman and four oarsmen, to each boat. The men had each a musket, and a supply of ammunition, all of which were snugly secured from the weather in boxes alongside their seats. The whole could be protected in wet weather by a tarpaulin which each boat carried.

The following extract from the letter of instructions of Major Isaac Craig, to Elijah Martin, Captain of mail boat No. 1. will explain the arrangements.

"You are to proceed immediately with the mail in "your charge to Limestone, touching on your way there "and back at Wheeling, Marietta and Gallipolis, at "each of which places a Post Office is established, and "a Postmaster appointed, who will give you further "instructions, if necessary. The time appointed for "your trip from this place to Limestone and back to "Wheeling, is from this time, (July 5th,) till the 24th "instant, at 12 o'clock, P. M. at which time you are "to be at Wheeling. You are, therefore, to proceed "without delay, both going and returning, so that the "mail may be delivered at Wheeling at the time above "stated, to enable the postrider to reach Pittsburgh "before the eastern mail is closed. After your return "to Wheeling you are to carry a weekly mail from that "place to Marietta and back."

Charles Mills, Captain of mail boat No. 2, was to leave Pittsburgh on the 11th of July, and was to return only as far as Marietta, at which place he was to be at 12 o'clock, A. M. of the 27th of July, to exchange mails with Captain Martin of boat No. 1, and then ply back and forth between Marietta and Gallipolis. Similar instructions were given to the Captain of mail boat No. 3 to ply between Limestone and Gallipolis.

This mode of carrying the mail was continued until 1798, and the conductors of the boats were so careful, that in all that time, but one attack was made upon them by the Indians.

While this arrangement for the transportation of the mails was in progress, before the mail boat No. 1 made her first trip back to Wheeling, and at the time when Gen. Wayne was advancing from Fort Greenville to the Maumee, the troubles which had long been brewing here in opposition to the excise on whiskey, broke out into open hostility, in repeated attacks on, and the final destruction of, the property of Gen. John Neville, in this vicinity, and in the occupancy of our town by armed insurgents.

This first insurrection against the laws of the Union occurring at our very door, cannot be overlooked in a work proposing to give a history of our city. The general histories of the country notice it; Brackenridge and Findley have both written *apologies* for their conduct in it, which have been looked upon as histories, and Alexander Hamilton, Secretary of the Treasury, has given a very dispassionate account of it. The late Judge Wilkinson, of Buffalo, New York, who grew to manhood on a farm in the immediate vicinity of the field of the greatest outrage, has, in some notes published in the Western Pioneer, borne just testimony to the virtues and services of the principal sufferers in the insurrection, but has fallen into some errors in his account of the family connection, while he has given them all credit for patriotic services. He says, "John Neville, a man of the most deserved pop-"ularity, was appointed collector, (inspector it should "be,) for Western Pennsylvania; he was one of the "few men of great wealth who had put his all at hazard "for independence. Besides his claims as a soldier "and a patriot, he had contributed greatly to the re-"lief of the suffering settlers. If any man could have "executed this odious law, Gen. Neville was the man. "He was the brother in law of the distinguished Gen. "Morgan, and father-in.law to Majors Craig and Kirk-"patrick, officers highly respected in the western coun-"try." Judge Wilkinson, from his residence, saw the ascending flames from the negro huts, the stables, the large well filled barn, and the comfortable mansion of Gen. Neville, and manifests in his article all that kindly feeling which a good neighbor might be expected to entertain. His kind heart had not changed in the half century which had elapsed between the destruction of the property, and the writing his account of it; but his memory, or his information of the family relations, was not so faithful as the kindness of his heart. John Neville was not the brother-in-law of Gen. Morgan, nor the father-in-law of Major Kirkpatrick. John Neville and Abraham Kirkpatrick married sisters of the name of Oldham, of as sound and true hearted a Whig family as any in the country, one of whose brothers yielded up his life in the cause of his country at Eutaw Springs, in South Carolina; the other at St. Clair's defeat.

Presley Neville, the only son of John Neville, married the daughter of Gen. Morgan, and Isaac Craig married the only sister of Presley. John Neville was, as Judge Wilkinson states, a man of great wealth for those days. He was the descendant of a lad who, at a very early day was kidnapped in England and brought to Virginia, and who subsequently accumulated a good property there. John Neville, was a man of good English education, of plain, blunt manners, a pleasant companion, and the writer well recollects how eagerly he listened to his well told anecdotes, and how, by his manner he could give interest to trifling incidents. He was born on the head waters of the Occoquan river, Virginia, on the direct road from Washington's paternal estate, to Winchester and Cumberland, and the residence of his father is laid down in Spark's map illustrative of "the operations in Virginia," during the war of 1754. From this circumstance, probably it was, that he became an early acquaintance of Washington, both of whom were of about the same age, and thus with the ardor of a young man, he engaged in Braddock's expedition. He subsequently settled near Winchester, in Frederick county, where he for some time held the office of Sheriff. Prior to 1774 he had made large entries and purchases of lands on Chartier's Creek, then supposed to be in Virginia, and was about to remove here when the Revolutionary troubles began. He was elected in that year a delegate from Augusta county, i. e. Pittsburgh, to the Provincial Convention of Virginia, which appointed George Washington, Peyton Randolph and others, to the first Continental Congress, but was prevented by sickness from attending. Subsequent to the Revolution he was a member of the Supreme Executive Council of Pennsylvania. Presley Neville, his son, was an accomplished gentleman, having received the best education the country could afford, was a good classical and French scholar, had served throughout the Revolution, part of the time as an aid to La Fayette. He and his father had together a princely estate on Chartier's Creek, besides large possessions elsewhere in Virginia, Ohio and Kentucky. He had, also, large expectations from his father-in-law. But unfortunately for the comfort of his latter days, his heart was ten-fold larger than his estate and all his expectations. In recently looking over some old letters from him, written while he was yet in exile, and while the ashes of his father's destroyed mansion, and barns, and stables, and negro huts were yet warm, I was struck with the following kind hearted expression.

" The prisoners arrived yesterday, and were, by the " ostentation of Gen. White, paraded through the dif- " ferent parts of the city, (Philadelphia,)—they had " large pieces of paper in their hats to distinguish them, " and wore the appear- ance of wretchedness ; I could " not help being sorry for them, although so well " acquainted with their conduct."

Major Abraham Kirkpatrick, a Marylander by birth, a soldier of the Revolution, as brave a man as drew his sword in the struggle for Independence, of but ordinary English education, but of strong native intellect, kind and even chivalric, though rather by fits and starts, shrewd in argument, and so fond of it, that he would rather change sides than let discussion cease.

Isaac Craig, an Irishman, born near Hillsborough, in the County Down, of reputable protestant parents, as certified in a paper in my possession, emigrated to Philadelphia in 1767, where he carried on his trade of house joiner, until the commencement of the Revolutionary war. He was, then, appointed by the authorities of Pennsylvania, a Captain of Marines, and as such in the sloop of war *Andrew Doria*, Capt. Nicholas Biddle, sailed in Commodore Hopkins' squadron, along with Paul Jones, Barney and others, to the Isle of New Providence, in the West Indies, where they seized and brought safely home, a large amount of arms and munitions of war, then much needed. Soon after his return he received an appointment as Captain in Proctor's regiment of artillery, just in time to be present at the capture of the Hessians at Trenton. Subsequently he was in the battles of Princeton, Brandywine and Germantown, and about the time of Brodhead's expedition up the Allegheny, accompanied General Sullivan in his most successful expedition up the Susquehanna against the hostile tribes of the Six Nations. He was, then, ordered to Pittsburgh, which after the war he made his home. He was of but common school education, but having a good mind for mechanics and mathematics, had in these branches added largely to his school acquirements and was at an early day, a member of the American Philosophical Society. His position here, during the insurrection, when his presence was so necessary to the supply and intercourse with Wayne's army, and yet continually exposed to insult and danger, was exceedingly unpleasant and trying.

Alexander Hamilton, in a letter to him, says: "Your

care of the interests confided to you, is, in every event, depended upon, according to circumstances. The keeping the arms and stores out of the hands of the insurgents is a matter of great importance. It is hoped that you will personally, in the worst issue of things, find safety in the Fort."

Major Craig never left Pittsburgh during that trying time, except for a few hours on the day of the last attack on General Neville's house. Then he, with David Lenox, the Marshal, Presley Neville and two others went out to get into the house, but were intercepted, detained some time, treated with much contumely and many threats, but finally escaped.

CHAPTER XI.

Apologetic; additional revenue necessary; duties on distilled spirits recommended by Hamilton, favored by Madison; law passed; unpopular; resistance would not have taken place had not designing demagogues encouraged and then cowered before their own work; Federal revenue officers insulted; first meeting at Redstone; Convention in Pittsburgh; first outrage on Robert Johnson; process against rioters; Deputy Marshal afraid to serve it; other outrages committed; Excise law amended; new law more favorably received in other parts of the country, not so in this region; Convention in Pittsburgh, violent resolutions; President's Proclamation; attack upon the house of a collector of revenue; additional outrages; additional amendments to the law enacted rendering it more effective; factious leaders deem it necessary to adopt more daring measures of opposition; Marshal of the district and the Inspector fired at; Inspector's house attacked; description of the place; second attack, house, stables, barn and all destroyed.

The writer of this work has deemed his brief notice of persons who were prominent here, at the time of the first outbreak against the laws of the country, a desirable ingredient in his history. He may be mistaken—his partialities for them, his knowledge of their virtues and services may have misled him in this respect, but be that as it may, he could not persuade himself to overlook them.

In December, 1790, when Congress assembled the nation was burthened with the debt contracted during the seven years struggle for Independence, the country was involved in war with some of the Western Indians; Harmar had just returned from his fruitless expedition against them, the expenses of the Government were necessarily large and the revenue but small, so that additional taxes became indispensible.

No tax seemed more proper than upon spirits both foreign and domestic. A memorial from the college of Physicians of Philadelphia advocated such a tax as desirable both to the morals and health of the people.

Such a bill was reported in the House of Representatives, in January, 1791, in conformity with the suggestions of Alexander Hamilton, as advocated by James Madison, and passed. It imposed a tax of from nine to twenty-five cents per gallon, according to their strength, upon spirits distilled from grain. To secure the collection of these duties, suitable regulations were made. Inspection districts were established, one or more in each State, and an Inspector for each. Distillers to furnish at the nearest inspection office full descriptions of their buildings, which were always subject to examination, by a person appointed for that purpose, who was to guage and brand the casks. Duties to be paid before removal. But to save trouble to small distillers not in any town or village, they were allowed to pay an annual tax of sixty cents per gallon on the capacity of the still.

Such bills taxing the greatest luxury of a large portion of our population would, of course, be unpopular. But it could scarcely have been foreseen that a large mass of citizen would be excited to resist, even to the extent of civil war, the execution of laws passed by the representatives of the people. Possibly had the ignorant and misguided portion of the people been left to themselves matters might not have been carried to extremities. But unfortúnately for the peace of the country, there were here some men of property and intelligence, destitute of sound principles of integrity or genuine love of country, who contributed to kindle the flame of opposition, hoping that they would be able to control its violence and thus use it for their own base purposes. These very men became alarmed by the fury of the storm which thay had aided to create, and were rejoiced to escape from its ravages. So soon as the law passed, opposition manifested itself by the circulation of opinions unfavorable to its execution, and calculated to prevent citizens from accepting the offices necessary to carry the law into effect. Soon, however, more direct means were resorted to, the officers of excise were treated with marks of contempt and insult; public meetings and conventions were adopted as means of promoting and fomenting discontent, and to encourage violence by a show of strength.

The first meeting was held at Redstone, (Brownsville,) on the 27th of July, 1791, when it was arranged that county committees should be convened at the different county seats of Allegheny, Fayette, Washington and

Westmoreland counties. On the 23d of August, one of these committees assembled at Washington, and passed some most intemperate resolutions, which were afterwards, probably very reluctantly, published by the editor of the Pittsburgh Gazette, in that paper. Popular clamor was, however, too strong to be resisted by ordinary men, and it was easier then to yield unresistingly to a vicious public opinion than to stand up manfully for the right. Among the resolutions was one strongly condemning the excise law, and declaring that any one who accepted office under it was inimical to the best interests of the country, and recommending the citizens to treat all such officers with contempt, to refuse to have any intercourse with them, and to withhold from them aid and comfort.

The meeting also appointed three of their number to meet delegates from Fayette, Allegheny and Westmoreland counties on the first Tuesday of the ensuing September to express the sentiments of the people of those counties, in an address to Congress, in relation to the excise law and *other grievances.* The last mentioned expression leads to a strong suspicion that some at least of the leaders were not influenced by a mere desire to get rid of the tax on whiskey, some of them were perhaps secretly hostile to the existing form of government, while others were merely seeking popularity, by a course of conduct, which produced more serious results than were probably anticipated.

The meeting appointed for the early part of September, took place at the appointed time, in Pittsburgh, and each of the twelve delegates seems to have brought with him a new list of grievances, a fresh supply of fuel for the growing excitement. The complaints against government were greatly multiplied and urged with increased venom. The outcry against the excise on whiskey was repeated, but it was accompanied by complaints about the exorbitant salaries of officers, the unreasonable interest of the public debt; the want of discrimination between the original holders and the assignees of the certificates of debt, and finally against the establishment of the United States Bank. A representation to Congress and a remonstrance to the Legislature of Pennsylvania, against the excise on whiskey, were adopted by the meeting, published with the other proceedings in the Gazette, and afterwards presented to the Legislature.

"These meetings," says Alexander Hamilton, in his report, "composed of very influential persons, and "conducted without moderation or prudence, are justly "chargeable with the excesses which have from time to "time been committed, serving to give consistency to "an opposition, which has at length matured to a point "that threatens the foundations of the Government "and the Union, unless speedily and effectually sub-"dued."

In the same month of September, the first act of violence against the enforcement of the law was committed on the person of Robert Johnson, collector of the revenue for the counties of Allegheny and Washington. A party of armed men, in disguise, met at a place on Pigeon creek, in Washington county, cut off his hair, tarred and feathered him, deprived him of his horse, and thus compelled him in that unpleasant condition to travel a considerable distance on foot.

Process was subsequently issued from the District Court of Pennsylvania against three of the persons concerned in this outrage, viz: John Robertson, John Hamilton and Thomas McComb. The Marshal, Clement Biddle, confided the execution of the warrants, to his deputy, Joseph Fox, who, in October, came to this county to serve them. Upon his way here, however, and after his arrival, he heard such alarming accounts of the state of excitement and irritation in the country, that he became convinced that he would place his own personal safety in great peril if he attempted to execute the processes. Under these circumstances he most unwisely adopted the expedient of sending the processes by a private messenger, under enclosures. The Deputy Marshal, in his report to his principal, mentions several facts to show the excited state of feeling in this quarter, inducing the belief that he could not safely execute the processes.

The Marshal, in transmitting the report of his Deputy to the District Attorney, uses the following language: "I am sorry to add, that he (the Deputy,) found the "people in general in the western part of the State, "and particularly beyond the Allegheny mountains, "in such a ferment on account of the act of Congress, "for laying a duty on distilled spirits, and so much "opposed to the execution of said act, that he was not "only convinced of the impossibility of serving the "process, but that any attempt to serve it, would have "occasioned the most violent opposition from the "greater part of the inhabitants; and declares that, "if he had attempted it, he believes he would not have "returned alive."

The messenger sent with the processes was whipped, tarred and feathered, and his money and horse taken from him, was then blindfolded and tied, and then left in the woods where he remained about five hours.

A very momentous state of affairs now existed, and one which well merited the most careful and deliberate consideration of the Government, which, was then, in its very infancy, and its strength and vigor entirely untried. The chief magistrate of that day, was really a man for that or any other crisis, his character for prudence and firmness was earned by long, severe and frequent trials, and he was not likely to shrink from the performance of his duty under any circumstances. But the law was a new one, as yet untried, strong prejudices existed against it in other sections of the country, which might ripen into open opposition and thus multiply difficulties. Besides Congress had not then provided the means by which the Executive could come in aid of the judiciary when found to be unable to enforce the execution of the laws. Finally, too, in addition to the foregoing considerations, it was desirable, in a government like ours, to avoid the resort to extreme measures, until all others had been tried in vain.

Under the united influence of these considerations it appeared advisable to forbear the adoption of coercive measures, until further time for reflection and experience of the law elsewhere had served to correct false impressions, and inspire greater moderation; and until Congress had an opportunity, by a revision of the law, to remove as far as possible, objections to it, and to reinforce the provisions for its execution.

In the meantime other instances of mal-treatment occurred; Mr. Wells, collector of the revenue for Westmoreland and Fayette counties, was illtreated at Greensburgh and Uniontown. Other instances of violence took place, but I pass them over. Designs of personal violence against the Inspector of revenue, were repeatedly attempted to be executed by armed parties, in order to compel him to resign, but by different circumstances were frustrated.

Congress assembled in October, 1791, and by an act, passed during that session, and approved on the 8th May, 1792, material alterations were made in the law. Among these the duty was reduced to a rate so moderate, as to silence complaints on that head, and a very favorable change was made, which allowed the distiller to pay a monthly, instead of a yearly rate, according to the capacity of his still, with the privilege of taking a license for the precise term which he meant to run his stills, and to renew the license for a further term or terms. The amending act was carefully prepared and considered, objections were calmly examined, and great pains taken to obviate all that had the appearance of reasonableness. This course seems to have operated well in other parts of the country, where objections existed and hopes were entertained that even the four western counties of Pennsylvania would be pacified. But notwithstanding these favorable signs, the hope of peaceable submission to the laws entirely failed.

It soon became a very prominent point in the policy of the opponents of the law, to intimidate the well disposed citizens, so as to prevent their acceptance of offices under the excise law. After considerable exertions, the Inspector of revenue prevailed upon Captain Faulkner, of the army, to permit his house in Washington county, to be used as an office for inspection. A short time after he, being in pursuit of some deserters, was encountered by a number of persons in the same neighborhood where Mr. Johnson had been ill used the year before, who reproached him for permitting his house to be used for an office of Inspection, drew a knife upon him, threatened to tar and feather him, and destroy his property if he did not promise to prevent the longer use of his house. He was thus driven to make the required promise, and on the 20th of August, wrote a letter countermanding the permission he had given, and next day published a note in the Gazette giving notice that his house should no longer be used by the revenue officers.

On the 21st of August, 1792, agreeable to previous notice, a number of persons styling themselves "A meeting of sundry inhabitants of the western counties of Pennsylvania," assembled in Pittsburgh and passed a series of resolutions, not less exceptionable than those adopted at previous meetings. After denouncing a tax on spirituous liquors they conclude by declaring that they consider it their duty to persist in remonstrances to Congress and every other *legal* measure that may *obstruct the operation of the law.*

On the 16th September, 1792, the President of the United States issued his proclamation earnestly exhorting and admonishing all persons to refrain and desist from all unlawful combinations and proceedings whatever, having for their object or tending to obstruct the operation of the excise laws, inasmuch as lawful measures would be put in operation to bring to justice the infractors thereof, and for enforcing obedience to the same, and moreover charging and requiring all courts, magistrates and officers, according to the duties of their several offices, to exert the powers in them respectively invested by law, for the purposes aforesaid, also enjoining all persons whomsoever, as they valued the welfare of their country, the just and due authority of the Government, and the preservation of the public peace, to be aiding and assisting therein, according to law, and likewise directing prosecutions to be instituted against, the offenders in all cases where the requisite evidence could be had.

Pursuant to these instructions, the Attorney General, with the District Attorney, attended a Circuit Court, held at York, in October, 1792, for the purpose of bringing forward prosecutions in the proper cases. Measures were also taken to procure the necessary evidence.

George Clymer, the Supervisor of the Revenue, was sent into the disaffected region to obtain evidence of the persons concerned in the Faulkner case, and of those who composed the Pittsburgh meeting, to uphold the confidence and to encourage the perseverance of the officers acting under the law, and finally to induce the inhabitants of that part of the district which appeared least malignant, to come voluntarily into obedience to the law.

The result of the visit of the Supervisor, was merely the ascertaining who composed the Pittsburgh meeting; also, the discovery of two persons concerned in the Faulkner case; and the discovering that there was an enmity existing in the minds of many, not merely to the excise, but the Government itself.

The Attorney General, Edmund Randolph, thinking it doubtful whether the proceedings of the meeting at Pittsburgh formed an indictable offence, no prosecution was entered against those who were actors in it. Prosecutions were entered against the two persons supposed to be concerned in the Faulkner affair, but it being afterwards discovered that they were not concerned in that outrage, the prosecutions were discontinued.

In April, 1793, a party of armed men, in disguise, made an attack in the night, on the house of a collector of the revenue, who resided in Fayette county, but he happening to be from home, they contented themselves with breaking open his house, threatening, terrifying and abusing his family. Warrants were issued by Isaac Meason and John Findlay, Associate Judges, for the arrest of some of the rioters, but the Sheriff refused or neglected to serve them.

In June of the same year, the Inspector of the Revenue, was burnt in effigy in Allegheny county, at a place, and on a day of a public meeting, in the presence of, and without interruption by, some of the magistrates.

On the night of the 22d of November, another party of men, some armed, and all disguised, called at the house of the same collector, which had been visited in April, broke it open, demanded a surrender of his papers and official books, and by threats compelled him to give them up, and also extorted from him a promise to publish his resignation of his office.

The administration had about this time adopted a scheme of policy in relation to the opponents of the excise law, which promised at first to be effectual.

1st. To prosecute delinquents in cases where it could clearly be done for non-compliance with the laws. 2d. To intercept the markets for the surplus produce of the distilleries of the non-complying counties, by seizing the spirits in the way to markets, in places where it could be done without opposition. 3d. By purchasing for the use of the army only the spirits, in relation to which there had been a compliance with the law. There were two difficulties, however, in the way of the effective operation of these measures. In the first place the law required an office of inspection and there could be no violation of the law where there was no such office, and the existence of such offices in some of the counties was prevented by violence and threats. The next difficulty was the non-extension of the law to the territory North and West of the Ohio, where a large portion of the surplus spirits were consumed.

These defects in the law could only be remedied by Congress, and measures were taken to obtain a further revision at the session which began in November, 1792. A bill amending these defects and others was brought in, but owing to more urgent matters, this was deferred until late in the session, and then in the usual hurry of the close of a session, remained unacted upon.

Notwithstanding the failure of these amendments, the laws appeared rather to be gaining ground in 1793. Several considerable distillers, who had before resisted, complied with the requisitions of the law, and others manifested a disposition to comply and were only prevented doing so by fear of the lawless.

These favorable appearances, seem to have alarmed the lawless leaders, and they determined to adopt more daring measures, to subdue the growing spirit of compliance.

The Inspector of Revenue, in a letter of the 27th February, 1794, stated that he had received information, that persons living near the line of Allegheny and Washington counties, had thrown out threats of tarring and feathering one William Cochran, a complying distiller, and burning his distillery; and that it had also been given out that there would not be a house left standing in Allegheny county which was owned by a person complying with the law; in consequence of which he had been induced to call upon several leading individuals in that quarter to ascertain the truth of the information, and to endeavor to avert the attempt to execute those threats.

It appeared afterwards, that the Inspector, on his return from the above named visit, had been pursued by a collection of disorderly persons, threatening vengeance against him, as they passed along. On their way these men called at the house of James Kiddoo, who had lately complied with the law, broke into his still-house and scattered fire over and about it.

Letters from the Inspector, in March, announce an increased activity on the part of the disorderly; and among other proposed measures was one to seize the Inspector, compel him to resign his office, and detain him prisoner, perhaps as a hostage.

In May and June new violences were committed. James Kiddoo, the person before mentioned, had parts of his grist mill carried away at different times; and Cochran, who had for some time been threatened, had his still destroyed, his saw-mill stopped by taking away his saw, and his grist-mill much injured. Several other persons were misused and injured for compliance with the law. Indications of a plan to proceed against the Inspector of the Revenue, as before indicated, continued. In a letter of the 10th of July, he said that the threatened visit had not been made yet; though he had still reason to expect it.

In the session of Congress which met in December, 1793, a bill for amending the law, as before stated, was brought in, and became a law on the 5th of June, 1794. The passage of this law was well calculated to render more effective the measures adopted by the Executive to secure obedience to the laws; and the factious leaders of the opposition, perceiving this tendency of matters, deemed it expedient to adopt more daring measures. The increased boldness of the lawless rendered it necessary for the Executive to adopt more vigorous means for sustaining the law. Complaints, too, were made by those who had peaceably complied with the law, that others were suffered to escape untaxed. Under all the circumstances it was concluded that there was no alternative but to exert the vigor of the law against delinquents and offenders. Processes were issued against a number of non-complying distillers in Allegheny and Fayette counties, and indictments having been found at a court held in Philadelphia, in July, against Robert Smilie and John McCollough, two of the rioters who had attacked the house of a collector in Fayette, processes issued against them also.

The Marshal of the District went in person to serve these writs. He executed them without interruption in Fayette county, though under discouraging circumstances; but while he was performing his duty in Allegheny county, accompanied by the Inspector, on the 15th of July, 1794, he was beset, on the road, by a party of thirty or forty armed men, who after much alarming conduct, fired upon him, though without injuring him or the Inspector.

On the morning of the next day, the Inspector had just had his horse brought to the door for the purpose of riding into Pittsburgh; when he perceived at a distance about one hundred armed men, approaching the house, suspecting at once their purpose, the horse was turned loose, the doors closed and secured, and the best practicable means adopted for defence. A vigorous attack was made, but finding a more resolute and effective resistance than was anticipated from a single person, the assailants soon withdrew to prepare for a more formidable attack.

The traveler who is going from Pittsburgh to Washing by the turnpike road, at about eight miles from the former place, passes by the house of Mr. John Wrenshall, the present owner of a portion of that beautiful tract of land formerly known as *Woodville.* If when he is just in front of the house on that place, he turns his back upon it and looks over a beautiful, fertile bottom between him and Chartier's Creek, and up a gently rising ground beyond the creek, he will overlook a fine tract of land formerly called *Bower Hill.* On this tract was situated the mansion house of John Neville. The Woodville farm was owned and occupied by Presley Neville, the son of John. Between the two residences and up the rising ground, a broad avenue was cut through the intervening forest, by which communications could be had by signals, and often were invitations to meet company or other messages sent through that vista. A few years since, this avenue was still perceptible, but may now be grown up, as the writer has not lately noticed it.

I have thought this brief allusion to, and indication of the *locale,* of the outrage which occurred there, might possess some interest to persons here, who have often heard of those occurrences, but had no definite notion of the place where they happened.

After the attack of the 16th, the Inspector apprehending that another and more formidable attack would be made upon his house, made a written application to the judges, General of militia, and the Sheriff, for protection. A reply to this application was made by John Wilkins, Esq., a magistrate, and Gen. John Gibson, of the militia, stating that owing to the too general combination of the people against the excise law, protection could not be afforded to him. They added, however, that they would do all in their power to bring the lawless persons to punishment, and would be glad to receive information of the persons concerned in the attack upon his house; that prosecutions might be commenced against them, and expressing their belief that if the *posse comitatus* were ordered out, very few persons would be found who were not of the party of the rioters.*

Upon this information being communicated to Major Thomas Butler, the commandant at Fort Fayette, one of several gallant brothers, who distinguished themselves during the Revolution, he detached eleven men from his feeble garrison, to aid the Inspector. These soldiers were joined by Major Abraham Kirkpatrick, whose wife was a sister-in-law of the Inspector, in whose family she had been brought up, and in whose house she had been married.

* So general was the combined influence of actual disaffection upon one portion of the community, and dread of the violence of the turbulent among the others, that the writer has often heard Major Craig say, that out of the family connection of Gen. Neville, and out of the *employees* of the Government, James Baird, a blacksmith, and James Robinson, the father of Wm. Robinson, jr., were the only persons in Pittsburgh on whom reliance could be placed, under all circumstances.

CHAPTER XII.

Second attack upon General Neville's house; meeting of insurgents at Mingo creek; robbery of mail; meeting at Parkinson's Ferry; large assemblage at Braddock's Field; Bradford's purpose to take Fort Fayette; prompt intimation by Major Butler; Democratic Societies; requisition on Governors of New Jersey, Pennsylvania, Delaware and Maryland for fifteen thousand militia; Commissioners appointed to arrange submission to the laws; meeting of insurgents at Braddock's Field; negociations and manœuvrings among the leaders; militia volunteers from New Jersey, Maryland, Pennsylvania and Virginia, promptly assemble at Bedford and Cumberland, unite at Uniontown; various arrests made; submission of the insurgents; flight of Bradford; Fauchet, the French Minister, and Secretary Randolph; influence of the insurrection upon the growth of Pittsburgh; Wayne's Victory.

I find the narrative of subsequent proceedings of the insurgents so well related in *Hildreth's History of the United States*, that I have concluded to adopt his account.

"The next morning, (July 17th,) the assailants reappeared, five hundred strong, led on by one John Holcroft, who, under the assumed name of Tom the Tinker, had been deeply concerned in stiring up previous outrages against officers who attempted to enforce the law, and distillers who were disposed to submit to it. On the approach of this force, Neville escaped from the house, leaving his kinsman, Major Kirkpatrick, with the soldiers, to make such defence or capitulation as might seem expedient. The assailants had appointed a committee of three as directors of the enterprise, and they had chosen as commander one

M'Farlane, formerly a lieutenant in the Continental service. The surrender of Neville was demanded, and, on information that he was gone, the admission of six men to search the house for the papers connected with his office was claimed. This being refused, a flag was sent for the women to leave the house, soon after which an attack was commenced. M'Farlane was killed and several other of the assailants were wounded; but they succeeded in setting fire to the out-houses, and, as the flames threatened to spread, the garrison, three of whom had been wounded, found themselves obliged to surrender. The men were dismissed without injury, but all the buildings were burned to the ground. The marshal and the inspector's son, who came up just after the surrender, were made prisoners.* The marshal was subjected to a good deal of abuse, and was only dismissed after a promise, extorted by threats of instant death, and guaranteed by young Neville, not to attempt to serve any more processes west of the mountains. The next day a message was sent to Pittsburgh, where the inspector and the marshal had taken refuge, requiring the one to resign his office, and the other to give up the warrants in his possession. This they refused to do. The means of protection at Pittsburgh were small; and as the roads eastward would most likely be guarded, as the only means of escape, they embarked on the Ohio, descended as far as Marietta, and thence set out by land for Philadelphia, the greater part of the way through a wilderness.

The next decided step seems to have been a public meeting, held at Mingo Creek meeting-house, in the neighborhood of which most of the late rioters resided.

* Also, Major Craig, Ensign Sample, and another name not recollected.

Bradford and Marshall were both present; also Brackenridge, a lawyer of Pittsburgh, a leading member of the Democratic club of that town, and who attended, according to his own account, by special invitation. Bradford was for making common cause with the rioters. Brackenridge suggested that, however justifiable in itself, their conduct was nevertheless illegal, and that it was bad policy to draw into the same position those who might otherwise act as mediators. It was finally agreed to call a convention of delegates from all the townships west of the mountains, and from the adjoining counties of Maryland and Virginia, to meet in three weeks at Parkinson's Ferry, on the Monongahela.

Two or three days after this preliminary meeting, anxious to ascertain how the late proceedings had been represented, Bradford caused the mail from Pittsburgh to Philadelphia to be intercepted. Letters were found in it, from young Neville and others, giving accounts, by no means satisfactory to the parties concerned, of the burning of the inspector's house, and of the late meeting at Mingo Creek. Without waiting for the proposed convention, a circular, signed by Bradford, Marshall, and four or five others, was forthwith addressed to the officers of the militia of the western counties, stating that, by the interception of the mail, important secrets had been discovered, which made necessary an expression of sentiment, not by words, but by actions. The officers were therefore called upon to muster as many volunteers as they could, to assemble on the first of August at the usual place of rendezvous, at Braddock's Field, on the Monongahela, with arms and accoutrements, and provisions for four days.

Meanwhile, the mail, with its contents, except the intercepted letters, was sent back to Pittsburgh, and the citizens of that town, to pacify the excitement, went through the form of expelling the obnoxious letter-writers.

The summons to the militia, though it had only three days to circulate, and that among a population scattered over a wide extent of country, drew together not less than seven thousand armed men. Many afterward alleged that they went out of curiosity, and others, that their sole intention was to prevent mischief; and this was certainly the case with some who were present, among whom was Ross, the United States senator. But the very fact of this prompt obedience to their orders could not but inspire the leaders with a high idea of their power and influence, while it tended also to increase the mischief, by giving the impression to the public at large of a general unanimity of sentiment. Colonel Cook, one of the judges of Fayette county, a member of the first popular convention held in Pennsylvania at the commencement of the Revolution, distinguished for his opposition to the excise, having repeatedly presided at the public meetings called to protest against it, was chosen president of this armed assembly. Albert Gallatin, the late rejected senator, was appointed secretary. Bradford, to whom every body cringed, assumed the character of major general, and reviewed the troops. A committee, to whom matters of business were referred, resolved that two more citizens of Pittsburgh should be expelled. The troops then marched into the town, and after receiving refreshments, which the terrified inhabitants hastened to furnish, the greater part marched out again. The more orderly dispersed; but several parties kept together, one of which destroyed a barn belonging to Major Kirkpatrick, and another attempted, but without success, to burn his house in Pittsburgh.

It was Bradford's design, in calling this armed body together, to get possession of Fort Pitt, and the arms and ammunition deposited in it; but, finding most of the principal militia officers unwilling to co-operate, that design was abandoned.* Immediately after this armed assembly, the remaining excise officers were expelled even from those districts in which the opposition had hitherto been less violent. Many outrages were committed, some of the officers being cruelly treated, and their houses burned. The same spirit began to spread into the bordering counties of Virginia, and, as the day for the meeting at Parkinson's Ferry approached, things assumed a very threatening aspect. However opposition to the excise law might have been countenanced by the great body of the population, including the principal political leaders, the measures

* The following extract of a letter from Major Craig to General Knox, dated August 8th, gives, perhaps, the true explanation. It was, no doubt, a fortunate circumstance that Major Butler commanded at that time:

"On the 1st instant, a numerous body of armed men assembled at "Braddock's Field, and continued there till yesterday, their number in-"creasing, it is asserted, to four thousand five hundred, being joined by "a number of the inhabitants of Pittsburgh, and commenced their march "about nine o'clock, as it was confidently reported, with a design of at-"tacking the Fort. But some of the leaders being informed, that every "possible means had been taken for its defence, they prudently conclud-"ed to postpone the attack, and sent a flag to inform the commandant "that they intended to march peaceably by the Fort into Pittsburgh, "cross the Monongahela and return home. Major Butler intimated to "the flag bearer, that their peaceable intentions would be best mani-"fested by passing the Fort at a proper distance, they, therefore, took "another road into town."

of actual resistance to it had been chiefly in the hands of a few violent and reckless individuals, who, sometimes by outrages and sometimes by threats, had kept in awe not only the excise officers, but such of the distillers also as were disposed to submit to the payment of the tax. This reign of terror was now extended and completely established. No one dared utter a word against the recent proceedings for fear of banishment, personal violence, or the destruction of his property.

News of the burning of Neville's house, of the meeting at Mingo Creek, and of the robbery of the mail soon reached Philadelphia. In the eyes of the President and his cabinet, these incidents assumed a very serious character. With the arrival of news of the great triumphs achieved by the French arms, and of the subsidence of internal revolt under the terrible discipline of the Reign of Terror, the Democratic societies, recovering from the temporary check growing out of the conduct of Genet and the disasters of the French republic, had become more vigorous and violent than ever, and very unsparing in their attacks upon the policy of the federal administration. The Charleston society, on their own application, and on motion of the celebrated Collot d'Herbois, had been recognized by the Jacobin Club of Paris as an affiliated branch. The Democratic society of Washington county, one of those involved in the present disturbances, had recently passed strong resolutions, copied from those of Kentucky, on the subject of the navigation of the Mississippi. The French agents were still active in Kentucky, and a secret understanding was suspected between all these parties. The Democratic society of

Philadelphia hastened indeed to pass resolutions, in which, after execrating the excise law, they declared, however, their disapproval of violent resistance. But no great faith was placed in their sincerity, or in the concurrence of the affiliated branches. In a cotemporary letter to Governor Lee, of Virginia, Washington speaks of the leaders of these societies—the great body of the members knowing little of the real plan—as artful and designing men, whose great object was, under a display of popular and fascinating guises, to destroy all confidence in the administration, and likely, if not counteracted and their real character exposed, to shake the government to its very foundation.

In the present inflammatory state of the public mind, the resistance to the laws in Western Pennsylvania, if not immediately checked, might find many imitators. Hamilton, Knox, and Bradford, Attorney General, advised that the militia be called out at once. But upon a suggestion to Governor Mifflin to that effect, he expressed apprehensions that a resort to force might inflame and augment the existing opposition, and, by connecting with it other causes of complaint, might produce such an excitement as to make it necessary to call in aid from the neighboring States—a step by which jealousy and discontent would be still further aggravated. He even questioned whether the militia would "pay a passive obedience to the mandates of the government." He doubted also his own authority to make a call; for, whatever might be the case with the federal judiciary, it did not yet appear that the ordinary course of the state law was not able to punish the rioters and to maintain order. He was therefore disposed to be content for the present with a circular letter already dispatched to the state officers of the western counties, expressive of his indignation at the recent occurrence, and requiring the exertion of their utmost authority to suppress the tumults and to punish the offenders.

Mifflin's refusal removed all pretense for alleging that opportunity had not been afforded to the State of Pennsylvania to vindicate the authority of the laws by her own means. As the case seemed to require immediate interference, Washington resolved to take the responsibility on himself, and to act with vigor. A certificate was obtained, as the statute required, from a judge of the Supreme Court, that in the counties of Washington and Allegheny the execution of the laws of the United States was obstructed by combinations too powerful to be suppressed by the ordinary course of judicial proceedings. A proclamation was put forth requiring these opposers of the laws to desist, and a requsition was issued to the governors of Pennsylvania, New Jersey, Maryland, and Virginia for a body of 13,000 men, raised afterward to 15,000. The insurgent counties could bring into the field about 16,000 fighting men. It was judged expedient to send a force such as would quite discourage any resistance.

This calling out the militia was not entirely approved by Randolph, the secretary of state. He seemed to apprehend, with Mifflin, that an attempt to enforce the authority of government might lead to a general convulsion; and he appeared to be greatly impressed by a letter of Brackenridge's to a friend in Philadelphia, communicated to the cabinet, in which the writer maintained the ability of the western counties to defend themselves, suggesting the indisposition of the midland counties to allow the march of troops for the West, the possibility of application to Great Britain for aid, and even of a march on Philadelphia.

The movement of the troops was fixed for the first of September. Meanwhile, three commissioners, appointed by the President, Senator Ross, Bradford, the attorney general, and Yates, one of the judges of the Supreme Court of Pennsylvania, were dispatched to the insurgent counties, with discretionary authority to arrange, if possible, any time prior to the 14th of September, an effectual submission to the laws. Chief Justice M'Kean and Gen. Wm. Irvine were appointed commissioners on the part of the state. Simultaneously with this appointment, Mifflin issued two proclamations, one calling the Legislature together, the other requiring the rioters to submit, and announcing his determination to obey the President's call for militia.

The two boards of commissioners crossed the mountains together, and, on arriving in the disturbed district, found the convention, called by the meeting at Mingo Creek, already in session at Parkinson's Ferry. It consisted of upward of two hundred delegates, including two from that part of Bedford county west of the mountains, and three from Ohio county, in Virginia. Almost all the townships of the four western counties were fully represented. Cook was chairman, and Gallatin secretary. The delegates were convened on an eminence, under the shade of trees, surrounded by a collection of spectators, some of them armed. Near by stood a liberty-pole, with the motto, "Liberty, and no excise! No asylum for cowards and traitors!"

A series of resolutions was offered by Marshall, of

which the first, against taking citizens out of the vicinity for trial, passed without objection. The second resolution proposed the appointment of a committee of public safety, empowered "to call forth the resources of the western country to repel any hostile attempts against the citizens." After a speech, in which he denied any danger of hostilities, the only danger being that of legal coercion, Gallatin proposed to refer this resolution to a select committee. But, though there were many persons present whose chief object, like Gallatin's, it was to extricate the people from the disastrous consequences of a violent opposition to the laws, which they themselves had done much to stimulate, no one dared to second the motion. Marshall, however, already began to waver; and he presently offered to withdraw the proposition provided a committee of sixty was appointed, with power to call another meeting. This was readily agreed to, as was also the appointment of a sub-committee of fifteen, to confer with the federal and state commissioners. For the purpose of being remodeled, the resolutions were referred to a committee, consisting of Bradford, Gallatin, Brackenridge, and Herman Husbands, then a very old man, a leader formerly among the North Carolina Regulators. The determination expressed in one of those resolutions, not to submit to the excise, was struck out on Gallatin's motion. But neither he nor any body else went so far as to advocate obedience to it. A promise to submit to the state laws was, however, inserted. This business being disposed of, the exercise of some address secured a dissolution of the meeting, the assembly of the committee of sixty being fixed for the 2d of September.

A few days after, as had been arranged, the committee of fifteen met the commissioners at Pittsburgh. Among the members of this committee were Bradford, Marshall, Cook, Gallatin, and Brackenridge, the whole, except Bradford, being inclined to an accommodation. A candidate for Congress for the Pittsburgh district, in his anxiety to secure votes, Brackenridge had hitherto gone so far as to make the insurgents believe he was on their side. But he was well aware of the folly and hopelessness of their cause, and at bottom not less anxious than Gallatin to escape out of the present dilemma. In a book which he afterward published, he excused the part he had taken as necessary to protect himself against the violence of the insurgents. The demands of the commissioners were exceedingly moderate. They required from the committee of sixty an explicit declaration of their determination to submit to the laws, and a recommendation to the citizens at large to submit also, and to abstain from all opposition, direct or indirect, and especially from violence or threats against the excise officers or the complying distillers. Primary meetings were required to be held to test the sense of the citizens in these particulars. Should satisfactory assurances be given on or before the fourteenth of September, the commissioners promised a suspension till the next July of all prosecutions for offenses prior in date to this arrangement; and in case the law, during that interval, should be generally complied with, in good faith, a final pardon, and oblivion of all such offenses.

The committee of fifteen pronounced these terms reasonable; and, to give more time to carry out the arrangement, they agreed to anticipate by four days the calling together of the committee of sixty. Meanwhile a report spread that the conferees had been bribed; indeed, that charge was made in express terms in a letter of Tom the Tinker to the Pittsburgh Gazette, which the printer, as was the case with other communications of that anonymous personage, did not dare to omit to publish. While the members of the committee of sixty were collecting at Brownsville, the place appointed for the meeting, an armed party of horse and foot entered the town with drums beating. The friends of submission were so intimidated that, but for Gallatin, they would have abandoned all thoughts of urging an accommodation. Bradford insisted on taking the question at once; but, by the exercise of some address, the matter was postponed till the next day, and meanwhile the armed party were persuaded to return to their homes.

Gallatin opened the business the next morning in a speech, in which the motives to submission were judiciously urged. He was followed by Brackenridge, who now came out strongly on the same side. Bradford, in an extravagant harangue, urged continued resistance, and the organization of an independent state. Not daring to expose themselves by an open vote, the friends of submission had prevailed that the decision should be by secret ballot. They were thus enabled to carry, by a very lean majority, a resolution that it would be for the interest of the people to accede to the terms offered by the commissioners. But they did not dare to propose what the commissioners had demanded, a pledge from the members of the committee themselves to submit to the law, and arrangements for obtaining, in primary meetings, a like pledge from the individual citizens. After appointing a new committee of conference, the committee of sixty adjourned without day.

The new conferees asked of the commissioners further delay till the 10th of October, to ascertain the sense of the people; but this was declined as being beyond their authority. They now required that meetings should be held in the several townships on the eleventh of September, any two or more members of the late committee of sixty, or any justice of the peace to preside, at which the citizens should vote yea or nay on the question of submitting to and supporting the law, all those voting in the affirmative to sign a declaration to that effect, which was to secure them an amnesty as to the past offences. The third day after the vote, the presiding officers were to assemble in their respective county court houses, to ascertain the number of votes both ways, and to declare their opinion in writing whether the submission was so general that excise inspection offices could be re-established with safety; all the papers to be forwarded to the commissioners at Uniontown by the sixteenth of the month.

Meetings were held under this arrangement in many of the townships, but the result, on the whole, was quite unsatisfactory. Most of the more intelligent leaders were careful to provide for their own safety by signing the required submission; but many of those who had taken no active part in resisting the law refused to attend, or to pledge themselves to obedience. As they had committed no offence, such was their argument, they ought not to be required to submit—as if winking at the violation of law and neglecting to assist in its enforcement were not among the greatest of offences. In some townships the meetings were violently broken up and the papers torn to pieces. Such was the case in the town in which Findley resided, who, it seems, was personally insulted on the occasion. From Allegany county no returns were received. The judges of the vote in Westmoreland expressed the opinion that excise inspection offices could not be safely established in that county. In the other two counties the expression of any direct opinion was avoided; but these counties had always been more violent than Westmoreland. The better disposed part of the population had begun to form associations for mutual defense, and the opinion among them was quite universal that the presence of the troops was absolutely necessary.

Notwithstanding the timidity and alarms of Randolph and others, real or pretended, the President's call for militia, as on the former appeal to the people in the case of Genet, had been responded to with a spirit that gave new strength and confidence to the government. The Pennsylvanians at first were rather backward, and a draft ordered by Mifflin seemed, likely, by reason, it was said, of defects in the militia laws, to prove a failure. But the Legislature, on coming together, having first denounced the insurgents in strong terms, to save the delays attendant on drafting, authorized the government to accept volunteers, to whom a bounty was offered. As if to make up for his former hesitation, and with a military sensibility to the disgrace of failing to meet the requisition, Mifflin, in a tour through the lower counties, as in several cases during the Revolutionary struggle, by the influence of his extraordinary popular eloquence, soon caused the ranks to be filed up. As a further stimulus, subscriptions were opened to support the wives and children of the volunteers during their absence. The quotas of the other states were promptly furnished, composed in a large part of volunteers. The troops of Virginia, led by Morgan, and those of Maryland by Smith, the Baltimore member of Congress, forming together the left wing, assembled at Cumberland, thence to march across the mountains by Braddock's road; those of Pennsylvania and New Jersey, led by Governors Mifflin and Howell in person, and forming the right wing, had their rendezvous at Bedford, to cross the mountains by the northern or Pennsylvania route. The command-in-chief of the expedition was given to Governor Lee, of Virginia.

The commissioners having returned to Philadelphia and made their report, the President the next day issued a new proclamation, given notice of the advance of the troops—which, in anticipation of the failure of the mission, had already been put in motion—and commanding submission to the laws. There was the more need of decisive measures, as the spirit of disaffection was evidently spreading. At Greensburg, in Westmoreland county, a house in which the state commissioners lodged on their way home had been assailed by a mob, who demanded entrance, broke the windows, and were only driven away by threats of being fired upon. The same feeling had also spread to the east side of the mountains. At Carlisle, while on their way home, Judges M'Kean and Yates had required bonds of certain persons charged with seditious practices in erecting whiskey or liberty poles. Hardly had they left the town, when two hundred armed men marched in, and being disappointed in seizing the judges, burned them in effigy, and committed other outrages. There were also signs of similar disturbances in the neighboring counties of Maryland; but these were soon suppressed by a party of horse, who made more than a hundred prisoners, most of whom were committed to Hagerstown jail.

Calmer thoughts, and the news that the troops were marching against them, soon produced a change of feeling in the western counties. Bradford and others of the more violent fled the country. Encouraged by these symptoms of returning reason, the better disposed caused a new convention to be held at Parkinson's Ferry. Resolutions of submission were passed, and a declaration was agreed to, that the late failure in obtaining written pledges was principally owing to want of time and information, to a prevailing sense of innocence, and to the idea that to sign the pledge required would imply a confession of guilt. Findley at last had mustered courage to take a decided part on the side of order; and he was dispatched, with one Reddick, to convey these resolutions to the President, and to stop, if possible, the march of the troops. At Carlisle these commissioners encountered the advance of the right wing, five or six thousand strong. Findley, who has left us a very labored apology for himself and his political friends, under the title of a "History of the Insurrection," found the troops, as he tells us, in a high state of excitement against the rebels. Two persons had been killed already; a man, run through the body by a soldier, whose bayonet he had seized when ordered to arrest him for insulting an officer, and a boy, accidentally shot by one of a party of light horse sent to arrest those concerned in the late riot at Carlisle. But in both these cases—and this was the only blood shed during the expedition—the parties concerned had been delivered over to the civil authorities for trial, and every effort was made by the President and the Secretary of the Treasury, both of whom had followed the troops to Carlisle, to preserve the strictest discipline, and to impress the necessity of avoiding all unnecessary violence and harshness. Findley, however, who was but just beginning to recover from the terror of having his buildings burned, or being himself tarred and feathered, by men whose violence he had found it much easier to stimulate than to control, seems to have been not a little frightened, on the other hand, at the swagger, bluster, and loud words of some of the militia officers against the whiskey rebels, whose insolent resistance to the laws had made necessary so long and fatiguing a march.

The President treated Findlay and his brother embassador with courtesy, and admitted them to several interviews; but did not see fit, from any evidence which they exhibited, to countermand the march of the troops. They hastened back, therefore, to procure more general and unequivocal assurances, which they hoped to transmit to Bedford, where Washington was again to meet the right wing, after inspecting the troops on the left. The Parkinson Ferry Convention, augmented by many discreet citizens, was again called together for the third time. Resolutions were passed declaring the competency of the civil authorities to enforce the laws, recommending all delinquents who had not already secured an indemnity to surrender for trial, and expressing the conviction that offices of inspection might be opened with safety, and that the excise duties would be paid. Findley hastened back with these resolutions, but before he reached the army the President had already returned to Philadelphia; Hamilton, however, remained behind, and was believed to act as the President's deputy. The troops crossed the Alleganies in a heavy rain, up to their knees in mud, and not without severe suffering, which occasioned in the end a good many deaths. The two wings formed a junction at Uniontown, and, as they advanced into the disaffected counties, the re-establishment of the authority of the law became complete. Having arrived at Parkinson's Ferry, Lee issued a proclamation confirming the amnesty to those who had entitled themselves to it, and calling upon all the inhabitants to take the oath of allegiance to the United States.

A few days after, arrangements having been previously made for it, there was a general seizure, by parties detached for that purpose, of persons supposed to be criminally concerned in the late transactions. But as those against whom the strongest evidence existed had either fled the country or taken advantage of the amnesty, this seizure fell principally on persons who, without taking an active part, had been content with encouraging and stimulating others. Many were dismissed at once for want of evidence; and of those who were bound over for trial at Philadelphia, the greater part were afterward acquitted. Among those thus bound over, Brackenridge was one; but, instead of being tried, he was used as a witness against the others. These people complained loudly of the inconvenience to which they had been put, and of the harsh treatment which, in some few cases, had been experienced at the hands of the military parties by whom the arrests had been made. But such evils were only the natural consequences of lying quietly by and allowing resistance to the laws to aggravate itself into rebellion.

Shortly after the seizure of prisoners, the greater part of the troops were withdrawn; but a body of twenty-five hundred men, under Morgan, remained through the winter encamped in the district. The advances necessary to sustain the troops in the field had been made out of a sum in the treasury of about $800,000, the unexpended balance of the foreign loans, Congress being trusted to for making good the deficiency.

About the time that the troops entered the disaffected counties, an election had taken place, at which were chosen not only members of the state Assembly, but members of Congress also. When the Legislature of Pennsylvania met, a question was raised as to the validity of these elections. Of those returned to the Assembly, Gallatin was one; and he had the greater interest in the question, since he had been elected at the same time a member of the fourth Congress, and that body might be influenced, perhaps, by the example of the Pennsylvania Assembly. In the course of an able speech, Gallatin confessed his "political sin" in having been concerned in the preparation and adoption of the Pittsburgh resolutions of August 24th, 1792, which, though not illegal, he admitted to have been "violent, intemperate, and reprehensible;" but all the rest of the opposition made to the Excise Law by means of public meetings he was inclined to justify, and to shift off the blame of the whole affair upon a few obscure rioters. Order, he maintained, had been substantially re-established before the elections took place. The Assembly, however, judged differently, and a new election was ordered.

Of all the prisoners tried before the Circuit Court at Philadelphia, only two were found guilty of capital offenses, one of arson, and the other of robbing the mail, both of whom, from some palliating circumstances, were ultimately pardoned by the President. According to Findley, Hamilton made great efforts to obtain evidence against himself, Smilie, and Gallatin. But, however reprehensible their conduct might have been in encouraging and stimulating the original opposition to the excise, the late outbreak, as Gallatin maintained in his speech, and Findley afterward at great length in his History, seems to have been a sudden, unpremeditated, and, in its particular circumstances, an accidental thing, with which they had no immediate concern. They had only prepared the combustibles to which others set the torch; and they seem to have exerted themselves with good faith, and Gallatin at some personal risk, and with a good deal of courage, in quenching the flame when actually kindled.

The vigor, energy, promptitude, and decision with which the federal authority had been vindicated; the general rally in its support, even on the part of many who had leaned more or less to the opposition; the reprobation every where expressed against violent resistance to the law; and the subdued tone, especially of the Democratic societies, made a great addition to the strength of the government. The Federalists exulted in this energetic display of authority, and Hamilton declared that proof at last had been given of the capacity of the government to sustain itself. In that point of view, both he and Washington considered the outbreak, however much to be lamented in other respects, as a fortunate occurrence.

In due proportion to the exultation of the Federalists was the vexation of the chief leaders of the opposition; a vexation the keener, because, to a great extent, it was necessary to withhold the expression of it. This vexation was largely shared by Fauchet, the French minister, whose communications on the subject to his own government contained statements and reflections sufficiently remarkable. In his private dispatch, No. 6, the precise date of which does not appear, but which must have been written some time in August, was given, according to an extract afterward furnished by himself, the following extraordinary piece of information. "Scarce was the commotion known"—the disturbances, that is, in the western country—"when the Secretary of State came to my house. All his countenance was grief. He requested of me a private conversation. It is all over, he said to me; a civil war is about to ravage our unhappy country. Four men, by their talents, their influence, their energy, may save it. But debtors of English merchants, they will be deprived of their liberty if they take the smallest step. Could you lend them instantaneous funds sufficient to shelter them from English persecution?" "This inquiry," the dispatch continued, "astonished me. It was impossible for me to make a satisfactory answer. You know my want of power, and my defect of pecuniary means. I shall draw myself from the affair by some common-place remarks, and by throwing myself on the pure and disinterested principles of the republic."

To this subject Fauchet returned in his dispatch, No. 10, dated the 31st of October. It commenced with a sketch of the rise of parties in the United States, in substantial accordance with the views of Jefferson as exhibited in previous chapters, and evidently derived from some one of the Republican party, who had undertaken, as Jefferson himself had in Genet's case, to initiate Fauchet into "the mysteries" of American politics. In this initiation, Mr. Secretary Randolph would seem to have had a principal share, since Fauchet speaks, in the commencement of the dispatch, of his "precious confessions" as alone throwing "a satisfactory light upon every thing which comes to pass." The disturbances in western Pennsylvania were represented by Fauchet as having grown out of political hostility to Hamilton, and Hamilton himself as taking the advantage which they afforded to make the President regard as a blow at the Constitution what, in fact, was only a protest against the minister. Hence the persistence in enforcing the excise, it being Hamilton's intention—and this piece of information was ascribed expressly to Randolph—"to mislead the President into unpopular courses, and to introduce absolute power under pretext of giving energy to the government." Such, according to Fauchet, was the origin of the expedition into the western counties of Pennsylvania. His disgust at the general co-operation it had called forth, and at the behavior in the matter of certain professed Republicans, is sufficiently evinced in what follows. "Of the governors whose duty it was to appear at the head of the requisitions, the Governor of

Pennsylvania alone enjoyed the name of Republican. His opinions of the Secretary of the Treasury and of his systems were known to be unfavorable. The secretary of this state [Dallas] possessed great influence in the popular society of Philadelphia, which, in its turn, influenced those of other states; of course, he merited attention. It appears that these men, with others unknown to me, were balancing to decide on their party. Two or three days before the proclamation was published, and, of course, before the cabinet had resolved on its measures, Mr. Randolph came to see me with an air of great eagerness, and made to me the overtures of which I have given an account in my No. 6. Thus, with some thousands of dollars, the republic could have decided on civil war or on peace! Thus the consciences of the pretended patriots of America already have their prices!

"Such, citizens, is the evident consequence of the system of finances conceived by Mr. Hamilton. He has made of a whole nation a stock-jobbing, speculating, selfish people. Riches alone here fix the consideration, and, as no one likes to be despised, they are universally sought after. Nevertheless, this depravity has not yet embraced the mass of the people. Still there are patriots of whom I delight to entertain an idea worthy of that imposing title. Consult Monroe—he is of this number; he had apprised me of the men whom the current of events has dragged along as bodies devoid of weight. His friend Madison is also an honest man. Jefferson, on whom the patriots cast their eyes to succeed the President, had foreseen these crises; he prudently retired in order to avoid making a figure in scenes the secret of which will, sooner or later, be brought to light.

"As soon as it was decided that the French republic purchased no men to do their duty, there were to be seen individuals about whose conduct the government could, at least, form uneasy conjectures, giving themselves up with a scandalous ostentation to its views, and even seconding its declarations. The popular societies soon emitted resolutions stamped with the same spirit, which, although they may have been prompted by love of order, might nevertheless have been omitted, or uttered with less solemnity. Then were seen coming from the very men whom we have been accustomed to regard as having little friendship for the system of the treasurer, harangues without end, in order to give a new direction to the public mind."

We shall have occasion to state hereafter the joint explanation, lamely attempted by Fauchet and Randolph, of the unofficial intercourse between them, disclosed in these extraordinary dispatches. They are given here, not for any weight to be attached to their allegations or conjectures, but as going to show the opinions which Fauchet had imbibed of the state of politics and the character of individuals, and as tending to throw light upon subsequent events, by exhibiting the position in which Randolph really stood to the policy of the administration and his colleagues in it. It certainly must be confessed that Washington was at least very unfortunate in the Virginia members of his cabinet.

Among numerous other bugbears suggested by those who had opposed the use of force against the Pennsylvania insurgents, the danger had been much dwelt upon that they might cut off the supply of provisions for the army in the West, thereby exposing it to disbandment or destruction. But as the militia were crossing the mountains, news arrived of a complete victory gained by Wayne over the Indians.

Thus far from Hildreth's History.

Of the leading actors in this insurrection, Gallatin, Findley, Smilie and Brackenridge, all foreigners by birth, all subsequently partook largely of Democratic popular favor; and Bradford alone, a native born, the bravest, and perhaps the best, among them, fled to Louisiana, then a Spanish possession.

This outbreak against the law of the land, though very objectionable both in its origin and purpose, and though suppressed without bloodshed, was expensive and rather burdensome to our young country, with its new and untried constitution, but was certainly not injurious to Western Pennsylvania. Among the volunteers who came out to suppress the insurrection, were many young enterprising mechanics, young men just passing out their apprenticeships, and on the look out for homes. Many of them were well pleased either with Pittsburgh or the country around, and at this day, large numbers of our citizens are the descendants of persons who made their first visits here as volunteers against the whiskey insurgents.

The victory of Wayne on the 20th of August, 1794, over the combined forces of the Indians, his pursuit of them even to the gates of the British fort, the destruction of McKee's house and the Indian cornfields close to that fort, and his very decided correspondence with the British commandant, broke the spirit of the Indians, and led to the treaty of Greenville, by which the Indian title to the eastern portion of the State of Ohio was ceded to the United States. This removed all danger of hostile incursions in this neighborhood, and thus, also, contributed to the advance of this place.

CHAPTER XIII.

Letter from Cornplanter; preparations by James O'Hara and Isaac Craig to erect first Glass-works; letter from Major Craig on the subject; First paper-mill west of the mountains; winter 1796–7 very severe; river long closed by ice; death of General Wayne; stormy weather at Erie; death of Shawanese chief Mio-qua-coo-na-caw at Pittsburgh; inscription on his tomb stone; number of inhabitants in Pittsburgh, in 1796, according to a statement in the Gazette, probably erroneous and exaggerated; list of houses in the place, in 1796, made out from memory; houses in Pittsburgh in 1786; population in 1800; description of the appearance of the ground fifty years ago; James O'Hara introduces Onondaga Salt; changes in Salt trade; two armed gallies built; yellow fever in Philadelphia; contribution here for relief of dis tressed poor in that city; impeachment of Judge Addison; ship building here; branch of Pennsylvania bank here; first stage line; Turnpike road proposed; Steam Flouring mill erected; the first Steam-boat built here; Pittsburgh Rolling mill erected; Bank of Pittsburgh chartered; Pennsylvania canal began and finished; the great freshet; improvement of the Monongahela by Locks and Dams; improvement of the Youghiogany in the same manner; Pennsylvania and Ohio Railroad began and twenty eight miles finished.

In the winter of 1795, a correspondence took place which, though not connected immediately with the history of our place, may merit preservation on account of one of the parties concerned in it. Major Thomas Butler, then commanding at Franklin, had informed Major Craig, that the very worthy and excellent Seneca chief, *Cornplanter* or *Gyantawachia*, as his name was spelt, in signing a treaty, had at his Saw-mill, a large quantity of boards; an article much wanted for the service of the public. The Major, therefore, immediately dispatched Marcus Hulings, an experienced waterman, with three bags of money, and some other articles, up the river to his place, to purchase all his lumber. Hearing, next day, that some private persons had gone on the same errand, the Major dispatched James Beard, a trusty person on horse back with a letter, informing Cornplanter of Huling's object. Beard arrived in time and secured the lumber. The following is the reply of Cornplanter, given *verbatim et literatim :*

GENESADEGO, 3d December, 1795.

I thank the States for making me such kind ofers. We have made peace with the United States as long as watter runs, which was the reason that I built a mill in order to suport my family by it. More so, because I am geting old and not able to hunt. I also thank the States for the pleashure I now feel in meeting them again in friendship, you have sent a man to make a bargain with me for a sertain time which I donot like to do· But as long as my mill makes boards the United States shall always have them in preference to any other, at the market price, and when you want no more boards I cant make blankets of them. As for the money you have sent if I have not boards to the amount, leave it and I will pay it in boards in the Spring.

I thank you kindly for the things you have sent me, I would thank Major Craig or Col. Butler to let Col. Pickering and Gen. Washington know that there is a grate deal of damage done in this country by Liquor, Capt. Brant has kiled his son and other chiefs has done the same, and when the drink was gone and they began to think on the horid crime they had comited, they resigned their comand in the Nation; two Chiefs has been kiled, the one at fort Franklin the other at Genesee, I have sent a speech to the States conserning the Chief killed at Franklin, and has been waiting all sumer to receive pay for him, but can see no sign of its coming, I am by my self to bear all the burden of the people. Now father take pitty on me and send me 40 dollars worth of black Wampum and 10 of of white, and I expect to see it in two monthes and an half, as I must make new Chiefs with it again that time, to help me. I wish to hear from my son and what progress he is making in his learning, and as soon as he is learned enough I want him at home to manage my business for me, I will leave it all to my father, Gen. Washington, to judge when he is learned enough. My compliments to my father and the United States, and I wish it was posible for me to live forever in the United States.

his
Capt. X O. BEAL.
mark.

In the spring of the following year, arrangements began to be made by James O'Hara and Isaac Craig, for the erection of the first Glass-works here. Wm. Eichbaum, Superintendent of Glass-works at the Schuylkill, near Philadelphia, was engaged to direct the erection of works. As this was an important experiment, the following letter from Major Craig giving an account of the very first movement, may be worth preserving.

PITTSBURGH, June 12th, 1797.

After your departure, I furnished Mr. Eichbaum with laborers and the necessary tools for digging and probing the hills near the Saw-mill and up the run as high as the manor line; considerable time and labor were spent without any other discovery than a stratum of coal from twelve to thirteen inches only. I then took Mr. Eichbaum up the Coal-hill and showed him the coal pits called Ward's pits, and the lots on which they are, with all of which, he was well pleased, both as to situation and convenience of materials for building. I, therefore, immediately purchased of Ephraim Jones, the house and lot near the spring for one hundred pounds and have made application to Ephraim Blaine for the two adjoining lots, which no doubt, I will get on reasonable terms. These three lots are quite sufficient, and we are now quarrying lime and building stone, both of which are found on the lot. James Irwin is engaged to do the carpenter work; scantling for the principal building is now sawing, four log-house carpenters are employed in providing timber for the other buildings, and I am negotiating with a mason for the stone work.

"Col. James O'Hara, Detroit."

The saw-mill referred to in the above letter must have been up the run at the upper end of Allegheny city, for in no other direction near Pittsburgh could they have failed to find a vein of coal of a proper depth. The line called the "manor line," was, no doubt, the line of the reserved tract. The lots spoken of were those now owned by Frederick Lorenz.

Such was the commencement of that business, which is now carried on so extensively here. Major Craig, who embarked so promptly in the work, did not partake of its profits, the reason why has never been generally known. The extracts from his correspondence, which our task has called forth, proves him to have been a man of energy and enterprise, and his means, then were very ample; but his brother-in-law, Presley Neville, by no means a man of business, became alarmed at the uncertainty of the result, and this alarm very naturally extended itself to his sister, the wife of Major Craig, and thus lead to an abandonment of his interest in the Glass-works, after a partnership of seven years.

In the year 1796, Samuel Jackson and Jonathan Sharpless, both mechanics of the Society of Friends, who had been raised near the paper-mill on the Brandywine, erected and put into operation the "Redstone paper-mill," near Brownsville. This was the first manufactory of the kind west of the mountains. The Pittsburgh Gazette was immediately published on paper from that mill and was no longer subject to the uncertainty of supplies from east of the mountains.

The winter of 1796–7, was one of uncommon severity, the rivers here closed with ice on the night of the 23d of November, 1796, and remained closed until the 3d February, 1797.

On the 15th of December, 1796, General Anthony Wayne died at Erie, and a letter from Major Kirkpatrick, who attended at his death bed, speaks of the weather as stormy and severe beyond example.

On the 25th of December, Captain Shaumburgh, with a party of Shawanese and Wyandot chiefs and their interpreters, arrived here on their way home from Philadelphia. Among these chiefs were *Red Pole* and *Blue Jacket*. They were detained here by the ice, and during their stay the former was taken sick and though faithfully attended by Dr. Bedford and Dr. Carmichael of the army, he died on the 28th of February, greatly regretted by the other chiefs and all who knew him. He was buried in that portion of the ground on Wood street which now forms the Episcopal grave yard, and the following inscription was placed upon his tomb stone by the order of Government:

MIO-QUA-COO-NA-CAW
or
RED POLE;
Principal Village Chief
of the
Shawanese Nation;
Died at Pittsburgh the 28th January, 1797,
Lamented by the
United States.

In the Pittsburgh Gazette, of January 9th, 1796, we find the following statement:

"The number of inhabitants in the borough of "Pittsburgh, as taken by the assessors last week, "amounts to *one thousand three hundred and ninety-"five.*"

This is the earliest authentic account of our population, and it may be well to tarry a while and notice the condition and appearance of this place at that time. The number of inhabitants at six to each house upon an average, would give two hundred and thirty-two houses, and although the writer's memory goes back pretty distinctly to that time, he cannot conceive where that number of houses could then be found. I have tasked my own memory severely, and with the aid of one whose recollection is more distinct than my own, have made out the following enumeration of the houses in Pittsburgh, about the time above mentioned:

On Penn street, East of Fort Pitt—Colonel Wm. Butler, Jas. O'Hara, Daniel M'Henry, 3

Liberty street—Cecils and Dr. Bedford, 2

On the Diamond—Blackbear tavern, Geo. M'Gunnigle, Wm. Denning, 3

Market street—Old jail corner of 4th, John Irwin, Molly Murphy, Brady's smith shop, corner of 3rd, Horner's, corner of 2nd, Brackenridge's, Mowry's; Ewalt's and Christy's, corner of Water, 10

Water street—P. Neville's, M'Intire's, Seull's, Wilmer's, Duncan's, J. Irwin, John Ormsby's, S. Sample's, John Neville's, Craig's, Redout, Kirkpatrick's, O'Hara's, Tannehill's, green tree tavern, Ferry house, Ross', Audrain's, 18

Wood street—John Wilkins, jr., John Wilkins, sr., Henderson, Sturgeon's, Palmer's log house, Rody M'Kinney, 7

Ferry street—Devereux Smith, Diehl's, Funk's, Charles Richards' and two other log houses, Willock's, 7

Front street—Ward's, M. Adams, Geo. Adams, Hanlon's, stone house, Larwills', Cooper's, Watson's log tavern, Delany's, 10

Second street, (East of Market,)—McNickle's, Mrs. Elliot, H. Reed, Nicholson's, Hanna's, Addison, 6

Second street, (West of Market,)—Fox Gibson's, Chambers', Gen. Gibson's, (the first brick house,) Turnbull's stone house, M'Laughlin's, Jinny Lang's, Ben. Askins, Major Irwin's, 9

Third street—Ben. Richard's, 1

Fourth street, (West of Market,)—Hamshers', M'Cord's, 2

Fourth street, (East of Market,)—2 one story log houses, where Larimer's office now stands, two story log house where Beale's house stands, small log house East of Pittsburgh Bank, Granny Irwin's log house, Engleman's, David Hogg, Jones, Marie's, still standing, now Ross', 9

Fifth street—(Battle Row between Wood and Smithfield,) Riley, Cogan, Tom Vaughan and two or three more, 5

Fifth street, (West of Wood,)—Leightenberger and two others, 3

Marbury street—Gen. Richard Butler, 1

Bouquet's old Redout, 1

In Fort Pitt, four or five, 4

102

In this list, I do not think, there are five houses overlooked; and allowing eight to a house, the population would be a little over eight hundred.

In Nile's Register, vol. 30, page 436, it is stated, but no authority given, that "Pittsburgh, in 1786, contained thirty-six log houses, one stone and one frame house and five small stores." The detail and particularity of this statement would seem to give it some credibility.

The census of 1800, gives Pittsburgh fifteen hundred and sixty-five inhabitants; thus showing an increase from 1796, of only one hundred and seventy, in four years, and yet in the next ten years, to 1810, the increase was three thousand two hundred and three.

We would be pleased if we could give our readers an adequate conception of the situation and appearance of the plain on which our city stands, at the time of the first assessment, or even many years later. Those who see Pittsburgh in its present, not very pleasant aspect, can scarcely imagine its former ragged and broken appearance. We shall attempt to describe it.

The ramparts of Fort Pitt were still standing, and a portion of the officer's quarters, a substantial brick building was used as a malt house, the gates were gone, and the brick wall called the revetment which supported two of the ramparts facing towards the town, and against which the officers and soldiers used to play ball, were gone; so that the earth all around had assumed the natural slope. Out side of the fort on the side next the Allegheny river, was a large deep pond, the frequent resort of wild ducks. Along the south side of Liberty street and extending from the foot of Diamond alley to the foot of Fourth street was another pond, from which a deep ditch lead the water into a brick arch way, leading from Front street just below Redout alley into the Monongahela.

By whom this arch way was built, I have never learned. It was no trifling work. The writer when a boy has often passed through it. The sides, which were from three to four feet high, and the top, were of hard burnt bricks; the bottom of flag stones. Before it was made, there must have been a deep gully extending up from the river below Redout alley; and I have supposed, that when Colonel Grant built the Redout on the bank of the river just above that gully, he probably had the arch way or culvert constructed to facilitate the communication between the Redout and Fort Pitt.

South of Market street, between Front and Water

streets, was another pond, and still another in the square in front of the St. Charles Hotel. Finally, there was Hogg's Pond, extending along the north side of Grant's Hill from Fourth street up to Seventh. From this last there was a low, ugly drain extending down nearly parallel to Wood street to the river. A stone bridge was built across this gully in Front street, probably soon after the borough was incorporated; because without it the gully would be very difficult to pass.

We have now a beautiful landing along the Monongahela from the bridge to the Point. Fifty years, nay even thirty years ago, nothing could be less pleasing to the eye than the rugged, irregular bank. From the bridge down to near Wood street, the distance from the lots to the break of the bank was from sixty to seventy feet. Wood street was impassable, when the river was moderately high. From Wood to Market, the distance from the lots to the break of the bank was fifty or sixty feet. At Market street, there was a deep gully worn into the bank, so that a wagon could barely pass along. At the mouth of Chancery lane, there was another chasm in the bank, so that a horse could not pass between the post at the corner of the lot and the precipitous bank. At the mouth of Ferry street, there was another similar contraction of the way, so that it required very careful driving for a wagon to pass along. At Redout alley there was quite a steep and stony descent down to the level of the covered archway of which I have before spoken. Below that archway the space between the lots and the break of the bank, nowhere exceeded twenty feet, and between Short and West streets it varied from fifteen feet to five. Between West street, Water street was closed by a fence, extending to the foot of the bank; so that persons, going to Jones' ferry from any place on Water street, had either to climb down the steep bank and go along the beach, or else turn up from Water to Front and pass along it to Liberty.

Such was Pittsburgh less than fifty years ago. No doubt, the next fifty years will produce as much improvement as the last.

About the beginning of the year 1796, James O'Hara, who was then Quarter Master General, and had occasion to visit Niagara, there ascertained that Salt from the Onondaga works, in New York, could be furnished on the Ohio cheaper than from Baltimore. Salt from New York was subsequently brought in large quantities by the way of the Lake, to Erie, and thence by Le Bœuf and French creek to Pittsburgh and the Ohio. This supply was continued until about 1810, when the Kenhawa salt began to come into competition with the product of the New York works, and finally the war of 1812 cut off entirely the supply from the latter.

Finally the opening of salt works on the Allegheny and Kiskeminitas, has produced another revolution in the salt trade and that article once more finds its way down the Ohio.

In 1797, our affairs with France assumed a very alarming aspect, the hostile and insolent deportment of the Directory of that country seemed to be fast driving matters to the last resort of an injured nation. Congress, therefore, found it necessary to make preparations for an appeal to arms, and under the provisions of the laws then passed, the first vessels competent to a sea voyage were built here. We find the following notices of them written at that time.

Extract of a letter from Major Craig, dated 25th May, 1798. "On the 19th instant, the Gally, *President Adams*, was launched and is now at anchor in the Allegheny. She will be completely equipped in a few days, and will, I am confident, be as fine a vessel of her burthen and construction as the United States possess.

"The keel of the second galley is laid and other materials all prepared."

Extract from same, dated 8th June, 1798. "The Commander-in-Chief (Gen. Wilkinson,) and his suite have embarked this morning, and will be under way in a few minutes. The galley to lead the van, followed by six large flat bottom boats and several small craft."

Same, dated 27th July, 1798. "The Gally (Senator Ross,) is ready to launch, but not water enough to float her. The river is said to be lower than ever known at this season. I am sorry that the Senator Ross is not on the Mississippi with the President Adams."

Same, dated 13th October, 1798. "The rivers here still continued to fall, and are now said to be twelve inches lower than ever before known."

The river continued low until closed by ice, so that the Galley, *Senator Ross*, was not launched until the spring of 1799, of which we find the following notice in a letter from Major Craig to James M'Henry, the Secretary of War, dated 5th April, 1799.

"The Galley, Senator Ross, has been launched, and is now rigged, and will in a few days be fully equipped for the Mississippi. She is anchored in the Monongahela abreast of the town. She is certainly a fine piece of naval architecture, and one which will far exceed anything which the Spaniards can show on the Mississippi."

During the summer and fall of 1798, the yellow fever raged in Philadelphia. It was, therefore, gratifying to find the following intelligence in a letter from Major Craig to Samuel Hogdon, of that city, dated November 9th, 1798. "The inhabitants of our little town have not been unmindful of the distresses occasioned by that awful scourge to your poor citizens. A subscription paper has been set on foot and sums collected for their relief amounting to nearly five hundred dollars, which will shortly be remitted."

In 1802, Pittsburgh and the country around it were greatly excited by the impeachment of Alexander Addison, the President Judge of the Judicial District, a man of great talent, of extensive learning, and undoubted integrity. He was, perhaps too impatient in his temper, not sufficiently courteous to his demagogical colleague, and thus afforded ground for an impeachment.

In the very able and manly speech of the Judge in his own defense, we find the following passage:

"A gentleman, of whose praise even a proud man "might be vain, handed me the following note:

"During the twelve years of your presidency, there "has been no bill of exceptions, no writ of error on a "demurrer, or case put upon the record, no second "ejectment, except in two instances, (one of which has "been affirmed, the other not yet tried,) though on an "average more than forty ejectments are tried every "year. Perhaps this evidence of confidence in the "opinion of the Court cannot be found in any other "part of Pennsylvania, of the United States or of "any other country."

Party spirit, then ran exceedingly high, and a pretext was only wanting to the Democratic party, to get rid of an honest man and able judge, whose charges had received the emphatic approval of Washington.

The Legislature of Pennsylvania, therefore, under the influence of a most intolerant spirit inflicted the highest penalty in its power upon an offence of the most venial character, and where there was no imputation of a want of integrity. For a mere want of courtesy, was a worthy man prosecuted and found guilty, and the citizens of the Judicial District deprived of the services of a man of most peculiar fitness for his station, and of integrity so bright and clear, that, even, his most bitter enemies never doubted it.

It was within the power of the Pennsylvania Legislature to make the most emphatic commentary on its own conduct, and to exhibit in the strongest light their own harsh and arbitrary decision in the case of Judge Addison; and this commentary and exhibition were afforded in the acquittal of Judge Franks a few years after.

From 1802 to 1805, four ships: *Pittsburgh*, *Louisiana*, *Gen. Butler* and *Western Trader;* three brigs, *Dean*, *Nanina* and *Black Walnut*, and three schooners, *Amity*, *Allegheny* and *Conquest*, were built here.

About the same time the *Monongahela Farmer* and *Ann Jane*, were built at Elizabethtown.

On the first day of January, 1804, a branch of the Bank of Pennsylvania was established here, in the stone building on the east side of Second street, between Ferry street and Chancery lane. In this same year the first Iron Foundry was erected here, by Joseph McClurg.

In May, 1805, the first stage started from Pittsburgh to Chambersburgh, and in the beginning of May, 1806, the first advertisement of the Commissioners for the construction of a Turnpike road, from Pittsburgh to Harrisburgh, appeared in the Pittsburgh papers.

In 1809, the Steam Flouring Mill was erected at the corner of Water street and Redout alley, by Oliver and Owen Evans.

The first steamboat built here was the *New Orleans;* she was built under the superintendence of Mr. Rosevelt, for Messrs. Fulton & Livingston of New York. She was a boat of one hundred and thirty-eight feet keel and calculated for about four hundred tons burthen. She was launched in March, 1811, and landed at Natchez in December, where she took in loading and passengers for the first time, and proceeded to New Orleans.

In 1812, the Rolling Mill, on the corner of Penn street and Cecil's alley, was erected by Christopher Cowan.

In 1814, the Bank of Pittsburgh was incorporated.

On the 18th of March, 1816, the act was passed erecting Pittsburgh into a city and body corporate, by the name and style of the "Mayor, Aldermen and citizens of Pittsburgh."

In 1819, the Monongahela Bridge was built and the St. Clair street Bridge over the Allegheny. Since that time two other bridges and an aqueduct have been built over the Allegheny river. The first aqueduct has also been taken down and a new one on the suspension principle built in its stead. The Monongahela bridge was burnt in the great fire of April 10th, 1845, and a new and very substantial one, on the suspension principle, erected in its stead.

The Pennsylvania Canal was commenced in 1826, and the first canal boat arrived at Pittsburgh on the 10th day of November, A. D. 1829.

In February, 1832, was the great freshet in the Ohio, when it rose to a greater height at Pittsburgh than was ever before known by the oldest inhabitants, and committed great destruction along its banks.

In the year 1843, the improvement of the Monongahela river, by locks and dams, was commenced, and on the 13th day of November, A. D., 1844, it was formally opened to the National road, at Brownsville, and has ever since formed the route of a large amount of travel and transportation.

On the 7th day of November, 1850, the improvement of the Youghiogany river, in a manner similar to that which has been so thoroughly tried and approved on the Monongahela, being previously completed, a great celebration of the opening of the navigation to West Newton took place. Since that time the navigation has been interrupted but a few days by the ice, and the work promises to be of great advantage to our city, and especially after the completion of the plank road from West Newton to the Baltimore and Ohio Railroad, at Cumberland.

In 1848, the Pennsylvania and Ohio Railroad was begun, and in July, 1851, it was opened to New Brighton, in Beaver county, twenty-eight miles, with most encouraging prospects up to this time, September, 1851.

CHAPTER XIV.

Ejectments against O. Ormsby and Snowden, Barclay and Cotter. Proceedings for the removal of Obstructions on Water street below West street.

I have reserved for the last chapter of this history, some transactions which have exercised a very important influence upon the interests and the growth of our city. These transactions extended over a series of years from about 1814 down to about 1835 or 6. I have preferred not touching upon these matters at all until I could devote to them a separate chapter and thus dispose of them continuously.

In the month of May and June, 1784, as I have before stated, the town of Pittsburgh was laid out in lots, streets and alleys. On the face of the plat, the lots were all numbered, and the size of each stated, the width of the alleys was given, as was that of all the streets, except Water street. On one side of that were the lots commencing at the point or junction of the rivers and extending up to Grant street, between these lots and the Monongahela river, there was no line drawn or laid down on the plat, nothing at all to indicate, that there was to be a street of any regular, definite width between these lots and the river. There was an irregular space, wide up at Grant street, but gradually and irregularly growing narrower towards the point.

On this long, straggling, ragged strip, were written the words "WATER STREET." At Grant street, the space between the lots and the break of the high bank was seventy or seventy-five feet, sufficient for a wide street; but at Ferry street the space was not fifty feet wide, and from Redout alley it gradually decreased from about twenty feet to four or five or less. Such was the appearance of Water street as shown on the plat of the town made by the proprietaries' surveyor, and approved by their agent. A copy of that plat was kept in the office of the Penns, in Philadelphia, and all the deeds to purchasers referred to it for the numbers and boundaries of the lots purchased.

The agent of the proprietaries had also a list of all the property of the Penns in the Manor of Pittsburgh, mentioning the lots and farms, in which there was not the slightest intimation of any spot of ground between Water street and the river. For about thirty years from 1784 to 1814 or 1815, the proprietaries or their agents never pretended to have any such claim.

About the time last mentioned, however, some greedy, unprincipled speculators, went to John R. Coates, the agent of the Penns, and induced him to execute to them a deed for all the land between Water street and the Monongahela river, without mentioning any length or breadth, for the consideration of ten thousand dollars. Of this ten thousand dollars not one dime was paid; but a mortgage was given on the purchased property. Upon this title suit was brought against Oliver Ormsby, who happened to have a hoisting machine extending over the bank in front of lot number 183. The city of Pittsburgh assumed the defense in that case; it was tried in Pittsburgh before the late judge Walker. It was very ably argued by the late judge Baldwin for the plaintiffs, and by James Ross, Esq.

for defendant. A verdict was rendered in favor of defendant. A second Ejectment was soon after instituted in the same court, against the Mayor, Street Commissioner and Wharfmaster of the city of Pittsburgh; and William Wilkins being the judge, a pretext or reason for its removal was furnished, and the cause was taken to the Eastern District of Pennsylvania. The case was tried before judge Washington, in Philadelphia, in April, 1829. Baldwin, Sergeant and cey for plaintiffs; Joseph R. Ingersol and Charles Smith for defendants.

The ground of the plaintiffs' claim was in substance as follows: That the public had a right of way of reasonable width along the bank of the river Monongahela, although the title to the soil remained in the proprietaries, that sixty feet was a sufficient width, and that they (the plaintiffs) had a title upon which they could sustain their ejectment for the ground between the river and a line sixty feet from the line of the lots.

In support of their claim the plaintiffs offered in evidence a Deed from the proprietaries to Craig and Bayard, for the thirty two lots between West, Liberty and Marbury streets and the rivers. In this deed the lots were all distinguished by the numbers given on the plat, but instead of Water street, the Monongahela river, was given as the southern boundary.

They also read in evidence the deed of John Ormsby, for lot "marked number 183, in the plan of said town," but the southern boundary, instead of Water street, is said to be the Monongahela river.

On the part of the defendants, several plats of the town made out by Vickroy, at the time of the survey, and also the plat kept in the office of the agent of the proprietaries were offered in evidence. The depositions of Ewalt and Finley, who were present when the survey was made, both of whom stated that at the time, objections were made by the inhabitants that Water street was too narrow and that George Woods, the principal Surveyor, declared that "Water street would be left open to the river, that the citizens might use it as landings, &c. That the people would be digging cellars, &c., and that they might extend the street out to low water mark."

The defendants, also, offered in evidence the article of agreement between the proprietaries and Craig and Bayard, executed *before* the town was laid out; and argued that although this article might preclude the grantors from cutting up the ground previously sold, *without the consent of the purchasers*, yet it would not prevent them from cutting up the balance of the town scite as they pleased. The first sale to Craig and Bayard, embraced only a portion of the seventeen lots along the Allegheny, from the Point to about Marbury street. The deed embraced the whole of those lots besides fifteen others, extending from Penn street to West, and from Marbury street to Water street, or as the deed expressed it to the Monongahela river.

There was much other evidence, but the foregoing summary embraces the most material. The cause was argued with extraordinary zeal and spirit by Mr. Baldwin, and with remarkable ingenuity by Mr. Sergeant for plaintiffs, and with great ability by Mr. Smith and Joseph R. Ingersol for defendants.

The charge of Judge Washington, which, I believe, was the last he ever delivered, was strongly in favor of the plaintiffs, and a verdict and judgment were given accordingly.

Various exceptions were taken to the charge and the cause was taken by writ of error to the Supreme Court of the United States.

In January term, 1832, the case was argued in that Court, and the opinion of the Court was given by Judge McLean, reversing the judgment below and remanding the cause for further proceedings.

This opinion can be seen at large in Hazard's Register, vol. 9, page 202 to 206, to which we refer our readers.

The case, then, went back to the Eastern district of Pennsylvania. In the mean time Judge Washington had died and Joseph Hopkinson, who had been employed originally as counsel for the defendants, was appointed the successor of the deceased Judge. Thus again a pretext or a reason for another removal was afforded, and the case was transferred to the Maryland district, where Chief Justice Taney presided.

It is not at all probable that the plaintiffs entertained any hopes of success in opposition to the very clear and decided opinion of the Court. It is most likely that they wished to keep the case pending with a faint hope of a compromise or with a reliance upon the chapter of accidents. The case, however, was vigorously pressed by Wm. Wilkins, the counsel for defendants, and finally this claim was for ever exploded by the plaintiffs taking a non-suit.

Thus our city, after a long and very vexatious, as well as expensive litigation, foiled a band of greedy speculators in an attempt to contract Water street, to interpose a line of lots between lots, which had been purchased in the belief that they were to have open fronts to the river, and the Monongahela river, and to deprive us forever of that landing place which is now so beautiful and commodious, so convenient for commerce, and so productive of revenue to our city.

While the before mentioned cases were pending in the United States Court, other proceedings arising out of the condition of Water street, were taking place in Pittsburgh and our State courts. Under the equivocal description of the western boundary of the lots embraced in Craig and Bayard's purchase; the owners of those lots, subsequent to the first purchasers, had encroached upon Water street. James O'Hara, for instance, had extended his fence over the bank and down to the beach of the Monongahela. Samuel Black, had a large frame house and John McDonald, Esq., a brick house on the north side of Liberty street, both of which encroached far upon Water street; so that that street seemed to end at West street, and persons desiring to go to Jones' Ferry, at the end of Liberty street, with wagons or carriages, were compelled to get into Liberty street, and then follow it to the river.

In 1827, the Councils of Pittsburgh passed a resolution directing the City Solicitor to take measures to open Water street to the Point. In obedience to these instructions the Solicitor took with him the Street Commissioner and some of his hands and cut down and removed that portion of the fences which encroached upon the street, and then entered prosecutions against McDonald and Black for nuisance, in obstructing the public highway. In contempt of the vulgar adage, "that dog will not eat dog," the Solicitor urged on the prosecution against Mr. McDonald, it was tried before Judge Duncan and a verdict rendered against defendant and judgment entered. It was then taken to the

Supreme Court of Pennsylvania, where the judgment was affirmed, and immediately after John McDonald, with characteristic promptitude and manliness, set hands to tear down all that portion of his house which extended beyond the line of Water street. Black, soon after did the same, and thus Water street was permitted to stretch itself out to that full length which the proprietaries intended to give it.

These cases, the ejectments, and the prosecutions for obstructing the street, were such important events in in our history, and in their results were so beneficial to our city, that I have considered it advisable to give full accounts of them, believing that they will be read with interest.

CHAPTER XV.

Advantages of the City of Pittsburgh and vicinity for Manufacturing and Commercial purposes.

In the course of our history, it has been shown that the position of Pittsburgh, at the head of the Ohio river, and the most convenient to the sea board, of all on that great tributary of the mighty Mississippi, was at a very distant day regarded both by France and Great Britain, as well as by Pennsylvania and Virginia, as a very important one. Scarcely had the white man shown his pale face in the great western valley, before this position became a bone of contention between the European States and neighboring colonies.

Any intelligent man who has before him a map of the United States, who casts his eye over it and fixes his attention upon the point at the head of the Ohio, will at once feel that it must be a very advantageous location for a great city, unless there exist some natural obstruction, such as lofty precipitous mountains, or insuperable, miasmatic swamps. Neither of these exist at the head of the Ohio. We have, it is true, some lofty hills, but they do not so entirely cover the ground, as to exclude the sites of one or more great cities; and even those hills contain veins, of rich bituminous coal, limestone, and extensive quarries of building stone, while their sides are covered with valuable timber and their surfaces, not only with timber, but a most luxuriant soil.

As to miasma, there is not and never has been any thing of the kind; probably no city in the country is more healthy than Pittsburgh and Allegheny. Cholera has visited our city four or five different years; but in all that time the deaths from that disease have not equalled those of a single week in one of our more western cities. Deeming this a matter of great interest, I have procured a communication upon the subject from a physician of much experience here.

These, then, are four of the natural advantages of our city, a commanding position at the head of the great valley of the Mississippi, a luxuriant soil, valuable materials for the use of the inhabitants and a most salubrious climate.

The intelligent man who has cast his eye over the map of the United States, and who has, at first sight, been struck with the commanding point at the head of the Ohio, cannot, upon further examination, fail to notice the remarkable manner in which nature herself has created for this place avenues of trade and intercourse with all the country around.

The small diagram of the country around the head of the Ohio, exhibits to the reader more distinctly than a general map can do, the remarkable manner in which the country around us is intersected by navigable streams. At this point the Monongahela river, bearing its tribute of water from the South, comes to meet the lovely Allegheny flowing from the North, and by their union form the magnificent Ohio. There these two streams, one coming from the cold North, the other from the balmy South, seem like too long arms extended at their full length to draw hither all the products of their extensive valleys. A few miles south of their junction, the Youghiogany river pours its waters into the Monongahela, a few miles northward the Kiskeminitas bears to the Allegheny the drainage of an extensive valley; while a few miles westward the Beaver river, collecting its tribute from the vicinity of the lakes and from the fertile plains of eastern Ohio, aids to swell the current of the already magnificent river, produced by the union of the Allegheny and Monongahela. Look again at our diagram, notice how all these various rivers, and other streams, which elsewhere would be called rivers seem to converge to this point, thus cutting up the region around us, affording ready and cheap means of intercourse with our cities and towns, and forming convenient routes of artificial improvements either by canals, locks and dams, rail roads, plank roads or other works.

I ask the attention of distant readers, to the little diagram, while I point out a few of the more important artificial works which have been constructed to multiply the means of intercourse with our "*City of three rivers*," meaning to include in that name, both our cities and the adjoining boroughs.

One of the most important of these artificial improvements is the Pennsylvania canal. This great work has a double terminus, one in the city of Pittsburgh into the Monongahela river; the other in the city of Allegheny into the Allegheny river, uniting in the upper end of the latter city, the canal thence pursues its course along the western bank of that river twenty-nine miles, to a point, a short distance above the mouth of the Kiskeminitas river, where it passes by means of a substantial aqueduct, to the eastern bank of the Allegheny, and then follows the Kiskeminitas and Conemaugh to Johnstown, about seventy-two miles. From the latter place by means of rail roads and canals, easy communication is afforded with Baltimore, Philadelphia, and all the other sea-board cities, and by this route a very large and annually increasing business is carried on.

Up the Allegheny river itself for more than one hundred miles above the Kiskeminitas, fine steamboats, of a smaller class than those running on the Ohio, regularly ply and carry on the business of exchanging the products of the mines, the fields and the forests of the rich valley of the Allegheny, for those of the shops and manufactories of our cities and of foreign countries.

Along this same river, descend immense rafts containing many millions of feet of the beautiful white and yellow pine, hemlock and other timber, and hundreds of large flat boats laden with the blooms, the metal and the agricultural products of the great region watered by that stream and its many extensive tributaries. Returning to Pittsburgh, we ascend the Monongahela by its excellent slackwater improvement, eighteen miles to M'Keesport, at the mouth of the Youghiogany river, passing on our way dozens of coal mines and railroads, all busily engaged in supplying to consumers the rich and valuable bituminous coal with which the entire region is filled. At M'Keesport, we have a choice either to follow the Monongahela, by the same slack-water improvement, thirty-eight miles farther to Brownsville, the point at which the National road crosses that river, and from whence there is an easy and rapid communication with the Baltimore and Ohio railroad, at Cumberland, or we may follow the Youghiogany river, which is also improved by locks and dams, to West Newton, from which place a plank road is now being rapidly constructed to Cumberland.

The Monongahela river in its slight descent and gentle current presents great facilities and strong inducements for the extension of the slack-water improvement far above Brownsville, and exertions are now making to carry the improvement up to Fairmount, in Virginia, where the Baltimore and Ohio railroad crosses it. Upon both sides of the river from Brownsville up, the country is well settled, several towns and many villages are dotted along its bank, and there can be no reasonable doubt, that the improvement will, ere long, be extended to Fairmount.

From Pittsburgh we sally forth once more, descending the Ohio, on the south side, about three miles distant, we come to Chartier's creek, a small, but valuable stream, which in some countries would be called a river, and which passes through a region of unsurpassed fertility, abounding in coal, and inhabited by a wealthy and prospering people. Along the stream an enterprising company have almost completed a rail road, and will in a few weeks be the first in this region to start a locomotive to convey coal to market.

Along this stream too, a railroad is projected to cross the neck of land formed by the Monongahela and Ohio rivers, and thus reach the heart of central Ohio, by a short and direct route through a very fertile, well settled and highly cultivated region of country. Already the Pittsburgh and Steubenville Railroad Company has been organized by the election of a very able, enterprising and wealthy board of directors—liberal subscriptions of stock made and sanguine expectations entertained by its active and zealous friends of its speedy completion.

Descending the Ohio still farther at the distance of twenty-five miles on the north side of that river, we reach the Big Beaver river. Ascending this river by slack-water of the Erie Canal Company, we may pass along that canal to the town of Erie, on Lake Erie, or we might diverge from that canal twenty-two miles up and pursue the Ohio and Pennsylvania canal to Cleveland, on the same lake, and one hundred miles west of Erie, passing through the rich and lovely region so well known, as the Western Reserve.

Again descending the Ohio, still on the north side, at the distance of twelve miles, we reach the Little Beaver, up which the Sandy and Beaver canal runs, and passing through the rich and fertile counties of

Columbiana and Starke, enters the great Ohio canal at Bolivar, and thus gives us access to the very heart of the great State of Ohio.

About ten miles still farther down the Ohio, we reach Wellsville, a very flourishing town on the north bank of that river, from whence a railroad is now being constructed to Cleveland on Lake Erie, about one half of which is already completed and in profitable use. From Wellsville, the route of a railroad has been surveyed up the Ohio to the mouth of Big Beaver, there to connect with the Pennsylvania and Ohio railroad, of which we will shortly take notice.

Descending still farther about sixteen or seventeen miles, we reach Steubenville, the western terminus of the direct road west from Pittsburgh, of which I have before spoken, and also the eastern terminus of the Steubenville and Indiana railroad, for the construction of which a large amount of stock has been subscribed, a board of directors elected, and an advertisement has for some time been published calling for proposals for constructing a considerable portion of the road.

The Cleveland and Pittsburgh railroad have authority under their charter to construct a railroad from Wellsville through Steubenville to Bridgeport, and many intelligent persons believe that when a railroad is completed from Wellsville, and from Wellsville to Steubenville, it will be a cheaper and speedier route than the Pittsburgh and Steubenville railroad. Experiment which is the best test of such matters may perhaps settle this one, and to that we are content to leave it.

Below Steubenville, the beautiful Ohio and the vast Mississippi, and their innumerable navigable tributaries are open to the visits of our many steamboats, but our design is not to travel beyond the limits of our little diagram of the country around and adjacent to the head of the Ohio.

Returning to the "head of the Ohio," once more, we find in the city of Allegheny the eastern terminus of the Pennsylvania and Ohio railroad—a work chartered by both those great States and extending from the city of Allegheny along the Ohio, to the borough of Rochester, at the mouth of the Big Beaver river, thence up that river, through the thriving manufacturing town of New Brighton, and Old Brighton, and from thence gradually ascending the table land between the waters of the Ohio and Lake Erie, and passing along the same to the village of Crestline, distant one hundred and eighty-five miles. Twenty-eight miles of this road, to New Brighton, has been in very successful and encouraging operation since the latter part of July, the portion of the road from New Brighton to Alliance, where it connects with the Cleveland and Wellsville railroad, is already graded and the contractors for laying the rails are activity at work from Alliance towards Brighton, and also from Brighton towards Alliance, and sanguine hopes are entertained that the road will be completed between those places, and the cars running to Cleveland in October next. From Brighton to Alliance is fifty-four miles, and the entire distance to Cleveland by railroad will be one hundred and thirty-eight miles. The road from Cleveland to Alliance is so far completed that the rails for the Pennsylvania and Ohio railroad are transported upon it to Alliance. Thus, in October we will have a continuance railroad from Pittsburgh by Cleveland to Cincinnati, on which travelers will pass from the Queen City to the Iron City in nineteen hours.

From Alliance to Crestline is one hundred and four miles, passing the entire distance through a very highly cultivated country, and through or by many thriving towns and villages, among others are Canton, Wooster and Mansfield, the county towns of the populous and wealthy counties of Starke, Wayne and Richland, and also through Massillon, the greatest wheat market in the State of Ohio.

The grading of the entire distance is now under contract, and rapidly advancing to completion. From Alliance to Loudonville, the most southern bend of the railroad is seventy-one miles, and from that place to Springfield one hundred and ten miles, a railroad has already been located, and thirty miles of it is now under contract, and from Springfield to Cincinnati, eighty-four miles, is already in use. Total distance from Pittsburgh by Alliance, Loudonville and Springfield to Cincinnati, three hundred and forty-two miles.

Thirty-three miles west of Loudonville, is Crestline, the western terminus of the Pennsylvania and Ohio railroad, at this point passes the railroad now in operation from Cleveland to Cincinnati.

From Crestline to Terre Haute, on the Wabash, a line of railroads is already under construction by different companies.

Eastward of Pittsburgh the great central road from Philadelphia is rapidly advancing to completion. Already the cars leaving the latter city can reach a point, distant from Pittsburgh only fifty miles, while from Pittsburgh the rails are already advancing eastward; so that the time of completion cannot be very distant.

This road gives us speedy access to the heart of Pennsylvania and to all the seaboard cities. We have neither time nor space, even, to enumerate the various turnpike and plank roads, the latter of which are now being made in all directions, and are proved to be the most convenient neighborhood roads.

Finally, the abundance and cheapness of fuel of a very superior quality, is an advantage, in which no western city can compete with the cities at the head of the Ohio. We are situated in the very heart of the great basin of bituminous coal and the rivers intersecting the country in all directions gives us the easiest and cheapest access.

Mr. Lyell, the very distinguished English Geologist, the author of several valuable works on Geology, was much struck with the abundance, and richness and the easy accessibility of stone-coal on the Monongahela, and in his "Travels in North America," fully manifests his appreciation of the present, and still greater *prospective* value of the abundant supply of coal.

I conclude with a few extracts from Lyell's "Travels in North America." His first impressions are given as follows:—

"From Uniontown we went to Brownsville on the Monongahela, a large tributary of the Ohio, where the country consists of coal-measures, like those at Uniontown, both evidently belonging to the same series as those more bent and curved beds at Frostburg before described. *I was truly astonished*, now that I had entered the hydrographical basin of the Ohio, at beholding the richness of the seams of coal, which appear every where on the flanks of the hills, and at the bottom of the valleys, and *which are accessible in a degree I never witnessed elsewhere. The time has not yet arrived,* the soil being still densely covered with the primeval forest, and manufacturing industry in its infancy, *when the full value of this inexhaustible supply of cheap fuel can be appreciated;* but the resources which it will one day afford to a region capable, by its agricultural produce alone, of supporting a large population, *are truly magnificent.* In order to estimate the natural advantages of such a region, we must reflect how three great navigable rivers, such as the Monongahela, Allegheny, and the Ohio intersect it, and lay open on their banks the level seams of coal. I found at Brownsville a bed ten feet thick of good bituminous coal, commonly called the Pittsburgh seam, breaking out in the river cliffs near the water's edge."

Again he says: "So great are the facilities for procuring this fuel that already it is found profitable to convey it in flat-bottomed boats for the use of steamships at New Orleans,* 1,100 miles distant, in spite of the dense forests bordering the intermediate river-plains, where timber may be obtained at the cost of falling it."

* This should be two thousand miles. The coal is also used for making Gas, for which purpose there is none better.

SALUBRITY OF PITTSBURGH AND VICINITY.

BY WILLIAM H. DENNY.

Pittsburgh is in latitude 40° 35′ North, situated seven hundred and fifty feet above the level of the ocean, two hundred miles distant from its nearest tide marshes. It is one hundred and eighty feet above the level of Lake Erie, and more than one hundred miles from its south-west coast. From both these sources of malaria, it is divided also by mountain ridges or plateaus of great elevation.

Although nearly surrounded by hills, more than four hundred feet in height, the valleys of the Allegheny and Ohio are open to the free ventilation by the north-east and north-west winds. The summer winds from the South, which visit other western cities from low and paludal grounds, here descend upon the town from a terrace four hundred and fifty feet high, after passing for a long distance over a well drained, cultivated, broken and mountainous region.

Of all the great western towns, Pittsburgh is the farthest removed from the baneful exhalations of the swampy borders of the Mississippi, and accordingly enjoyed a greater exemption from those diseases, which during the summer and autumn prevail even as high up as Cincinnati.

That exemption is supposed to be aided by an artificial cause. The combustion annually of ten millions of bushels of bituminous coal fills the atmosphere with carburetted hydrogen, sulphurous gas, and the all-pervading impalpable dust of carbon. The smoke is thickest in the calm, cool and foggy morning of autumn. It is *anti-miasmatic:* and hence it is, that formerly the natural ponds, and latterly the foul and stagnant artificial basins, have never generated remittent or intermittent fever.

Dropsies, dysenteries, diarrheas and cholera, diseases which are influenced by causes of a malarious origin, have never prevailed to any extent. The *goïtre* or swelled neck, has disappeared; the few cases, which formerly excited the apprehensions of the stranger, no longer exist to gratify his curiosity. Their locality was in no respect remarkable, and by no means supported the hypothesis of the first Professor Barton, that the goitre was produced by the same causes which produced intermittent fever: nor could it be accounted for in the water which was drunk at that time by the inhabitants; which differed in nothing from what they drank after it began to disappear. In a few instances it was connected with cretinism, and in many cases it was followed by consumption, and in every case, where the experiment was tried, the swelling was lessened or removed by a journey and change of air.

It is not improbable that the presence of iodine in our peculiar atmosphere, so charged with particles of soot, or some other unknown element in our smoke, has had a salutary effect, as well in preventing the disease of the thyroid gland, as in arresting the tendency to the formation of tubercles in the lungs, and thus account both for the disappearance of goitre and the comparative *rarity of phthisis pulmonalis.*

The water which was drunk by the inhabitants before, and after the disappearance of goitre, was well water, slightly impregnated with carbonate of lime. Since 1827, the water used has been pumped into a reservoir directly from the running stream ; the clear and pure Allegheny—unobstructed in its entire rapid course, over pebbles and bowlders, from their common source and origin in the sandstone rock.

Strangers with weak lungs, for a while, find their coughs aggravated by the smoke, but nevertheless asthmatic patients have found relief in breathing it.

In this account, coal is our creditor in another way : its abundance, cheapness and consequent general and profuse use by the poorest inhabitants, is undoubtedly a great cause of our superior healthfulness.

The low fevers, so prevalent in the large cities, among the poor, during a hard winter ; and the ague and fever, so common in the eastern counties where wood is scarce, are here in a measure prevented by the universal practice of keeping good coal fires, late in the spring, and early in the autumn, and indeed at all seasons when the weather is damp and inclement.

The prevailing complaints are those which characterise the healthiest situations of the same latitude, elsewhere in America ; in winter pneumonia and sore throat, and in summer bilious affections.

In comparison with the eastern cities, there is much less pulmonary consumption, less scrofula, and less disease of the skin. There is scarcely any ague and fever, and no yellow fever. In comparison with the western cities, including Cincinnati, there is less bilious fever, less ague and fever, less cholera infantum and far less malignant cholera.

We are the intermediate link of disease, as well as

of commerce: we have less hepatic disease than the west, and less pulmonic disease than the east.

As so large a portion of our population is engaged in manufactures, it is expected that as these establishments increase, they will add to the bills of mortality, but not to the same extent which similar employments have done in Europe. Our youth are not so early introduced into factories, the confinement is not so great, and the food is more nutritious; but few, if any, dwell in cellars or crowded apartments; and none labor under the continual apprehension of being, by the fluctuations of trade, thrown out of employment and wanting bread.

On the whole, with regard to the health of Pittsburgh, it may be said that no city in the union is more healthy, and that none resists better the malarious diseases, to which, during the autumn, the whole great valley is more or less subject. Indeed of the adjacent country, including nearly all western Pennsylvania, it may be said, that no part of the United States, is better suited to a European constitution, and that the greater part will bear no comparison with it in point of salubrity.

BUSINESS OF PITTSBURGH.

The following account of manufactories here, is taken from the Directory of Pittsburgh, for 1850, prepared by Samuel Fahnestock, Esq.

There are in Pittsburgh and vicinity, thirteen Rolling mills with a capital of about $5,000,000, and employing 2,500 hands. These mills consume about 60,000 tons of pig metal, and produce bar iron and nails amounting to $4,000,000 annually.

There are also 30 large Foundries, together with a great many smaller ones, having a capital in all amounting to about $2,000,000, and employing not less than 2,500 hands. These Foundries consume 20,000 tons pig metal annually and yield, with the labor employed, various articles amounting to about $2,000,000.

There are 2 establishments manufacturing locks, latches, coffee mills, patent scales, with a great variety of other malleable iron castings, with a capital of $250,000 and employing 500 hands, consuming 1,200 tons pig metal, and producing goods amounting to $300,000 annually.

There are 5 extensive cotton factories, besides many smaller ones, with a capital in all amounting to about $1,500,000, and employing 1,500 hands; these establishments consume some 15,000 bales cotton, and produce yarns, sheeting, batting, &c. amounting to upwards of $1,500,000.

There are 8 flint glass manufactories with a capital of $300,000 invested, employing 500 hands, consuming 150 tons lead and 200 tons pearl ash, and producing various articles of glass ware amounting to $400,000. There are 7 phial furnaces and 11 window glass manufactories, with a capital of $250,000, employing 600 hands, and producing $600,000 annually.

There is also a soda ash manufactory, producing 1,500 tons annually, employing 75 hands.

There is one copper smelting establishment, producing 660 tons refined copper annually, valued at $380 per ton, and amounting to $250,000.

There is also a copper rolling mill now in operation, producing 300 tons sheeting and braziers copper, amounting to $150,000 annually.

There are 5 white lead factories with a capital of $150,000 invested, and producing 150,000 kegs lead annually, worth $200,000, and employing 60 hands.

There are also a number of manufactories of the smaller sizes of iron, several extensive manufactories of axes, hatchets, &c. spring steel, steel springs, axles, anvils, vices, mill, cross cut, and other saws, gun barrels, shovels, spades, forks, hoes, cut tacks, brads, &c.

There also in full and successful operation an establishment manufacturing cast, shear, and blister steel, and files, all said to be of a very superior quality, besides a great variety of manufacturing establishments not enumerated in our list; and after a careful investigation we find that with our manufacturing and other business, taking all together the actual amount does not fall short of $50,000,000 annually.

There is consumed about 12,000,000 bushels of coal annually in our manufacturing establishments, valued at $500,000 and an equal number of bushels exported to the lower markets, giving employment to upwards of 4,000 hands.

www.ingramcontent.com/pod-product-compliance
Lightning Source LLC
LaVergne TN
LVHW020225110826
845151LV00003B/835

* 9 7 8 1 4 2 5 5 3 1 8 1 2 *